A Garland Series

OUTSTANDING DISSERTATIONS IN THE

FINE ARTS

Attic White-Ground

Its Development on Shapes
Other Than Lekythoi

Joan R. Mertens

Garland Publishing, Inc., New York & London

1977

Library of Congress Cataloging in Publication Data

Mertens, Joan R
   Attic white-ground.

   (Outstanding dissertations in the fine arts)
   Thesis--Harvard, 1972.
   Bibliography: p.
   1. Vase-painting, Greek. 2. Vases, Greek.
3. Slipware--Greece. I. Title. II. Series.
NK4649.5.M47 1977   738.3'82'0938   76-23641
ISBN 0-8240-2711-6

64469

Attic White-ground: Its Development

on Shapes Other than Lekythoi

A thesis presented

by

Joan R. Mertens

to

The Department of Fine Arts
in partial fulfillment of the requirements

for the degree of
Doctor of Philosophy
in the subject of
Fine Arts.

Harvard University
Cambridge, Massachusetts
April, 1972

P R E F A C E

The publication of this dissertation posed the problem of whether to leave it as submitted or to rewrite it extensively. In favor of the second alternative was the possibility, first, of taking into account recent articles and monographs like those of M. Eisman, D. Callipolitis-Feytmans, D.C. Kurtz and, second, of incorporating changes of mind. I should now, for example, make a more basic distinction between slip as a ground for decoration and as a means of emphasizing part of the shape of a vase. While maintaining the primacy of Andokides, I should revise Chapter I, especially as concerns the period between Nearchos and Andokides and the relation between Nikosthenes, Psiax, and the Antimenes Painter. I should also have shortened the chapter on cups considerably, since this material has been reworked for an article in the Metropolitan Museum Journal 9 (1974). That these and other modifications were not made is due to two decisive considerations. For present purposes, the result would have borne too little relation to the thesis and, furthermore, before having seen all major collections of pertinent material even these changes seemed premature. I have tried instead to reach a compromise. The original catalogue and text have remained as submitted, with few minor exceptions having to do with clarity of expression, the list of illustrations, etc. What follows in this preface, however, are corrections and additions to the catalogue. The additions consist of interesting vases newly come to my attention, lesser pieces that are in neither Beazley nor the CVA, and a number that I had deliberately omitted from my first lists. In the latter, some categories like the outline alabastra had been reduced to a minimum; I have reinstated the vases by significant artists and workshops so as to present their relative importance more accurately. This solution may weaken the connection between catalogue and text, yet of the two parts the former is the more basic.

The acknowledgements that I had made in the dissertation must, to a considerable extent, be repeated and re-emphasized here. Dietrich von Bothmer has continued to give Attic white-ground the benefit of his interest and he regularly discovers new examples in the remoter corners of museum storerooms. My debt remains as well to the Department of Fine Arts, Harvard University. A number of private collectors have generously allowed me to keep in this reprint vases of theirs that had been illustrated in the dissertation; I should like to thank Walter Bareiss, René Bloch, Jan Mitchell, Joseph V. Noble. Herbert A. Cahn has brought to my attention and allowed me to publish several more pieces in his collection. I feel particularly indebted to the curators who have given me access to material not on exhibition or to their storerooms: Dr. B. Philippaki (Athens, National Museum); Dr. E. Sakellarakis (Athens, Agora Museum); Dr. M. Raumschüssel (Dresden, Skulptursammlung); Dr. E. Paul (Leipzig, Karl-Marx-Universität); Miss K. Gorbunova (Leningrad, Hermitage); Mr. D. Haynes, Mr. B. Cook, Dr. A. Birchall (London, British Museum); Dr. D. Ohly, Dr. F. Hamdorf (Munich, Antikensammlungen); Dr. R. Moorey (Oxford, Ashmolean); Dr. F. Villard, Mr. A. Pasquier (Paris, Louvre); Mrs. I. Aghion (Paris, Cabinet des Médailles).

August, 1976

Addenda and Corrigenda

P. 33.C.2   WG: panel frame and decoration within.

P. 36.D.6   D. Callipolitis-Feytmans, Les Plats Attiques à
             Figures Noires (Paris, 1974) [hereafter Feytmans
             Plats], p. 377,5.

P. 49.A.13   RA 1972,1, 127 ff.

P. 49.A.17   Read Louvre Cp 10681.

P. 54.B.2   JdI 85 (1970), 49, fig. 13.

             To the Cape Town Class add

             -Berlin 3684. Herakles and the Lion. WG: body and
             shoulder panels.
             -Villa Giulia inv. 74912 (ex coll. Pesciotti).
             Herakles and the Lion. WG: body and shoulder
             panels. M. Moretti, Villa Giulia: Nuove Scoperte
             e Acquisizioni (Rome, 1975), pl. 63,16.

P. 58.C.23   WG: body and neck.

P. 56.C.   Antimenean add

             -Swiss market. Neck, A, Satyr mask; B, the like.
             Shoulder, ornament. WG: neck, shoulder zone with
             palmettes.

             To the Class of Cabinet des Médailles 218 add

             -Leipzig T 946a. A, Warrior's departure; B, battle
             with quadriga. Neck, A, hoplite; B, (hoplite).
             WG: body certainly. CV pl. 40, 1-3.
             -Basel market. A, Centaur and Lapith; B, the like.
             Neck, A, Dionysos; B, the like. WG: body and neck.
             MM 51 (1975), no. 130.

P. 57.C.   To the Light-make Class add

             -Mariani Painter. Schwerin 736. ABV 595, 1 bis;
             Para. 298. A, Dionysos and maenad, seated; B,
             the like. WG: neck and body. CV pl. 16,1-3 &
             pl. 17,4.
             -Mariani Painter. Rome, Villa Giulia inv. 74913
             (ex coll. Pesciotti). A, Dionysos between maenads;
             B, symposium. WG: neck and body. Moretti Nuove
             Scoperte pl. 62.
             -Group X. Leipzig T 50. Para. 300. A, Herakles and
             Apollo. B, Seated woman, departing man. WG: lotus

band. CV pl. 18, 3-4.
-Group X. Oxford 220. Para. 300. A, Ariadne
mounting chariot; B, Dionysos and maenad. WG:
lotus band. CV pl. 24, 4-6.
-Group X. Williams College CG 6. A, Fight; B,
the like. Under handles, sphinx. WG: neck and body.
-Munich 2216. A, Satyrs and maenad. B, Fight.
WG: neck and body.
-Munich 1664. A, Symposium; B, the like. WG: neck
and body.

P. 58.C.   Unattributed add

-London market. A, Maenad; B, the like. WG: body.
Sotheby 14 May 1973, no. 191.
-Munich 9007, fr. Satyr. WG: figure zone.

P. 64.D.15   Read Leipzig T 428. CV pl. 39, 1-2.

P. 64.D.17   Topside lip reserved.

P. 64.D.19   Collar reserved.

P. 64.D.   Add

Painter of Würzburg 351 [Cahn]. Swiss market.
Dionysos and satyr. WG: panel. M.M. A.S.V. (1964),
no. 78.

P. 73.D.68   Sèvres Class; Athena Painter, workshop.

P. 73.D.69   Gela Painter, compared with [Cahn, D.C.Kurtz].

P. 74.D.74   Painter of Vatican G. 49, by or near.

P. 74.D.75   Painter of Vatican G.49, by or near. Bochum
S.494. N. Kunisch, Antiken der Sammlung Funcke
(1972), no. 73.

P. 73.D.   Add

Painter of Vatican G. 49. Louvre F 338. ABV 536,35.
Herakles holding meat on spit at altar. WG: ivy.
Pottier pl. 85.

Unattributed add

-Göttingen [Hartwig] 51, fr. Herakles wrestling.
WG: picture surface.
-Heidelberg S 76, fr. Two warriors. WG: picture sur-
face. CV pl. 147,10.

-Louvre F 373. Quadriga. WG: neck, panel.
-Louvre Cp 10710. Komasts. WG: neck, body.

P. 81.E.   Unattributed add

-Athens 1081 (CC. 790). A, Quadriga racing; B,
the like. WG: side of lip.
-Bonn, Corneto 62 f, fr. Banqueters. WG: rim,
picture surface.

P. 82.F.7   Now augmented by Amsterdam 2162, fr. Bull. Besch.
50 (1975), 164.

P. 84.F.27 Theseus Painter, near. [Eisman]. AJA 77 (1973), 72.

P. 84.F.28 Hanfmann Painter. [Eisman]. AJA 77 (1973), 71.

P. 84.F.29 Psiax, recalling. [Eisman]. AJA 77 (1973), 71.

P. 82.F.   To Psiax, recalling add

-Munich 1984, from Vulci. ABV 295,1 below. Between
eyes, satyr on hands and knees; beyond eyes,
satyrs kneeling with halteres. WG: body.
Archaeology 26,2 (1975), 80.
-Louvre Cp 11054, frr. [Eisman]. (Seated figures
with vines). At handle, large eyes. WG: body.
AJA 77 (1973), 71.

To the Painter of London B 620, related ? add

Basel, Cahn, frr. Part of cock at handle and of one ey
WG: body. Possibly belongs to Heidelberg 263
& Amsterdam 2162.

P. 83.F.   To the Group of Vatican G. 57, of or near, add

-Leningrad b4472. [Frel]. Between eyes, Dionysos
seated. At handle, sphinxes. WG: body. AJA 77
(1973), 72.
-Munich 1990. [Eisman]. Between eyes, Dionysos
on donkey. At handle, Pegasoi. WG: body. AJA 77
(1973), 72.

P. 84.F.   To the Caylus Painter, follower, add

Louvre Cp 163 [Eisman]. Theseus and the Bull
between onlookers. WG: body. AJA 77 (1973), 73.

Unattributed add

-Louvre Cp 12110. Between eyes, hoplite. At handle,

panthers. WG: body.
-Heidelberg S 187, fr. Dionysos reclining. WG: body.
CV pl. 165,2.
-Östermundigen, Blatter, frr. Hen at handle. WG: body.

P. 87.G.   Add

-Swiss market. A, Negro with spears; B, youth.
WG: body. Apollo (May, 1975), advt. [Brought to
the attention of D. von Bothmer by D.C. Kurtz].
-Göttingen H 97, fr. WG: zone of ivy at lip.

P. 88.H.   Add two-handled mastoid

Louvre F 476. A, Men and youth; B, the like. WG:
picture zone.

Add handleless mastoids

-Louvre F 477. Fight. WG: picture zone.
-Dresden AB 185. Herakles and the Lion. WG: picture
zone.
-Dresden AB 280. Dionysos, maenad, satyr, and
centaurs (?). WG: picture zone.

P. 89.I.   To the Pistias Class M add

Louvre F 119. ABV 627, 10. A, Woman and hare;
B, woman dancing. WG: body. Ency. phot. III, 40,a.

P. 90.I.   Unattributed add

Thebes. A, Chariot departing; B, the like. WG:
picture zone.

P. 95.J.   To the Diosphos Painter add

-Athens, from Kolokotroni necropolis. Frieze with
athletes between patternwork. WG: frieze, palmette
and key zones. Delt. 23 (1968), pl. 29.
-Athens from Panepistimiou-Amerikis necropolis.
Circumscribed palmettes. WG: body. Delt. 25 (1970),
pl. 67δ.

P. 96.J.   Unattributed add

-Munich (Antikensammlungen), von Schoen 55. Men
and woman with mirror. WG: body.(Lullies Schoen
no. 55).
-Louvre MNC 477. A, Man and woman at tree; B,
flutist and woman with krotala. WG: net pattern
and picture zone.

-Athens, from Panepistimiou-Amerikis necropolis.
Frieze with combat between patternwork. WG:
whole body ? <u>Delt</u>. 25 (1970), pl. 67γ.

-Baltimore, Walters 48.232. Frieze of palmettes
between patternwork. WG: body.

P. 101.K.   To the Haimon Painter, manner add

-Heidelberg 65/16. Five deer. WG: picture zone on
lid. <u>CV</u> pl. 163,8-9.
-Athens 18703. Hounds pursuing hare. WG: picture
zone on lid.

Unattributed add

-London 1908.7.-20.1. Topside of lid: horsemen;
side of lid: horsemen, satyr, maenad. WG: side of lid.
-Eleusis. Billeting. WG: body.

P. 102.L.   Add

Athens, Agora A-P 3215, fr. Potter's shop. WG:
picture surface.

P. 103.M.   Thanks especially to D. Callipolitis-Feytmans'
<u>Plats</u>, a separate category should be made for the
black-figure plates with white ground.

1. Athens, Akropolis 457, fr. Lotus and guilloche.
WG: framing zone. (P. 300, A I, 9).
2. Copenhagen ABc 1017, bought in Athens. Tongues,
crescents, petal star. WG: petal star. (P. 310,6).
3. Athens, Agora P 26751, fr., from area of Eleusin-
ion. Tongues. WG: framing band. (P. 312,20).
4. Athens, First ephorate reserve, 1959 NAK 1012
& 498. Apollo with instrument between draped
figures. Reverse: gorgoneion. WG: picture surfaces.
(P. 320,31).
5. Athens, NM 18911, from Vari. Rosette and rays.
WG: obverse except rosette. (P. 367, B II, 2).
6. Athens, Akropolis 2442. Athena; exergue with
serpent. WG: picture surface. (P. 377,7).
7. Athens, Akropolis 2435, fr. Dionysos and satyr.
WG: picture surface. (P. 380, B II, 10).
8. Athens, NM, from Vari. Decoration in added red
gone. WG: whole obverse. (P. 382, B II, 37).
9. Brauron 239, fr. Satyr. Exergue formed by band
of oblique zigzags and filled with maeander. WG:
rim. (P. 382, B III, 1).

10. Brussels A 1962, from Attica. Woman at fountain.
WG: whole obverse. (P. 383, B III, 3).
11. Athens, NM, fr. (Woman). Exergue with dolphin.
WG: framing line; band on rim with ivy. (P. 392,
B I 10).
12. Yale 1913.127. Dionysos riding mule. Exergue
formed by key, and containing dog. WG: whole
obverse. (P. 392, B I 11).
13. Athens, Agora P 2766, frr. Herakles and Amazons.
WG: picture surface. (P. 395,1).
14. Athens, Akropolis 2463, fr. Theseus and Skiron.
Exergue with dolphins. WG: picture surface. (P.
396,3).
15. Athens, NM, fr. Archer. Exergue with figured
scene. WG: picture surface. (P. 396,4).
16. Athens, First ephorate reserve, 1960 NAK 192,
fr. Figure mounting chariot. Exergue. WG: picture
surface. (P. 396,5).
17. Athens, Akropolis 2455, frr. Kitharode between
draped figures. Exergue with dolphins. WG: picture
surface. (P. 396,6).
18. Athens, Akropolis 2447, fr..Winged figure with
wreath; framing band with double row of dots.
WG: picture surface and ornament. (P. 396,8).
19. Athens, Akropolis, fr. Man and seated woman.
WG: picture surface. (P. 396, 8 bis).
20. Athens, Agora P 17970, fr. (ostrakon), from
between Areopagos and Hill of Nymphs. Framing band
with double row of dots. WG: ornament. (P. 396,9).
21. Reggio di Calabria 4038, frr., from Lokri. Quadriga
and seated woman. Exergue. WG: rim with ivy. (P.
397,10).
22. Athens, NM, frr. Woman and armed man. WG:
framing band with double net. (P. 397, 10 bis).
23. Athens, NM 11558. Man and woman between seated
onlookers. Exergue formed by billeting and containing quadriga and post. WG: framing zone with
double row of dots, band on rim with ivy. (P. 397,12).
24. Athens, NM AP 322, fr., from the North Slope.
(Man's head). WG: framing band with double row of
dots. (P. 397,16).
25. Athens, NM AP 259, fr., from the North Slope.
Eros bringing hare to charioteer. WG: framing
band with double row of dots. (P. 397,17).
26. Athens, Akropolis 2448, frr. Quadriga before
palm tree and winged figure. WG: picture surface
and framing band with double row of dots. (P. 397,18).
27. Thasos, fr., from the Artemision. Framing zone
with double row of dots. WG: ornament. (P. 399,27).
28. Athens, Akropolis 2429, fr. Exergue formed by
key and containing horseman. WG: picture surface

and framing band with double row of dots. (P. 399,28).

29. Adria A 170, fr., from Adria. Dionysos and figure mounting chariot. WG: picture surface. (P. 399,31).

30. Eleusis 938, frr. Quadriga and kitharode. WG: picture surface and framing band with double row of dots. (P. 399,32).

31. Delphi 8656. Herakles and Apollo disputing tripod. WG: picture surface. (P. 400, 1a).

32. Brauron, fr., from the sanctuary of Artemis. Palmette chain. WG: centre of plate. (P. 400,2).

33. Athens, NM 18999, from Vari. Five swans. WG: whole obverse. (P. 402, B IV, 21).

P. 103.M.6   According to D. von Bothmer, from a dinos or stamnos.

P. 105.N.   Unattributed add

-Athens, Akropolis 2513. Athena. WG: projecting zone with inscription. Graef pl. 103.
-Athens, Akropolis 2581. Athena with snake and owl. WG: obverse. Graef pl. 110.
-Athens, Akropolis 2582. Athena. WG: obverse. Graef pl. 109.
-Athens, Akropolis 2592. Herakles in chariot with Hermes and Athena. WG: obverse. Graef pl. 111.
-Athens, Akropolis 1038. Athena. WG: obverse. Langlotz A. pl. 81.

P. 119.A.1   (Feytmans Plats p. 371,1).

P. 119.A.4   (Feytmans Plats p. 374,27).

P. 119.A.6   (Feytmans Plats p. 374,34).

P. 119.A.7   According to D. von Bothmer, fr. of a stemless cup not a plate.

P. 119.A.10 (Feytmans Plats p. 222).

Unattributed add

-Athens, Agora P 6500, fr. Toes. WG: whole obverse.
-Athens, Akropolis 40 a, frr. Palmettes. WG: ornament. (Feytmans Plats p. 374,26).
-Centre Island, von Bothmer, fr. Seated woman with lyre. WG: picture surface.

P. 122.B.   Unattributed add

Volute krater. Bologna 284, frr. A-B, Perseus and Medusa. WG: picture surface. Pellegrini

<u>Vasi felsinee</u>, fig. 75.

P. 126.C.1 Mug. Palermo inv. 2132. WG: picture surface.

Unattributed add

Swiss private. Horseman. WG: body. For shape and style compare Geneva 20300.

Also the mugs

-Diosphos workshop [E. Simon]. Würzburg H 5356. Death of Aktaion. WG: picture surface. E. Simon, <u>Führer durch die Antikenabteilung des Martin von Wagner Museums der Universität Würzburg</u> (Mainz, 1975), pl. 37.
-Palermo inv. 2139. Youths. WG: picture surface. <u>Du</u> (May, 1976), 33.

P. 129.D.10 Leningrad Б 2214.

P. 129.D.12 Leningrad Б 2633.

P. 130.D.19 On the topside of the mouth ΕΡΜΟΤΙΜΟ5 ΕΡΟΙΕΙ.

P. 130.D.24 WG: picture surface and maeander below.

P. 129.D. To the Group of the Paidikos Alabastra (b) add

-Athens 2207. ARV^2 99,4. Palmettes; on bottom, rf palmette. <u>WG</u>: body. <u>Mon. Piot</u> 26 (1923), 89, figs. 13-15.
-New York 06.1021.92. ARV^2 99,6. Palmettes; on bottom, black palmette. WG: body. Richter, <u>Handbook of the Classical Collection</u> 85,5.

To the Group of the Paidikos Alabastra (c) add

-New York 41.162.81, from near Bologna. ARV^2 101,29. Two naked women. On bottom, in silhouette, satyr dancing. <u>CV Gallatin</u> pl. 27,6 & 8.
-Eleusis, <u>fr.</u>, from Eleusis. ARV^2 101,31. (Maenad, little satyr ?). WG: body. <u>Delt</u>. 9 (1924-5), 6.
-New York 57.12.17. ARV^2 101,32. Two youths and woman. On bottom, in silhouette, komast. WG: body.

Group of the Paidikos Alabastra, remotely related

Berlin inv. 31390, from Athens. ARV^2 101,4. Youths, and boy with cat. On bottom, in silhouette, archer. <u>Vereinigung der Freunde: Bericht 1932-4</u>, 15.

To the Syriskos Painter add

-Athens, Vlasto, from Athens. ARV² 264,58. Woman
with flute and flower at altar. WG: body.
-Brussels R 397. ARV² 264,60. Woman with alabastron.
WG: body. CV Jb pl. 1,4.
-Gerona 5.337, from Ampurias. ARV² 264,62. Woman.
WG: body. G. Trias de Arribas, Ceramicas Griegas
de la Peninsula Iberica (1967), pl. 118,1-2.
-Athens, Akropolis Museum, fr. ARV² 264,64. (Woman).
WG: body. Delt. I, suppl., 49, fig. 15.
-Amsterdam inv. 2193, fr. ARV² 264,65. Archer. WG: body.

To the Group of the Negro Alabastra add

-Athens 13887. ARV² 268,31. Negro in chiton with
kylix. WG: body.
-Cambridge GR 5.1968. Negro with pelta. WG: body.
Archaeological Reports 1970-71, 73, fig. 8.
-Cambridge GR 6.1968. Negro with axe. WG: body.
Archaeological Reports 1970-71, 73, fig. 8.
-Karlsruhe inv. 69/34. Amazon. WG: body. Thimme
figs. 5-6.

P. 130.D. To the Painter of New York 21.131 add

-New York 21.131. ARV² 269,1. Amazon. Youth leaning
on stick. WG: body. Bothmer Am. pl. 73,4.
-Durham (N.C.), Ella Brummer. ARV² 269,3. Amazon.
WG: body. Bothmer Am. pl. 73,5.
-Palermo, from Selinus. ARV² 269,4. Amazon. WG:
body. Mon. Ant. 32 (1927), 330, fig. 140.

To the Group of the Cracow Alabastron add

Louvre C 10712, frr. ARV² 270,2. Amazon. WG: body.

To the Painter of London D 15 add

Athens 18570. ARV² 391,2. Two naked youths and
cock. WG: body. BCH 68 (1962), 431, figs. 13-14.

To the Villa Giulia Painter add

-Tarentum 4536, from Tarentum. ARV² 625,92. Youth
and woman. WG: picture surface, only ?
-Athens, Agora P 5233. ARV² 625,94. A, Woman; B,
woman. WG: picture surface, only ?

Villa Giulia Painter, near

-Athens, Vlasto, fr., from Athens. ARV² 626,4. A,

Woman; B, woman taking wool from basket. WG:
picture surface, only ?
-Tübingen E 50, fr. ARV² 626,5. A, Woman; B,
woman. WG: picture surface. .

Aischines Painter

-Athens. ARV² 717,228. A, Nike to right with sash.
B, Lost. WG: picture surface, only ?

To the Painter of Copenhagen 3830 add

-Cabinet des Médailles 507. ARV² 723,2 below. Youth
leaning on stick; woman. WG: picture surface, only ?
De Ridder 372, fig. 88.
-Once Arlesheim, Schweizer. ARV² 727,3 below. Women.
WG: picture surface, only ?
-Heidelberg. ARV² 724,4. Youth with dog; woman.
WG: body. AA 1916, 185-186.
-Palermo, Banco di Sicilia 796 [J. de la Genière].
Youth and woman. WG: body. CV Mormino pl. 1, 1-4.

P. 131.D.   To the Painter of Taranto 2602 add

Wuppertal, Funcke. [Kunisch]. Man and youth. WG:
body. Kunisch, Funcke, no. 93.

Unattributed add

-Athens, Akropolis 2288, frr. Palmettes. WG: body.
Graef pl. 96.
-Berlin 2257. Woman and seated youth. WG: body.
-Kerameikos. Satyr and maenad. WG: body. AA 1974,2,
193, fig. 23.
-The Hague, Schneider-Herrmann inv. 88. A, Nude
warrior in back view; B, nude man in back view.
WG: body. Bull. Besch. Suppl. 1 (1975), pl. 43, 105.
-Athens, from the Veikou-Aglaurou necropolis. A,
Woman. B, Unknown. WG: picture surface and orna-
ment below. BCH 96 (1972), 607, fig. 37.
-Athens, NM 480. Woman fluting and man. WG: body.
-Athens, Kanellopoulos. Woman and youth. WG: picture
surface, only ?
-Delphi 8713. A, Woman with kalathos; B, the like.
WG: picture surface.
-Louvre CA 2979. Two satyrs (very heavily repainted).
WG: body.

P. 138.E.20 Meidias Painter.

Unattributed add

-Berlin 3396. Women and man. WG: picture surface, rays.
-Athens, Akropolis 571, fr. Figure striding to right.
WG: picture surface. Langlotz A̲. pl. 42.

P. 142.F.3   Kerameikos inv. 1961.

Unattributed add

-Athens, Agora P 25017, fr. Horse. WG: picture
surface.
-Athens, Kerameikos. Youth. WG: picture surface.
(A̲A̲ 1940, 328-329).

P. 148.I.7   Geneva 20333

Add the oinochoai

-Sabouroff Class. Berlin 4032, from Greece. ARV^2
1545, 28. WG: stephane. JHS 49 (1929), 66, f̲ig. 17.
-Chairete Class. Oxford 1946.85. ARV^2 1546, 3 top.
WG: stephane. JHS 49 (1929), 69, f̲ig. 20.
-Basel Class. Berlin 2201. ARV^2 1549, 26. WG:
stephane. J̲H̲S̲ 49 (1929), 72, fig. 24.

From a plastic vase, though not definitely a head
vase, unattributed,

Louvre G 249, frr. A, Dionysos, satyr, and maenad.
B, Youth and a woman. WG: picture surface. E̲n̲c̲y̲.
T̲E̲L̲ III, 41 D.

P. 155.A.3   With new foot, Metropolitan Museum Journal [here-
after M̲M̲J̲] 9 (1974), 94, figs. 6-7.

P. 156.A.8   Now Stockholm, Medelhavsmuseet 1960:12.

P. 156.A.11   Now recovered.

P. 156.A.14   M̲M̲A̲ 9 (1974), 93, figs. 3-4.

P. 157.A.16   WG: exterior picture surface.

Unattributed add

-Segment Class. Basel, Cahn, frr. I, Satyr and
another. A, Herakles and Cerberus. WG: exterior
picture surface. M̲M̲J̲ 9 (1974), 96, figs. 10-11.
-Baltimore, Walters 48.34. I, Gorgoneion. A, Between
eyes, satyr and maenad; B, the like; beyond eyes,

satyr. WG: exterior picture surface.

P. 162.B.1   HSCP 76 (1972), 271 ff.

P. 164.B.   To the Painter of the Paris Gigantomachy add

Cabinet des Médailles 807. ARV² 422, 106. I,
(WG, black border). A, Back of youth's head.
According to D. von Bothmer, may belong to Cab.
Méd. 608.

P. 171.B.33   MMJ 9 (1974), 104, figs. 24-25.

P. 171.B.   Add

Villa Giulia Painter. [Vickers]. Oxford 1973.1. I,
Woman offering between two altars. A-B, Komasts.
WG: interior. JHS 94 (1974), pls. 17-18.

P. 181.B.63   RA 1972,2, 232 ff.

P. 183.B.85   From a covered cup, if at all.

Unattributed add

-Athens, Agora P 22326, fr. I, Snake and mound (?).
A, Black-figure palmette. WG: interior picture
surface.
-Athens, Agora. Woman at altar. WG: interior.
-Barcelona 488, fr. I, Man and figure in chiton.
A, Palmette and volute. CV pl. 17,1.
-Istanbul A6-3440, fr. I, Legs of man and horse.
A, Woman reclining, with phiale. WG: interior
and exterior picture surfaces. H. Metzger, Fouilles
de Xanthos IV (Paris, 1972), pl. 81, 361.
-Berlin 481x, fr., from Samos. I, Woman. A, Woman
striding to right. WG: interior picture surface.
AA 1964, 605-606, fig. 53, & 611.
-London 88.6-1.758, fr. I, Glaze. A, Head to left.
WG: exterior picture surface.
-Louvre SB 6786, fr., from Susa. I, (WG, black border).
A, palm tree
-Louvre SB 4778, fr., from Susa. I, (WG, black border).
A, Helmet bracket, and part of handle ornament ?
-Louvre SB (number unclear), fr., from Susa. I,
(WG, black border). A, Woman with arm raised.
-Würzburg H 5237, fr., I, (WG, black border).

P. 195.V.   note 1: now published, D.C. Kurtz, Athenian White
Lekythoi (Oxford, 1975).

P. 206.V.   For a third white lekythos by Douris see J.
Dörig, Art Antique: Collections Privées de
Suisse Romande (Genève, 1975), no. 205.

P. 219.V.   note 1: B. Cohen, "Observations on Coral Red,"
Marsyas 15 (1970-71), 1 ff.

TABLE OF CONTENTS

ACKNOWLEDGEMENTS

The preparation of this thesis has not only taught me much, but it has also brought me great pleasure. Both benefits result to a considerable degree from the facilities which I was able to use, those of the Fogg Museum, Harvard University, and of the Metropolitan Museum of Art, New York. Moreover, at each institution I worked with a teacher of exceptional generosity. I am deeply grateful to Professor G.M.A. Hanfmann for his personal interest and encouragement, for his willingness to read the dissertation while on sabbatical, and for his criticism which always falls lightly but very surely.

Professor D. von Bothmer kept a benevolent watch over the writing of the thesis and gave unstinting assistance at every stage. He allowed me to draw on his books, his notes, his photo archive, and most of all, on his unrivalled knowledge of Greek vases. He brought to my attention a great many of the principal white-ground pieces which are either unpublished or whose publications were unknown to me. As he promised, Dr. von Bothmer also vetted the text, and it owes much to his comments and suggestions.

This is a fitting place to thank the successive Chairmen of the Fine Arts Department, Professor S. Slive and Professor J. Rosenfield, as well as their assistant, Mrs. M. Sevčenko, for help in many forms over quite a few years.

I owe special thanks to Dr. Jiří Frel, whose comments

to the thesis I particularly appreciate, as well as to Professor D.G. Mitten from whom I first learned about vases and who has willingly and helpfully read my papers ever since.

Señora M. Braña, Mrs. K. Biosse Duplan, Mr. H. Giroux, Professor Lilly Kahil, and particularly Professors E.T. and C.C. Vermeule have very kindly made material and information available to me. Dr. Herbert Cahn brought several vases to my attention and provided me with photographs. In procuring photographs, I acknowledge the help of Mr. Brian Cook, Mr. J. Eisenberg, Dr. M. Schmidt, and Dr. N. Yalouris.

Miss D. Buitron helped me in many ways at the Fogg. Mrs. C.S. Springer has had at once the least and the most gratifying of tasks. With good-humored patience and skill, she has typed a much-corrected draft of the text into a thesis.

In conclusion, I gratefully thank the person through whom antiquity first became a reality and a friend whose unceasing interest and encouragement are but a very small part of my debt.

A NOTE ON PROCEDURE

This thesis depends heavily on the method of J.D.
Beazley not only in the discussion but also in the catalogue
portions of the text. While it follows the "Instructions
for Use" printed in Attic Red-figure Vase-painters (second
edition), a few specific points of procedure should be stated
here.

"Red-figure," "black-figure," and "white-ground" are
written out in the text but abbreviated in the catalogue.

The catalogue is adapted from the form introduced by
Beazley, but it contains only basic, essential information
for each object. Entries generally begin with the attribution
to a painter, to a stylistic group, or to a class of shapes;
in some cases, a vase is simply related to another, e.g.
"Kevorkian oinochoe, compared with." Next comes the present
whereabouts of the piece, according to city or major museum
(e.g. London, Louvre, Vatican, etc.); the accession, inventory,
or catalogue number follows. A vase in a private collection
typically appears as "Greenwich, Bareiss 23." The succeeding
reference to the relevant standard work of Beazley's or to
C.H.E. Haspels' monograph on Attic black-figure lekythoi is
to facilitate further investigation. After identification
of the subject matter, the entry defines the areas of the
vase with white slip. These indications must often be
considered tentative, for many published descriptions are
incomplete. At the end come significant inscriptions and

reference to a good and, where possible accessible, illustration. Where neither an illustration nor a readily available description exists (e.g. in the standard museum catalogues like those of Furtwängler or Pottier), an informative source of a different kind is cited; such works appear in parentheses.

Vases illustrated in the thesis have an asterisk preceding the entry and a plate reference enclosed by brackets at the end. In the plate section, every figure is identified by museum number. The bracket immediately following provides a cross-reference to the catalogue; it identifies the chapter (Roman numeral), the shape sub-section (capital letter), the list number, and the page on which the entry appears. Thus, II.A.9 p.49 refers to chapter II, section A on hydriai, number 9 which occurs on page 49. The list of illustrations identifies the source from which each photograph was taken.

In the catalogue, footnotes, and bibliography, "p." is omitted for page references, with only two exceptions. The abbreviation appears where necessary for clarity and wherever cross-references are made within the thesis.

The bibliography presents a list of important works consulted. It also serves as a list of abbreviations for periodicals and serials appearing throughout the thesis and for publications cited in the list of illustrations and in the catalogue. The bibliography comprises two parts. The first gives the list and abbreviations of journals, serials, and the standard books of Beazley and Miss Haspels. Although

a number of abbreviations follow the form given in <u>AJA</u>
74 (1970), they have been repeated here so that the bibliography contains all publications referred to in the catalogue.
The second part takes in all other works. The footnotes
follow standard procedure in having a first full bibliograph-
ical citation and subsequent references shortened to the
author's name.

LIST OF ILLUSTRATIONS

IX,3.   Berlin 1969.3. Sotheby 17-18 October 1949, pl. 6.

IX,4.   Villa Giulia. Stud. Etr. I (1927), pl. 32,b,1.

X,1.   Brussels, Bibliothèque Royale 6. Feytmans pl. 15.

X,2.   Basle market (M.M.). M.M. 22 (1961), no. 150.

X,3.   Harvard 1927.154. CV Fogg pl. 21,7.

X,4.   Osnabrück. M.M. 22 (1961), no. 151.

XI,1.   Karlsruhe B 32. Jacobsthal O. pl. 50,a.

XI,2.   Once Swiss market. Photo Dieter Widmer.

XII,1.   Leningrad, ex Botkin. Trésors d'Art en
         Russie (1902), 50.

XII,2.   Munich 1986. Frel Sborník pl. 1,2.

XII,3.   Munich 2003. Museum photo.

XIII,1. Frankfurt VF β 316. CV pl. 51,5-6.

XIII,2. London B 681. AM 77 (1962), pl. 29,3.

XIII,3. Copenhagen, Ny Carlsberg inv. 2759. Bruhn,
         From the Colls. 2, 125, fig. 10.

XIII,4. Once Geneva market. Photo Boissonas.

XIV,1.   Once Barcelona, Montaner. Garcia y Bellido
         Hallazgos pl. 83,3.

XIV,2.   Gerona 9. Garcia y Bellido Hallazgos pl. 84,2.

XIV,3.   Havana, Lagunillas. Photo supplied by the owner.

XIV,4.   Gerona 806. Garcia y Bellido H.G. pl. 89,82.

XIV,5.   London B 669. Museum photo.

XV,1.   Maplewood, Noble. Photo W. Pons.

XV,2.   Louvre. Photo D. von Bothmer.

XV,3.   London B 678. Museum photo.

XV,4.   Athens, North Slope A-P 2073 a-c and 1774 d.
         Hesp. 9 (1940), 235, fig. 46.

XVI,1.	Adria Bc. 64.10. Hoppin Rf I, 438.
XVI,2.	Athens, Akropolis 427. Langlotz A. pl. 32.
XVI,3.	New York 91.1.462. Museum photos.
XVII.	Cincinnati, Art Museum 1962.388. Metropolitan Museum of Art and Cincinnati Art Museum photos.
XVIII,1.	London D 13. Bieber Entw. pl. I,2.
XVIII,2.	London D 14. Museum photo.
XVIII,3.	London B 668. EAA V, 983, fig. 1198.
XVIII,4.	Louvre CA 1920. Mon. Piot 26 (1923), 87, fig. 10.
XIX,1-2.	Berlin inv. 3382. Thimme figs. 1 and 2.
XIX,3.	Louvre CA 2515. Photo Chuzeville.
XX,1.	Boston 98.887. Caskey-Beazley I, pl. 15,37.
XX,2.	Berlin 2261. CV pl. 136,1-2.
XX,3.	Dresden ZV. 54. Dresdener Kunstblätter 14, VI (1970), cover.
XXI,1.	New York 28.167. Richter and Hall pl. 76.
XXI,2.	Louvre CA 4194. M.M. 26 (1963), no. 153.
XXI,3.	Taranto 4553. Die Antike 1 (1925), 282, fig. 4.
XXI,4.	Boston 65.908. BMFA 67 (1969), 88, fig. 19.
XXII,1.	London D 8. Jacobsthal Pins fig. 203.
XXII,2.	Louvre SB 4138, SB 4151. Photo D. von Bothmer.
XXIII,1-2.	Boston 98.928. JHS 49 (1929), pl. V,2 and p. 48, fig. 4.
XXIII,3.	Tarquinia 6845. CV pl. 42,1.
XXIII,4.	Leningrad. Photo D. von Bothmer.
XXIV,1-2.	New York, Jan Mitchell. Photo D. von Bothmer.
XXIV,3.	Stockholm, Medelhavsmuseet 1960:12. A.A. II (1960), no. 143.
XXV,1-2.	London B 679. Museum photos.

XXV,3-4.	Athens 408. Collignon-Couve pl. 36.
XXVI,1.	Greenwich, Bareiss. Photo J.M.
XXVI,2-3.	Gotha 48. CV pl. 42, 1 and 2.
XXVII,1.	Florence PD 265. CV pl. 92,1.
XXVII,2.	Athens, Akropolis 434. Langlotz A. pl. 35.
XXVII,3.	Athens, Akropolis 432. Langlotz A. pl. 33.
XXVIII,1.	Berlin inv. 3240. CV pl. 108,4.
XXVIII,2.	Ruvo, Jatta 1539. Photo R.I.
XXVIII,3.	Cabinet des Médailles 608. Museum photo (detail).
XXIX,1.	Louvre G 276. Photo D. von Bothmer.
XXIX,2-3.	London D 1. Museum photo.
XXX,1.	Boston 00.356. Caskey-Beazley I, pl. 15,36.
XXX,2.	London D 6. Murray W.A.V. pl. 17.
XXX,3.	Brussels A 891. CV pl. 1,2.
XXXI,1.	Brauron. A.K. Beiheft I pl. 9.
XXXI,2.	Florence 75409. Hirmer Photo Archive, Munich.
XXXII,1-2.	Athens, Akropolis 439. Langlotz pl. 36; JHS 9 (1888), pl. 6.
XXXII,3.	London D 4. Photo Mansell.
XXXIII,1.	Athens, Akropolis 589. Langlotz A. pl. 45.
XXXIII,2.	Louvre G 109. Archives photographiques.
XXXIII,3.	Athens. Waldstein II pl. 68.
XXXIV,1.	Athens, Agora P 43. Hesp. 2 (1933), 225, fig. 5.
XXXIV,2.	Athens 2187. AM 6 (1881), pl. 4.
XXXV,1.	Palermo. ABL pl. 23,3.
XXXV,2.	Athens 1130. ABL pl. 29,3.
XXXVI,1.	New York 41.162.29. CV Gallatin pl. 44, 1 a-c.

XXXVI,2.	New York 66.11.4. Photo J. M.
XXXVI,3.	New York 06.1070. Richter ARVS fig. 71.
XXXVII,1.	Germany, private. Blümel no. 9.
XXXVII,2.	Princeton. Museum photo.
XXXVII,3.	New York 08.258.28. BMMA 4 (1909), 102, fig. 9.
XXXVIII,1.	Göttingen 21. Jacobsthal Gött. pl. 6,20.
XXXVIII,2.	Vienna 3644. ABL pl. 48,4,a.
XXXIX,1.	Athens, Agora A-P 422. Hesp. 4 (1935), 291, fig. 39
XXXIX,2.	Gela. Benndorf pl. 46,1.
XXXIX,3.	Palermo. Marconi pl. 57, 1-2.
XL,1.	Leningrad inv. 2363. Museum photo.
XL,2.	Berlin inv. 3262. Museum photo.
XL,3.	Basle, Antikenmuseum. Photo F. Bürki.
XL,4.	Munich 2797. Museum photo.
XLI,1.	Brussels A 1021. CV pl. 5,1.
XLI,2.	New York 31.11.13. BMMA 27 (1932), 105, figs. 1-3.
XLI,3.	Leningrad TG 19. Photo D. von Bothmer.

INTRODUCTION

The period around 530 B.C. marks a watershed in the
history of Attic vase-painting. It was a time of intense
experimentation, directed especially towards devising ways
of painting that would improve upon black-figure. The
innovation of greatest consequence proved to be red-figure,
but several other processes also emerged. The most important
were "Six's technique," decoration with opaque colors upon
a black glaze background;[1] "coral red" glaze, an alternative
to the usual black or to simple reserve;[2] and "white-ground,"
the use of a prepared white slip as a surface for figure-work
and ornament. Of these three subsidiary techniques, white-
ground seems to have been the most widely used; at least it
survives in the greatest quantity and on the widest variety
of shapes. It has, however, never been studied in detail,
and this is the objective of the present thesis. By way of
introduction, we shall define our subject and the scope
of our investigation, and briefly review the basic literature.

As indicated above, white-ground is a technical procedure.
It makes use of pure, "primary" clay which differs from
secondary clay in two major respects; it is virtually free
of minerals like iron and of other impurities and it remains
white after firing.[3] One source in Attica was situated near
Cape Kolias.[4] The special clay was prepared in the same way
as glaze[5] and applied with a brush to the surface of the vase.
It covers the whole surface or only a limited section. Drawn
in glaze upon this ground, the decoration gradually changed

in execution. At first, it followed the standard black-
figure conventions complete with incision and added red and
white. After the introduction of red-figure, black-figure
painters often adopted a technique combining figures or
details in black with others in outline.[6] Red-figure painters
working on white-ground drew in outline, using added color
sparingly at first, but then increasingly liberally.[7] These
colors also become increasingly varied in hue, matte in
texture, and impermanent in quality. The ground and the glaze
underwent comparable changes. The former evolves from dense
and greyish-orange in color towards flaky and white, owing
probably to better purification of the clay before use. The
glaze which begins as lustrous, and translucent when diluted,
gives way to a dull black paint. If applied before firing,
the latter often contains manganese;[8] if applied after firing,
the black is made of charcoal mixed with a medium like egg.
However much they determined the appearance of a white-ground
vase, these modifications did not affect the firing itself
which followed the standard oxidation-reduction-reoxidation
cycle.[9] In effect, then, the technical aspects of white-
ground differed little, in the beginning at least, from those
of added white in black-figure. As an innovation, white-ground
represents a new application of methods current c. 530 rather
than the actual invention of a technique, as with coral red,
for example.

The use of white slip occurs in various centres of Greek

ceramic production. An investigation restricted to the late
archaic and classic Attic examples might therefore call for
special justification. As we hope to show, Attic white-ground
forms a self-contained body of material with a discernible
history extending from c. 530 to the early fourth century.
While it can be isolated for analysis, this material is also
an integral part of the larger black-figure and red-figure
developments, the most intensively studied and best understood pottery sequences in Greece. White-ground constitutes
a sideline in the oeuvres of potters and painters whose
artistic personalities Sir John Beazley has done so much to
define. The incidence of white-ground in non-Attic fabrics
is a problem that leads far beyond the pale of our subject,
but use of this technique was fairly widespread and in some
regions it took firm root. An enumeration of the major centres
at which it occurs may be of interest.

From the evidence in Coldstream's <u>Greek Geometric Pottery</u>,[10]
a prepared cream-colored slip first appears on Middle Geometric
fabrics from Naxos[11] but becomes widespread only during the
Late Geometric period. One concentration of material comes
from the larger Cycladic area: Naxos, Thera, and Euboea,[12]
another comes from the eastern Aegean: Chios and Samos.[13]
On the Greek mainland, Boeotia[14] and especially Lakonia[15]
adopted the light slip, while the three major Geometric
centres, Attica, Corinth, Argos rejected it.[16]

During the succeeding period when Orientalizing and black-
figure were the dominant styles, the use of a prepared ground

became still more prevalent, and for practical reasons.
Since few Greek clays were so fine as the Attic in quality
or so carefully purified, a slip provided the smooth, dense
surface necessary for painted decoration. Furthermore, since
the prevalent decorative idiom was dark-on-light, a buff or
almost white slip enhanced the contrast with brownish-black
figure-work and ornament. In Attica, where their raison d'être
was primarily esthetic, light slips occur in Protoattic[17]
before white-ground came into its own during the first red-
figure generation. Corinthian potters avoided the technique,
but it makes a significant appearance on the painted wooden
plaques found at Pitsà.[18] In Boeotia,[19] Euboea,[20] and
Lakonia,[21] the Late Geometric tradition continues; indeed,
it acquires a certain artistic distinction with the cups of
Lakonian III and IV.

However commonly they may occur on the mainland, archaic
white-slipped fabrics seem to have originated in the island
workshops of the Aegean, ranging from Thasos[22] to Crete[23]
and Rhodes.[24] The attribution of certain Cycladic styles to
specific ateliers remains problematical,[25] nor has the Chian-
Naukratite dilemma been fully resolved.[26] Nonetheless, the
material evidence for island slipped wares is abundant,
and significant inasmuch as it introduces the possibility
of chronological priority over Protoattic.[27] This entrenched
light-slip tradition extends to Ionia where it emerged with
the early Wild Goat style and continued through the succeeding
archaic production.[28]

Even as summary a survey as this one will indicate the
relative frequency of a light ground in Orientalizing and
black-figure vase-painting. The situation changes during
the fifth and earlier fourth centuries when Attic white-
ground is the only noteworthy fabric of its kind. By Hellenistic times, the ceramic hegemony of Athens was over, although
the use of white-ground continued, e.g. for Panathenaics.[29]
Several of the regional schools which emerged developed white-
ground styles of their own.[30]   Apart from the lagynoi,[31]
the main groups are Hadra ware from the Egyptian Delta,[32]
Canosa ware from Apulia,[33]   and Centuripe ware from Sicily;[34]
as Dr. von Bothmer points out, however, the latter three
fabrics have a ground applied to the fired vase and made
with lime not clay.[35]   The foregoing overview was not intended
as a comprehensive analysis but as a reminder that the larger
setting for Attic white-ground comprises not only the Attic
tradition but also a variety of other local Greek fabrics.
Henceforth, however, our focus shall remain within the limits
of our subject.

Of these limits, one of the most important is that of
shape. The existing literature on Attic white-ground deals
almost exclusively with cups and lekythoi. The former attract
attention for their high quality, the latter exist in great
quantity and illustrate interesting subjects. Apart from an
occasional publication, other shapes have been neglected.[36]
Their fate is undeserved, for much of this material is

artistically fine and all of it is necessary for a proper
understanding of the white-ground technique. The present
thesis, therefore, deals with the less studied shapes and
with cups, for which new examples and conclusions can be
presented. For our own preparation, we have considered the
lekythoi in ABL, ABV, ARV[2], and Paralipomena; however, in
view of the latter catalogues and the many works describing
and interpreting lekythoi, we refer only to specific vases
where relevant and, in the last chapter, we emphasize the
lekythoi of artists who specialized in other shapes. The
catalogue accompanying our text comprises 522 items from a
total of about 1450;[37] many groups of vases occur in their
entirety, others only in representative selections.[38] Our
hope is to highlight the material hitherto ignored and to
convey an integrated picture of Attic white-ground with the
relative importance and frequency of its shapes and styles.

The first and primary task of this thesis is to present
the evidence. In so doing, however, we may also throw some
light on several special problems. For example, with white-
ground one can study the spread of an artistic innovation
as well as the tenacity of certain conventions. The technique
seems to have been rejected for some shapes, used sporadically
for others, while for lekythoi, it almost becomes identified
with the shape and its function.[39] A related question is
important for understanding workshop procedure in the Kerameikos. The production of a Greek vase required a potter and

a painter, and to each shape belonged a set scheme of subsidiary ornament. Did potter or painter lay out the decoration of a vase? Who allocated the areas of reserved ground,
black glaze, white slip? Our subject provides relevant
evidence because slips were the potter's concern and because
the implication of the preserved artist signatures is fairly
consistent.

Arising logically again from the preceding question is
that of the function of white-ground with respect to black-
figure and red-figure decoration. With black-figure, it
intensifies the existing contrast between dark painting and
lighter background. To red-figure, however, it added the
possibility of drawing in outline while preserving a light
ground; outline thus becomes a factor in the (re)introduction
and acceptance of white-ground. A final problem which bears
mentioning but will not be fully explored concerns the relation of white-ground to coral red and Six's technique.
While all three are associated with specific artists and
shapes, some artists produced several different combinations
of shape and technique. Moreover, each technique illustrates
in a different manner and degree the extent to which such
innovations continued to depend on the prevailing black-figure
or red-figure style. These, then, are a number of points
directly suggested by our material and contributing to an
understanding of it. While many other questions naturally
arise from them, they may indicate the main lines of our
investigation.

A study such as this one owes much to the earlier
literature. Without compiling a history of white-ground
scholarship, we should review the main works, which fall into
three categories. The first, and unquestionably the most
important, consists of Sir John Beazley's Attic Black-figure
Vase-painters (1956), Attic Red-figure Vase-painters first
(1942) and second (1963) editions, and Paralipomena (1971).
From Beazley's lists one derives the essential raw material:
a collection of vases, attributions to painters and potters,
and such additional information as important inscriptions
and proveniences, if known. Here also one finds the wherewithal
to reconstruct the larger ceramic setting.

The second category contains special studies, mostly of
lekythoi since they have attracted the most attention. Among
the early collections of material, Murray's White Athenian
Vases in the British Museum (1896) includes several important
pieces otherwise unillustrated[40] while Fairbanks' White
Athenian Lekythoi (1907,1914) and Riezler's Weissgrundige
attische Lekythen (1914) are worth consulting for parts of
the text as well as for illustrations. Two major publications
appeared in 1936. Written under Beazley's aegis, Miss Haspels'
Attic Black-Figured Lekythoi classifies these rather thankless
objects by painter, gives a sense of the development in shape
and decoration, and adds useful indications for iconography
when obscure. Les Coupes à Fond Blanc by Philippart is far
more limited in scope, but it collects, describes, and gives
bibliography for sixty-eight entire and fragmentary white-

ground cups; Beazley's review in Gnomon (June, 1937) contains
valuable corrections and addenda. Delivered in 1937 and
published in 1938, Beazley's Charlton lecture entitled Attic
White Lekythoi may well be the most recent essential work
that focuses on white-ground. This brief and lucid essay
concentrates on the purpose, shape, and style of the lekythoi,
but it also includes important observations concerning technique, the rise of white-ground, and its occurence on other
shapes.

The third category of publications comprises site reports
which include significant examples of white-ground; since
they generally contain many photographs, such reports are
frequently more useful than museum catalogues. For material
discovered in Greece, the two major sources are Graef-Langlotz,
Die antiken Vasen von der Akropolis zu Athen (1925-1933) and
the Hesperia articles concerning finds from the Agora itself,[41]
from the North Slope,[42] and from the Lenormant Street burials.[43]
Useful also are Lilly Ghali-Kahil's presentation of vases
from Brauron[44] as well as the Couve-Collignon and Nicole
catalogues out of which one may cull the pieces from Eretria.[45]
For excavated sites in Italy, the Monumenti Antichi publications of Megara Hyblaea (1892), Gela (1906), Cumae (1913),
and Selinus (1927) make available a considerable amount of
material. Zannoni[46] and Pellegrini[47] do the same for Bologna.
Finally, in his account of Greek pottery from Emporion,
Frickenhaus presents examples of white-ground that are un-

distinguished but noteworthy as exports to Spain.[48] The
literature consulted for this thesis is obviously more
extensive; however, the publications cited here have provided most of the entries in our catalogue and basic principles of classification and interpretation.

In this introduction, we have sought to delimit the
scope of our inquiry and to discuss briefly three major
aspects of our subject, i.e. the technique, the geographical limitation, and the range of shapes. The sections that
follow will comprise lists of vases integrated with the
text relevant to them. After the first chapter on the
establishment of Attic white-ground, we shall discuss the
black-figure and red-figure material proceeding in each
case by shape, but excluding cups and lekythoi. The latter
categories will be treated separately because they raise
special problems and because a juxtaposition of the two
produces significant conclusions concerning the artistic
quality, the uses, and the volume of Attic white-ground
ware.

INTRODUCTION: Footnotes

1   E.g. C.H.E. Haspels, "A Lekythos in Six's Technique," Muse 3 (1969), 24 ff; cf. J.V. Noble, The Techniques of Painted Attic Pottery (New York, 1956), 66.

2   E.g. A. Winter, "Beabsichtigtes Rot," AM 83 (1968), 315 ff; includes earlier bibliography. Cf. also Noble 64.

3   Noble 1.

4   Athenaios XI, 482b; also Suidas Κωλιάδος κεραμῆες ; Geoponica VI,3,1 enumerates various clays by color.

5   Noble 62, 36-37.

6   Miss Haspels (ABL 110) called the technique "semi-outline," a term which we have not adopted for two reasons. "Semi-outline" literally means "half outline" which may be misleading. Furthermore, it fails to indicate the technique--standard black-figure, black-figure with incision, or silhouette--used in conjunction with outline.

7   The use of a second white on white-ground is generally associated with outline lekythoi of the fifth century. However, the practice begins before the end of the sixth century, e.g. on the plaques of Paseas (see p.107).

8   P.J. Riis, Review of An Inquiry into the Forgery of the Etruscan Terracotta Warriors in the Metropolitan Museum of Art by D. von Bothmer and J.V. Noble (New York, 1961) in Gnomon 35 (1963), 712-713. I owe this information to Dr. von Bothmer.

9   Noble 77-78.

10   (London, 1968).

11   Coldstream 168. An important example is N.Y. 74.51.965.

12   Coldstream 172, 186, 190.

13   Coldstream 289, 294.

14   Coldstream 196.

15   Coldstream 215.

16   Professor Hanfmann brought to my attention the various types of light-slipped ware produced in Anatolia from the Early Iron Age on and well documented at Tarsus. Cf.

G.M.A. Hanfmann, "The Iron Age Pottery of Tarsus,"
Tarsus III (Princeton, 1963), especially 32 ff.

17   E.g. D. Burr, "A Geometric House and a Proto-Attic
Votive Deposit," Hesp. 2 (1933), 628; J.M. Cook, "Pro-
toattic Pottery," BSA 35 (1935), 195; J. Boardman,
"Painted Votive Plaques and an Early Inscription from
Aegina," BSA 49 (1954), passim; E. Brann, "Protoattic
Well Groups from the Athenian Agora," Hesp. 30 (1961),
314 -- note the phrase "characteristic white slip."

18   First published by A.K. Orlandos, "Pitsà," EAA VI, 200 ff.
Here the main plaque is dated 540-530, the other three
to the last quarter and very end of the sixth century.

19   E.g. P.N. Ure, Sixth and Fifth Century Pottery from
Rhitsona (Oxford, 1927).

20   E.g. J. Boardman, "Pottery from Eretria," BSA 47 (1952),1ff.

21   E:g. E.A. Lane, "Lakonian Vase-Painting," BSA 34 (1934),
99 ff; cf. also J. Boardman, "Artemis Orthia and Chronology," BSA 58 (1963), 1 ff. For two exceptional column-
kraters with white-ground: Antike Kunst aus wuppertaler
Privatbesitz (Wuppertal, 1971), no. 35; Louvre E 682.

22   E.g. L. Ghali-Kahil, La céramique grecque (Paris, 1960),
52,142.

23   E.g. H.G.G. Payne, "Early Greek Vases from Knossos,"
BSA 29 (1929), 280-281; J.K. Brock, Fortetsa (Cambridge,
1957), 143-144.

24   E.g. W. Schiering, Werkstätten orientalisierender Keramik
auf Rhodos (Berlin, 1957), 8, 10, 12, 13.

25   E.g. H.G.G. Payne, "Cycladic Vase-Painting of the Seventh
Century," JHS 46 (1926), 203 ff; R.M. Cook, Greek Painted
Pottery (London, 1960), 104-116; I. Ström, "Some Groups
of Cycladic Vase-Painting from the Seventh Century B.C.,"
Acta Archaeologica 33 (1962), 221 ff.

26   J. Boardman, "Chian and Naucratite," BSA 51 (1956), 55 ff;
J. Boardman, Excavations in Chios 1952-1955 (London, 1967),
157.

27   For the possibility of Cycladic influence on Protoattic,
cf. Brann 311 and references. Such problems as Attic-
Cycladic interconnections or the Cyclades as a centre
of artistic innovation have no place in this thesis.
However, the importance of these islands is gradually
being elucidated (for example, E. Homann-Wedeking,

Anfänge der griechischen Grossplastik (Berlin, 1950),
J. Boardman, Island Gems (London, 1963); the practice
of white slipping may be a further late geometric innovation that either began or developed in Cycladic workshops.

28 R.M. Cook Greek Pottery 118-126; R.M. Cook, CVA: B.M.
8 (G.B. 13), 1954. For the Lydian styles cf. C.H. Greene-
walt, Jr., "Orientalizing Pottery from Sardis," Cali-
fornia Studies in Classical Antiquity 3 (1970), 55 ff.

29 G.R. Edwards, "Panathenaics of Hellenistic and Roman
Times," Hesp. 26 (1957), 327-328, 345-347; H. Thompson,
"Activities in the Athenian Agora: 1959," Hesp. 29 (1960),
366. Dr. Jiri Frel kindly brought this material, and
these publications, to my attention.

30 Summarized Cook Greek Pottery 203.

31 E.g. G. Leroux, Lagynos (Paris, 1913); J. Schäfer, Per-
gamenische Forschungen II (Berlin, 1968), 101 ff.

32 E.g. B.F. Cook, Inscribed Hadra Vases (New York, 1966).

33 E.g. M. Jatta, "Tombe canosine del Museo Provinciale
di Bari," RM 29 (1914), 99 ff.

34 E.g. G. Libertini, Centuripe (Catania, 1926); G. Libertini, "Nuove ceramiche dipinte de Centuripe," Atti e
Memorie della Soc. Magna Grecia (1932), 187 ff.

35 B.F. Cook Hadra 11; Jatta 119-120; G.M.A. Richter,
"Polychrome Vases from Centuripe in the Metropolitan
Museum," Metropolitan Museum Studies 2 (1929-1930), 192.

36 H. Philippart drew attention to this situation in 1936
("Coupes Attiques à Fond Blanc," Ant. Class. 5 (1936)
6-7, n. 2). His plans for a broader study of white-ground
never materialized, nor has anyone else undertaken the
project during the past thirty-five years.

37 This figure represents a rough total of black-figure
white-ground vases (lekythoi and other shapes) and outline vases of other shapes. It does not include any
white outline lekythoi.

38 We present only part of a body of material when it comprises
a large number of mediocre or poor objects that are re-
dundant and when a full list occurs in one of Beazley's
reference works. In such cases, our catalogue represents
the various classes, groups or painters and includes a
sufficient number of examples to show the range of subjects
as well as the character of the ornament and figure style.

Our text always indicates where a selection has been
made and how many items each group actually contains.

39   With white lekythoi, one approaches the question of
"modes," styles which in themselves carry meaning, independently of the forms and subjects they depict.
A clear example in Greek vase-painting is the use of
black-figure on Panathenaic amphorae long after the
technique had gone out of use.

40   Some of the illustrations, however, are retouched, a
shortcoming that is worth noting and that does not
occur in Riezler.

41   L. Talcott, "Vases and Kalos-Names from an Agora Well,"
Hesp. 5 (1936), 333 ff.

42   M.Z. Pease, "The Pottery from the North Slope of the
Akropolis," Hesp. 4 (1935), 214 ff; C. Roebuck, "Pottery
from the North Slope of the Akropolis, 1937-1938,"
Hesp. 9 (1940), 141 ff.

43   C.G. Boulter, "Graves in Lenormant Street, Athens,"
Hesp. 32 (1963), 113 ff.

44   L. Ghali-Kahil, "Quelques vases du sanctuaire d'Artémis
à Brauron," A.K. Beiheft I (1963), 5 ff.

45   M. Collignon and L. Couve, Catalogue des vases peints
du Musée National d'Athènes (Paris, 1902); G. Nicole,
Catalogue des vases peints (Paris, 1911).

46   A. Zannoni, Gli scavi della Certosa di Bologna (Bologna,
1876-84).

47   G. Pellegrini, Catalogo dei vasi greci dipinti delle
necropoli felsinee (Bologna, 1912).

48   A. Frickenhaus, "Griechische Vasen aus Emporion,"
Anuari: Inst. d'Estudis Catalans 2 (1908), 195 ff.

CHAPTER I: THE ESTABLISHMENT OF WHITE-GROUND

The technique of white-ground was known in Athens before it became an established genre. As mentioned in the Introduction, it occurs on Protoattic vases. It makes another early appearance on a fragmentary kantharos by Nearchos dated to the latter part of the decade 560-550 B.C.[1] We shall preface the main body of this chapter with a discussion of the piece; not only is it the first in our series but its ties with the later material have not been sufficiently stressed.

A. Nearchos

*Kantharos. Athens, Akropolis 611, frr., from Athens. ABV 82.1 below. A, Harnessing of Achilles' chariot. B, (Gods). WG: tongue pattern.ΝΕΑΡΧΟϟΜΕ ΛΡΑΦϟΕΝΚΑ[ΓΟΙΕϟΕΝ] . Graef pl. 36; Robertson 59. [I,1].

As the main surviving fragment shows, Akropolis 611 was decorated in the standard black-figure manner except for the outside of the lip. A white slip, now worn, covers the lip zone whose lower limit is defined by a black glaze line. The slip provided a special ground for the subsidiary decoration of alternating black and red tongues possibly framed by additional lines; a bit of red remains above the name ΧΛΙΤΟϟ Originally, white happens also to have occurred beneath the heads of Achilles and the white horse where they overlap the tongue zone. The Nearchos kantharos is exceptional not only as the first known Attic work using white-ground but also as the first Attic representation of a harnessing scene and as one of the few with the chariot directed to left. Furthermore, in the white horse, it presents the unusual procedure of a narrow strip of glaze left exposed to set off the added color.²

On the basis of this vase, Nearchos may seem to have
specialized as painter; not only is it innovative in the
combination and application of colors but it also preserves
the artist's only extant signature as painter. However, he
has signed at least four times as potter, including the
satisfied ΝΕΑΡΤοϚ[ΕΓΟΙΕϚΕ]ΝΕΥ ³. The ratio of potter to painter
signatures and the fact that Nearchos both made and decorated
the kantharos are evidence to be used with caution, yet both
considerations are relevant to the basic question whether
potter or painter applied the white ground.

In discussing the Nearchos kantharos, Beazley wrote, "It
is the earliest Attic example of that white ground which had
a certain vogue in later black-figure... ."⁴ He isolates the
piece, implying that quite some time intervenes before the
next occurrence of related pottery. Beazley is right insofar
as he refers to the concentration of white-ground at the end
of the sixth century. On the other hand, a number of ties
bridge the chronological gap and bring into some relation the
material at either side of it. Of primary interest here is
the development of a black-figure outline style at exactly
the time when Nearchos was active. This style first becomes
current for the representation of a single female head⁵ on
the exterior of lip cups.⁶ While most often associated with
Sakonides, it occurs on the cups of Eucheiros, Hermogenes,
Phrynos, and others.⁷ Although Nearchos himself never used
outline, he must have been aware of its new application; he

made at least one lip-cup,[8] and of his two potter sons, Tleson
produced them in quantity.

The black-figure outline tradition continued to the end
of the sixth century in the work of the Amasis Painter.
According to the chronology drawn up by Bothmer, the Amasis
Painter began his career c. 560 B.C.[9] During the late 540's
or early 530's, he briefly experimented with the outline
style on one amphora type B,[10] two amphorae type A,[11] and a
neck-amphora.[12] In every case, he used it for full-length
figures of maenads. After an interval of some fifteen years,
the Amasis Painter reverted to outline on an eye-cup where the
eye displays a fragile contour disposed around the black and
white iris.[13] This interest in the outline style during the
third quarter of the sixth century has no direct relation to
the oeuvre of Nearchos; yet, in his day, it was an innovation
with which he was certainly familiar and, later on, it
is a factor in the establishment of white-ground.[14]

Nearchos' ties to the end of the century exist in another
form. The course of black-figure from c. 590 on was a diversified one, comprising various tendencies and "sub-styles."
In analyzing the decade c. 570, both Beazley[15] and Martin
Robertson[16] contrast the miniaturizing manner of Kleitias and
Ergotimos with a monumentality exemplified by Nearchos and
continued by such artists as Lydos and Exekias. A pupil of
the latter, the Andokides Painter,[17] brings us to the thresh-
hold of white-ground. Nearchos thus stands within a line of
painters and potter-painters who significantly intensified

the expressiveness of black-figure with new subjects and a
broader, graver manner of representation; indeed, after
Exekias, black-figure was exhausted and the rise of an alternative inevitable.

If our foregoing conclusions smack too much of art history
based on hindsight, one more concrete point may be made.[18]
The Nearchos kantharos came to light in the Persian debris
and it bears traces of fire; thus, it was still above ground,
and probably visible, at the Persian sack of 480-479 B.C.
Offered as a dedication on the Akropolis, the vase stood
there for seventy-five years and, in the beginning at least,
its novel subject and technique will have attracted attention.
For artists working later in the century, it may have provided
inspiration or a sanction for experimentation.

By the third quarter of the sixth century, a number of
preconditions seem to have existed that favored or fostered
the emergence of white-ground; these factors include earlier
or contemporary light-slip traditions in Attica and elsewhere,
the "equivalent effect" sometimes achieved with white added
to black-figure,[19] and the example of works like the Nearchos
kantharos. The actual introduction of white-ground, however,
was probably the achievement of one artist whose example and
reputation helped to impose the innovation. Four personalities
must be discussed in this context, Nikosthenes, Andokides,
Psiax, and the Antimenes Painter. They stand at the head of a
tradition which henceforth continued unbroken for almost a
century and a half.

B. Nikosthenes

*1. Oinochoe. Painter of Louvre F 117. Louvre F 117, from
   Vulci(?). ABV 230,1 top. Herakles in Olympos. WG: whole
   body; face of protome.N[I]KOSOEN[ESME]ΓOI[ESEN] . Hoppin Bf 255;
   Jacobsthal O. pl. 42,b. [I,2].

2. Oinochoe. Painter of Louvre F 117. Louvre F 116. ABV
   230,2 top. Herakles, Athena, Hermes. WG: whole body.[NIKOS-
   ΘENE]SMEΓOIESEN;...]S:KALOS . Hoppin Bf 254; Jacobsthal O. pl. 30,b.

In the literature of the later nineteenth and early
twentieth centuries, Nikosthenes is frequently credited with
the introduction of white-ground into Attic vase-painting;[20]
he may thus be considered first. The Louvre oinochoai are the
only known white-ground works attributable to him without
question. They show no sign of trial or error but relate
directly to other groups of oinochoai that may depend on the
Nicosthenic workshop.[21] The Louvre examples appear to form a
pair, owing to their comparable size,[22] the complementary male
and female plastic heads, and the painting attributed by Beazley
to the same hand. As a result, they are probably contemporary;
the subsidiary ornament of F 117 provides leads for determining
the approximate date. The zone of lotus buds with dots in the
lower interstices occurs on neck-amphorae and hydriai of the
later sixth century. After an early appearance on a plate by
Lydos,[23] it can be followed through neck-amphorae of Group E[24]
and Exekias,[25] and it occurs again with the Painter of Munich
1410.[26] The schematization and elongation of the lotus buds,
the imprecise shape and alignment of the dots, the irregularity
of the arcs joining the buds, and the two pairs of horizontal
lines framing the motif all relate the Nicosthenic dotted-

lotus to our later parallels. The very few examples from hydriai[27]
offer no contradictory evidence. Thus, one of the oinochoe's
ornaments indicates a date c. 530 B.C. or slightly later.

The spiral and palmette complex beneath the handle supports
our conjecture. In discussing the whole group of oinochoai
related to Nikosthenes, Jacobsthal associates a loosening and
resilience in their palmette decoration with the emergence of
red-figure.[28] He makes a point of placing the spiral motif of
F 117 after 530, when such forms disappear from neck-amphorae.[29]
It would seem legitimate, therefore, to assign Nikosthenes'
two white-ground works to the years c. 530.

Nikosthenes was a potter whose signature as such appears
on ninety-odd vases. He seems to have headed a large establishment specializing in export ware for Etruria, notably his own
brand of neck-amphora. The painters with whom he collaborated
indicate the length of his career, for they range from Lydos[30]
to Oltos[31] and Epiktetos.[32] The emphasis in his enterprise
was on variety. Nikosthenes left his name on vases of a dozen
different shapes decorated in black-figure, red-figure, the
"bilingual" combination of the latter two, white-ground, and
Six's technique.[33] These considerations are relevant in evalu-
ating the Louvre oinochoai. They are the signed work of an
"entrepreneur" who specialized as potter. In the handling of
white slip, they appear perfectly accomplished, creating no
impression of particular achievement. Just as the ornaments
are derived from different vase types, so Nikosthenes may

have adopted white-ground for its decorative effect and novelty.
He does not, therefore, seem to have developed white-ground;
on the other hand, the next chapter contains evidence that he
contributed materially to diffusing the technique, perhaps
even in conjunction with Psiax.

C. Andokides

*1. Amphora. Andokides Painter. New York 63.11.6. ARV^2 3,
2 bis (1617); Para. 320. A, Herakles and Apollo: struggle
for the tripod. B, Dionysos with maenad and satyr. Lip bf;
A and B, Herakles and the lion. WG: lip.ΑΝΔΟΚΙΔΕϟΕΓΟΕ. BMMA
Feb. 1966, 201, 203-205, 208, 209, 211. [II,1-2].

*2. Amphora. Andokides Painter. Louvre F 203. ARV^2 4, 13. A,
Amazons making ready. B, Women (Amazons?) bathing. WG:
special technique for figures.ΑΝΔΟΚΙΔΕϟΕΓΟΕϟΕΝ   . AJA 11
(1896), 2-3. [II,3-4].

The Andokides Painter is generally considered the inventor
of red-figure and Dr. von Bothmer has recently questioned
whether he may not also have introduced white-ground.[34] Two
amphorae type A constitute the evidence. The example in New
York combines red-figure pictures with black-figure ornament
framing the panels, on the handles, and on the lip. The treatment of the lip is unique, for a dense yellowish slip extends
from the outer edge of the topside over the entire side. This
surface is divided into two parts by a vertical black glaze
line centred above each handle. Rigorously symmetrical and
correlated with the figures below, the decoration on both A
and B consists of Herakles wrestling with the Nemean lion
between Athena and Iolaos; some passages are lost where the
black glaze failed to fuse with the slip. The New York amphora
gives the impression of a display-piece. The old and new

techniques are juxtaposed, but the former also subordinated;
in addition, the black-figure appears modernized through
its application to a light ground.[35]

The Louvre amphora proves equally unconventional. It
combines red-figure procedure with white-ground as the previous example combined black-figure with white-ground. A clay
surface limited to the actual panel was prepared with slip;
on it, the Andokides Painter drew his figures with glaze lines,
with added red for fillets, wreaths, other details of dress
and equipment, and twice with incision for the hair. He thus
reserved the forms in white instead of the usual clay color,
creating an effect that was traditional, and appropriate, for
the flesh of women. However remarkable, the technique employed
on this vase was not a complete innovation. In standard black-
figure, added white depicts elements that are light in color
or made of substances like metal or stone; it was also used
to ensure the distinctness of forms in scenes containing
overlapping horses or shields, for instance. Where details
were drawn over added white, the result corresponds to white-
ground. This situation occurs e.g. with the eyes[36] or jewelry[37]
of a female figure, the fillet of a white-haired old man,[38]
or the trappings of a horse.[39] The hetairai on a cup-skyphos
by the Amasis Painter[40] are particularly interesting counterparts to the Amazons on Louvre F 203.[41] In the works of his
teacher Exekias, the Andokides Painter could have seen all the
technical refinements of black-figure, including the "equivalent
white-ground effect." Apart from the slip, however, the figures

of the Louvre amphora, with their long curves and twisted poses, are eminently red-figure in character.

Unlike the oinochoai of Nikosthenes, the amphorae of the Andokides Painter give the impression of major undertakings. Significantly, both also have the signature of Andokides neatly incised on the foot. The chronology of the amphorae thus becomes particularly important. Knauer[42] and Szilágyi[43] follow Bothmer[44] in assigning the New York piece to the beginning of the Andokides Painter's career, and in dating his very earliest work between 540 and 530 B.C. Bothmer would give New York 63.11.6 second, if not first, place within the painter's oeuvre, implying a date c. 530 B.C. The Louvre amphora belongs somewhat later, in the middle third of the oeuvre, perhaps shortly before 520.[45] Nikosthenes, Andokides, and their painter collaborators worked contemporaneously, and on the basis of existing evidence, the matter of priority cannot be conclusively resolved. In our opinion, however, the Andocidean atelier was more decisively innovative, for its recognized contributions include not only red-figure but also the development of the amphora type A initiated by Exekias.

D. Psiax

*1. Lekythos. Paris, Jameson, from Greece. ABV 293,11. Women dancing, fluting. WG: body. AJA 45 (1941), 591. [III,1].

*2. Alabastron. Leningrad 381. ABV 293, 12. Dionysos with maenads and satyr. WG: body. Αἴστις καλός. AJA 45 (1941), 590. [III,2].

3. Alabastron. Munich 2294, from Vulci. ABV 293, 13. Herakles and Amazons. WG: body. Mon. Ined. I, pl. 26,21.

*4. Alabastron. London 1900.6-11.1, from Eretria. ABV 294, 25;

ARV^2 8, 13. Youths with horses. WG: ornament. ΚΑLΟϚ-
ΚΑΡΥϚΤΙΟϚ,ϚΜΙΚΡΙΟΝΚΑΙΟϚ,ΜΟΡΥΙΟϚ . JHS 85 (1965), pl. 14. [III,3].

*5. Kyathos. Würzburg 436, from Vulci. ABV 294,16. Between eyes,
Dionysos and maenad. At handle, sphinxes. WG: body; face
of protome. Langlotz W. pl. 118. [III,4].

*6. Plate. Basle no. 421, from Vulci. ABV 294, 21. Man dancing,
woman fluting. WG: obverse, rim of reverse. Schefold M.
158. [IV,1].

7. By or near. Lekythos. Athens, Agora P 5002, frr., from
Athens. ABV 295, 2 above. (Man smelling flower). Predella,
horsemen. WG: body.…ϚΕΝretro., end of signature on one
fragment. Hesp. 15 (1946), pl. 21, 1-3.

    During the period immediately after its introduction,

white-ground was used with black-figure more readily than

with red-figure or outline. For a while, the slip may have

posed a challenge great enough to discourage artists from

combining it with the new manner of drawing. As we have seen,

Nikosthenes took up white-ground early. Psiax worked at the

same time, and it was he who produced the first white-ground

oeuvre of any size. Known to us only as a painter, he deco-

rated vases of almost every important shape and in every

manner: black-figure, red-figure, bilingual, white-ground,

coral red, Six's technique. He specialized in black-figure

and in small vases like lekythoi, alabastra, plates, and

cups. However, the bulk of his standard black-figure occurs

on amphorae, neck-amphorae, and hydriai while the four new

techniques (red-figure, white-ground, coral red, Six's)

appear on alabastra and cups in particular. Through his

distinctive style and ornament, Psiax imposed a

stamp on this diversity and created an oeuvre so tightly-knit that its chronology poses an unusually difficult problem.

Among the six white-ground works attributed to Psiax
with certainty, the lekythos and alabastra form a loose group.
The Jameson lekythos is, in fact, the earliest preserved example with white-ground, thus transferring to Psiax the primacy hitherto held by the Edinburgh Painter.[46] The lekythos
and alabastra correspond in design, for their decoration
comprises a figured scene set between combinations of crenelle
patterns, wavy lines, rightward meanders, and ivy. Painted
with noteworthy precision on all vases, the ornament on the
alabastra occupies as much surface as the figurework. In
addition to being a virtuoso technical achievement, the piece
in London suggests a special interest in ornament; the latter
overlies a white-ground so that it both sets off and holds
its own next to the zone in Six's technique. Although the
importance of inscriptions should not be exaggerated, Psiax
chose to praise two youths and add the name of a third on
the London vase. He may have attached special importance to
it as to his red-figure alabastra which he signed with the
potter Hilinos.

The kyathos attributed to Psiax stands somewhat apart.
It resembles the aforementioned white-ground works in the
figure style, filling branches, coloristic effects, and
crenelle motif. However, the shape, including the female protome and the added handle palmette, is a special one; it
first appears during the second half of the sixth century
and may have been invented by Nikosthenes.[47] Psiax decorated

two kyathoi, Würzburg 436 and a plain black-figure example
in Milan;   furthermore, he influenced the Group of Vatican G. 57, which includes much white-ground.[49] With the evidence that exists for Psiax and Nikosthenes, one wonders
whether the two may not have collaborated, more and less
closely, in the production of certain kyathoi. The Würzburg example would not be one of their most successful
products, for it falls below the standard of Psiax' other
white-ground pieces.[50]

During the last two decades of the sixth century, the
plate enjoyed a period of particular popularity. Psiax
decorated five examples,[51]   all in a severe manner without
ornament or superfluous detail. The one in Basle is the most
elaborate, due to the white ground applied on both sides and
the two figures each with several attributes. Together with
London B 591, the piece leaves a strong impression of red-
figure influence. The composition filling the tondo, the use
of an exergue, the open pose of the animated figure, and
the precise detail are features that recur in the red-figure
plates of Paseas, a painter whose affinities to Psiax have
been recognized repeatedly.[52]

Despite an over-all consistency in the figure style, the
white-ground works of Psiax display different genres of decoration. The kyathos comes closest to the average late black-
figure effect with its little people, spreading branch-fillers,
and predisposition for details in relief. The alabastra reflect
a more accomplished style; the ornament remains within its

limits and the figures move within a relatively unencumbered space. The lekythos achieves even greater clarity, for the picture covers almost all of the actual cylinder while the few rows of patternwork provide a frame and articulate the areas of transition in the shape. For the adaptation of subject to surface, the plate ranks with the lekythos. However, the former creates a more forceful effect because the whole unembellished scene is visible at one time and because its composition is adapted to the concentric parts of the plate's form.[53]

In our discussion of these pieces, there is no implication of a chronological order, since factors like shape or the collaborating potter influenced the scheme of decoration. The style of Psiax certainly evolved with time, yet his white-ground works bring out another point. They suggest that, in the beginning at least, the new technique created a special inter-dependence between potter and painter. One potter, then a few, made use of white slip. The painter needed to respect the demands of the innovation as well as the decorative conventions traditionally associated with each shape. If Psiax actually began his career in the workshop of the Amasis Painter,[54] he may have acquired a predisposition for added white there. However, we may guess that he first encountered white-ground in the workshop of Andokides since they collaborated at least twice.[55] As one of the earliest who worked with slip, he may have been sought after by various potters and it is noteworthy that his white-ground production consists not of important pieces like amphorae but of small vases often produced in quantity. On the one hand, Psiax suggests something of a popularizer; on the other, he was one of the leading artists of the day whose inventiveness and skill produced works of superior quality. Indeed, his clientele extended beyond Greece to the knowledgeable collectors in Etruria.[56]

E. Antimenes Painter

1. Hydria, London B 304, from Vulci. ABV 266, 4. Harnessing chariot. Predella, boarhunt. Shoulder, fight with chariot. WG: side of foot. CV pl. 76,1 & pl. 77,1.

2. Hydria. Dresden ZV. 1779, from Greece. ABV 268,21. Frontal chariot. Predella, lion and boars. Neck, mourners. WG: neck. Diehl pl. 34, T 203.

*3. Hydria. Dresden ZV. 1780, from Greece. ABV 268, 22. Horseman and youths. Predella, swan and snakes. Neck, mourners. WG: neck. Diehl pl. 34, T 204. [IV,2].

4. Hydria. London B 316, from Vulci. ABV 268, 24. Herakles and Apollo: struggle for the tripod. Predella, lions and boars. Shoulder, warriors leaving. WG: sides of mouth and foot. ΕΥΟΙΕΤΟΣΚΑΛΟΣ   retro. on mouth. CV pl. 79,4 & 83,1.

*5. Neck-amphora. Basle, Bloch. ABV 270, 54 bis; Para. 120. A, Herakles and boar; B, centauromachy. WG: neck. [IV,3].

6. Neck-amphora. Villa Giulia 50626 (M. 487). ABV 270, 63. A, Herakles and Pholos. B, Apollo with divinities. WG: neck. Mingazzini pl. 69,5 & pl. 72.

7. Neck-amphora. Edinburgh 1887.211. ABV 271, 84. A, Dionysos with Hermes, maenads, satyr. B, Chariot wheeling round. WG: neck. C. Smith, Cat. Ed. pl. 3,2; B. Ap. XV, 39.

8. Neck-amphora. Boulogne 18. ABV 272, 91. A, Dionysos with satyrs and maenad. B, Chariot wheeling round. WG: neck.

Throughout Beazley's writings, the Antimenes Painter and Psiax are described as "brothers,"[57] and they complement one another in our context as well. The Antimenes Painter is best known from the decoration of neck-amphorae and hydriai and he

seems to have worked in black-figure exclusively. He has
left a less diversified oeuvre than Psiax, but he may be
credited with introducing white-ground to his two preferred
shapes. While the relation may not be direct, his vases
display the same principle as the Andokides Painter's New
York amphora where the slip sets off a distinct and subordinate part of the form.

The Antimenean works with white-ground fall into two
groups according to where the slip was applied. In the hydria
London B 304, it occurs on the side of the upper degree of
the foot; in London B 316, it occurs there as well as on the
side of the mouth, underlying a painted kalos inscription.
Both pieces have a considerable amount of decoration with
figured zones on the shoulder, over the body, and in the
predella; the thin white horizontals add a further coloristic
effect and, at the same time, mark the vertical limits. The
Dresden hydriai probably form a pair since they correspond
in height,[58] in the motifs on the body, in the plain shoulder,
and in the white-slipped neck showing a group of mourners;
decoration on the neck of a hydria is in itself exceptional,
but it becomes all the more so when painted over a prepared
surface. The latter feature associates the Dresden vases with
the Antimenes Painter's four neck-amphorae. These distinguish
themselves through the white ground that underlies the usual
neck ornament of a lotus-palmette chain; Villa Giulia 50626
has the additional refinement of a corrugated mouth.

The significance of the Antimenean white-ground seems
to lie in the principle rather than in the application.
The neck-amphorae did not undergo a basic change in kind
through the use of a slip; in their own day, they may have
appeared somewhat more modern than the standard black-figure
examples, but they do not show an especially successful accomodation to the new technique. Later on, neck-amphorae appear
that have slip over most of their surfaces[59] and they are an
innovation. However, in pieces like those of the Antimenes
Painter, the lotus-palmette would not seem to warrant a heightene
effect and, generally speaking, the neck seems to have been
chosen as a "safe" trial area. The hydriai present a somewhat
different situation. The pair in Dresden represent a bold, if
isolated, experiment. The white-ground on the other pieces is
logically motivated in that it picks out parts of the shape
that are visually and functionally prominent and often carefully profiled by the potter. As the slip varies in effectiveness from neck-amphora to hydria, it also varies in effect
between the oeuvres of the Antimenes Painter and Psiax. Its
selective application by the first tends to highlight elements
of structure and ornament while the all-over white-ground
in the works of Psiax subserves the decoration as a whole.

If our observations are to any degree accurate, then
the establishment of white-ground depends on Andokides, Psiax,
and the Antimenes Painter. It should be said that, although
we have been stressing the rôle of potters, we shall frequently
deal in terms of painters owing to our dependence on Beazley's

system of classification and to the uncertainties that remain regarding the division of labor between potter and painter. Allowing for these considerations, it would seem that Andokides produced the innovation and that Psiax and his "brother" demonstrated its possibilities, thus assuring its survival. As the next chapter will indicate, other artists worked with white-ground at the same time as the Antimenes Painter and Psiax, but the latter hold a special position because of their proximity to Andokides and the number and variety of their white-ground vases at a relatively early date.

CHAPTER I: Footnotes

1   H.G.G. Payne, Necrocorinthia (Oxford, 1931), 344; Pease
    North Slope 299; J.D. Beazley, The Development of Attic
    Black-Figure (Berkeley, 1951), 43.

2   Beazley Dev. 40-41.

3   Civitavecchia; and Rome, Marchesa Isabella Guglielmi
    (ABV 83, middle).

4   Beazley Dev. 40-41.

5   Among the exceptional pieces: New York 25.78.4 (ABV
    119,9); Berlin inv. 4495. J.D. Beazley, "Little-Master
    Cups," JHS 52 (1932), 175.

6   Outline had occurred earlier in Protoattic and on certain
    amphorae type B: Munich 1360 (ABV 16,2) and Athens,
    Agora P 17393 (ABV 16,2).

7   A list is given in Beazley LM Cups 174-175.

8   Civitavecchia; and Rome, Marchesa Isabella Guglielmi
    (ABV 83, middle).

9   D. von Bothmer, "New Vases by the Amasis Painter,"
    A.K. 3 (1960), 79-80.

10 Basle, Antikenmuseum (Para. 65).

11 Berlin inv. 3210 (ABV 151,21); Samos frr. (ABV 151,18).

12 Cabinet des Médailles 222 (ABV 152,25).

13 Vatican 369a (ABV 157,87).

14 See pp.107-108, 220-221.

15 Beazley Dev. 38.

16 M. Robertson, Greek Painting (Geneva, 1959), 61.

17 Beazley Dev. 75; J.D. Beazley, "The Antimenes Painter,"
    JHS 47 (1927), 91.

18 I owe the observation to Dr. von Bothmer.

19 See pp. 34-35.

20 E.g. G. Loeschke, "Dreifussvase aus Tanagra," AZ 1881,
    29 ff.; H.B. Walters, History of Ancient Pottery (London,

1905), I, 385; E. Pfuhl, Malerei und Zeichnung der Griechen (Munich, 1923), I, 281; M.H. Swindler, Ancient Painting (New Haven, 1929), 130, 181.

21 See pp. 66 ff.

22 F 117 0.365 m.; F 116 0.33 m. Dr. von Bothmer confirmed my guess that the feet could be alien; he attributes the foot of F 116 to a neck-amphora, of F 117 to a red-figured oinochoe. This explains the existing discrepancy in height.

23 Athens 507 (ABV 112,56).

24 Berlin 1716 (ABV 137,62); Group of London B 174: Naples 2498 (ABV 141,5).

25 London B 210 (ABV 144,7), London B 209 (ABV 144,8); Heidelberg S 178 (ABV 147,1); Naples Stg. 38 (ABV 148,II,3).

26 New York 98.8.14 (ABV 311,6).

27 E.g. Vatican G 45; Astarita 626.

28 P. Jacobsthal, Ornamente griechischer Vasen (Berlin, 1927), 53-54.

29 Jacobsthal O. 56.

30 Oxford 1966.768 (ABV 113,80 and 229,IV; Para. 45).

31 Florence 2 B 11 (ARV² 54,8); cf. also ARV² 55,10-11.

32 Würzburg 468 (ARV² 71,8), Odessa (ARV² 77,87).

33 Louvre F 114 (ABV 226 top).

34 D. von Bothmer, "Andokides the Potter and the Andokides Painter," BMMA (Feb., 1966), 207.

35 We have consciously avoided the question whether the Lysippides Painter may not have painted the lip. While important as regards the painting of the vase, it has little bearing on either the potting or the chronology.

36 In footnotes 36-39, I cite a few examples observed first-hand. Eyes: New York 98.8.14 (ABV 311,6); New York 59.11.17 (ABV 698,3 bis; Para. 192); New York 64.11.13 (ABV 169,4 bis; Para. 71); Harvard 1960.312 a&b (ABV 148,III); Harvard 1960.326.

37 New York 98.8.14 (ABV 311,6); New York 59.11.17 (ABV 698,

3 bis); Boston 61.195 (ABV 334,5 bis; Para. 147).

38 New York 17.230.8 (ABV 307,55); New York 17.230.9 (ABV 703 bottom); New York 56.171.21 (ABV 321,2); Boston 76.40 (Para. 144,1 bottom); Boston 86.155.

39 New York 17.230.8 (ABV 307,55); New York L.64.31 (ABV 253,I) Boston 76.40 (Para. 144,1 bottom). Other cases where "equiva lent white-ground" occurs include: the tongue of a gorgon (New York 01.8.6; ABV 51,4); a tress of a woman's hair (New York 21.88.76; CV III pl. 23,1-2); the belt of a charioteer (New York 56.171.29; ABV 362,30. New York 56.171.31 BMMA March 1957, 165 ff. Boston 63.473; ABV 362,31 bis; Para. 164); a baldric worn over a corslet (New York 56.171.1 ABV 87,14. Harvard 1960.318; ABV 86,4). A white shield with the device in outline or added color is very rare. The only certain example known to me is a fragment of a fourth century Panathenaic amphora, New York 60.92.5 (CV pl. 45,5); on the lekythos New York 41.162:256 (ABV 490,36) there may once have been a device painted in glaze.

40 Louvre A 479 (ABV 156,80).

41 D. von Bothmer, Amazons in Greek Art (Oxford, 1957), 153-154.

42 E.R. Knauer, Die Berliner Andokidesvase (Stuttgart, 1965), 3, 7, 21.

43 J.G. Szilágyi, "Une coupe du peintre d'Andokidès," Bulletin du Musée Hongrois des Beaux-Arts 28 (1966), 27, 29

44 Bothmer Andokides 202, 212.

45 Bothmer Andokides 212; H. Bloesch, "Stout and Slender in the Late Archaic Period," JHS 71 (1951), 30-31; W. Kraiker, "Epiktetos," JdI 44 (1928), 147-149; B. Schweitzer "Die Entwicklung der Bildform in der attischen Kunst von 540 bis 490," JdI 44 (1929), 130; E. Langlotz, Zur Zeitbestimmung der strengrotfigurigen Vasenmalerei (Leipzig, 1920), 23-24. An exception is Szilágyi 27 where Louvre F 203 is considered a late work.

46 ABL 88-89; P. Truitt, "Attic White-ground Pyxis and Phiale, c. 450 B.C.," BMFA 67 (1969), 72.

47 This seems to be one of the conclusions reached by M. Eisman in his unpublished doctoral dissertation on kyathoi; cf. AJA 74 (1970), 193.

48 Poldi-Pezzoli 482 (ABV 293,15).

49 See pp. 85 ff.

50 Miss Haspels (ABL 106) follows Langlotz, Griechische
    Vasen: Martin von Wagner — Museum der Universität
    Würzburg (Munich, 1932), 82 in doubting Beazley's
    attribution to Psiax.

51 ABV 294,17-21.

52 H.R.W. Smith, "New Aspects of the Menon Painter,"
    University of California Publications in Classical
    Archaeology I (1929), 34; C. Roebuck, "White-ground Plaques
    by the Cerberus Painter," AJA 43 (1939), 467; ARV² 163.

53 The plate is exceptional since composition was not one
    of Psiax's particular strengths; cf. Smith Menon Ptr,
    passim.

54 ARV² 6.

55 Madrid 11008 (ARV² 7,2), Castle Ashby (ABV 293,7).

56 Out of thirty-seven surely attributed works, thirteen
    came to light in Vulci.

57 Beazley Antimenes 91; Attic Black-figure: A Sketch
    (London, 1928), 25-26; Dev. 79; ABV 266,292.

58 0. 42 m. P. Herrmann, "Erwerbungsbericht der Dresdener
    Skulpturen-Sammlung," AA 1902, 116.

59 See pp.60 ff.

CHAPTER II: THE WHITE-GROUND VASES DECORATED WITH BLACK-
        FIGURE

In this chapter and the next, our approach has been
determined by the varied nature of the material and by the
uncertainties in the relation between painter and potter. As
a result, considerations of shape have taken precedence over
those of style and artistic personality. Thus, our first
concern includes placement and function of the slip as well
as the form, purpose, frequency, and quality of the shape.
For vases whose decoration is undistinguished, these are the
essential points; where relevant, the latter are supplemented
with observations regarding artists and the relation between
styles. In the catalogue given for each shape, the attributed
examples come first, in Beazley's order; this arrangement
keeps together material that has already been associated
and gives a sense of chronology. The unattributed examples
follow in a sequence that is roughly chronological and that
groups vases with the same slipped parts.

A. Hydriai

1. Euphiletos Painter. Munich 1703, from Vulci. ABV 324,26.
   Chariot. Shoulder, symposium. WG: side of mouth. Peters
   Pan. pl. 4,a.

*2. Euphiletos Painter. Copenhagen 111. ABV 324,29. Chariot.
   Shoulder, Achilles and Troilos. WG: floral band on neck.
   CV pl. 123,4. [V,1].

*3. Euphiletos Painter. Würzburg 312, from Vulci. ABV 324,35.
   Wedded pair in chariot. Shoulder, Dionysos with following.
   WG: side of mouth. Langlotz W. pls. 90,97. [V,2].

4. Euphiletos Painter. Louvre F 290. ABV 324,37. Achilles and
   Ajax playing. Shoulder, boar between lions. WG: side of

mouth. <u>CV</u> pl. 69, 6-7.

5. Euphiletos Painter, compared with. Louvre F 292. <u>Para</u>. 142. Herakles and Apollo: struggle for the tripod. Shoulder, between eyes, warrior. WG: floral band on neck. <u>CV</u> pl. 70,2&4.

6. Madrid Painter. Würzburg 313, from Vulci. <u>ABV</u> 329,3. Athena mounting chariot, with Herakles. Shoulder, chariot and warriors. WG: floral band on neck. Langlotz <u>W</u>. pls. 92,93,97.

7. Tychios (potter). Trieste S 405, from Tarquinia. <u>ABV</u> 350 top. Athena mounting chariot. Shoulder, Herakles and Triton. WG: side of mouth.ᵀⱽ⁺ⁱᴼ[ˢ]ᴱᴦᴼⁱᴱˢ[ᴱ]ᴺ on side of mouth. <u>CV</u> pl. 3.

8. Lykomedes Painter. Greenwich, Bareiss 23. Herakles and Apollo: struggle for the tripod; shoulder, Herakles and the Nemean lion. WG: sides of mouth and foot. <u>BMMA</u> June 1969, 432.

*9. Lykomedes Painter. Leningrad 2366. Chariot with Apollo & Hermes. Half of shoulder, cock fight; other half, palmettes. WG: one half of shoulder. Gorbunova fig. 11. [V,3-4].

10. Paris, Petit Palais 310, from Vulci. <u>ABV</u> 668,1. Hermes and Maia. Under handles, goat, ram, lion. WG: body.ᴷᴬᴸᴼˢᴷᴬᴾⱽˢᵀⁱᴼˢ . <u>CV</u> pl. 11.

*11. Darmstadt, Max von Heyl (lost); New York, Love, frr. Women at fountain. Shoulder, boar and panthers. Under handle, Dionysos. WG: body, shoulder. Langlotz <u>Heyl</u> pl. 21. [VI,1].

12. Ferrara T 867, from Spina. Amazons setting out. WG: panel, shoulder. Aurigemma ¹87,1 (²93,1).

*13. Louvre CA 4716. Hunters. Shoulder, chariots. Neck and mouth, birds amid palmettes. WG: outside and inside neck, topside mouth. (<u>AA</u> 1893, 192). [VI,2-3].

14. Athens, Agora A-P 306, A-P 309, frr., from Athens. (Citharode). Shoulder, (quadriga). WG: shoulder. <u>Hesp</u>. 4 (1935), 251.

15. Auxerre no. 45. Quadriga and hoplite. Shoulder, hoplite duel. WG: floral band on neck. (Rolley <u>Cat. Auxerre</u> no. 45).

16. Vatican G. 45. Warriors departing. Shoulder, horse race. WG: side of mouth. Beazley <u>RG</u> pl. 17.

17. Louvre CA 10681. Dionysos. Shoulder, hoplites. WG: side of mouth. <u>CV</u> pl. 148,1-2.

    The black-figure hydriai with white-ground belong to

the last third of the sixth century. Seven examples, forming

the largest group, have slip on the side of the mouth; on
this surface, all but one have an additional row of ornament
or an inscription. In the Bareiss hydria, the mouth corresponds
to the similarly slipped, but otherwise plain, foot. It is
interesting that six of the seven pieces also have an orna-
mental predella of lotus without dots and vertical panel
frames of ivy. A second group comprises four hydriai on the
neck of which appears a band of lotus and palmettes overlying
a white ground. Such a foliate zone proves exceedingly rare
on hydriai[1] and may have been adopted from neck-amphorae. Among
our examples, the bands differ in the vertical "lotus" element
as well as in the horizontal chain. Copenhagen 111 distinguishes
itself further through the plastic gorgoneion slipped white
and placed where the vertical handle meets the mouth. The
remaining works are in one way or another exceptional.

Petit Palais 310 represents a potter's phantasy, for it
combines an unparalleled globular body with a neck and handle
reminiscent of oinochoai. The decoration is equally noteworthy
due to the figure zone which covers the whole body, the precise miniaturistic style, and the plastic ornament at each
end of the vertical handle. Plaoutine associated the vase
with the Menon Painter,[2] an observation that deserves greater
consideration than Plaoutine gave it. The tongue, crenelle,
and ivy patterns are familiar from the works of Psiax discussed
previously;[3] the kalos name recurs only once, on the alabastron
London 1900.6-11.1; the figure e.g. of Hermes proves comparable

to those on the Jameson lekythos. Without proposing a definite attribution to Psiax, we should place the Petit
Palais hydria within his circle.

The hydria once owned by Max von Heyl[4] corresponds more
nearly to the standard form and again has slip and figure-
work over the entire body. It proves difficult to discuss
because of plaster restorations to the shape and the poor
condition of the figures. The decoration presents a conflation
of subjects popular c. 520-500; they include two fountain
houses, Dionysos with a kantharos and vines abandoned beneath
the handle, and three hydrophorai who recall the mourners
on the Antimenean hydriai in Dresden.[5] Of special interest
are the hydrophorai whose bodies are in silhouette with
flesh areas in outline. Generally speaking, the Heyl piece
is a curiosity displaying an ambitious iconography and
technique. Though unattributed, it prompts a number of
associations. The silhouette and outline women suggest an
influence of the Amasis Painter. The boar and panthers on
the shoulder recall hydria predellas of the Antimenes Painter;
the interest in fountain and Dionysiac subjects, in hydriai
and white-ground recall the same artist. A possible connection
between the Amasis and Antimenes Painters becomes significant as well.[6] One wonders, therefore, whether the Heyl hydria
may not represent an independent, and only partially successful, adaptation of certain subjects and procedures observed
in the Antimenes Painter's workshop.

The hydria Louvre CA 4716 presents no peculiarities in

shape or in the decoration of the body, but the treatment
of its neck and mouth are unique. A white ground covers
the entire concave surface of the neck, gives way to black
glaze on the underside and rim of the mouth, and then extends
over the topside of the mouth into the neck. In both areas
where it occurs, the slip underlies a motif of palmettes
interspersed with fronds and birds; the latter peck, strut,
look back, stretch up, showing off a variety of positions
even without a surface to stand on. The conception here is
remarkable even though Attic vases may have several zones of
apparently unrelated subject matter.[7] On its body and shoulder, the Louvre hydria shows two departure scenes, each
filled with figures and enlivened with added color and
inscriptions. Directly juxtaposed, the palmette and bird
motif with its sparseness and stark tonal contrast creates
an incongruity seldom equalled in Attic vase-painting.[8]
On the other hand, the palmettes as applied strengthen the
architectonic qualities of the vessel; furthermore, decoration on the mouth provided something to look at for the water
carrier at the well and for bystanders when the water was
poured. The Louvre hydria may well be attributed to the
Leagros Group. Characteristic of the latter are the shape
and the predella ornament of circumscribed palmettes up
and down at a forty-five degree angle; other indicative
details include the articulation of the horses and dogs,[9]
the intent round-backed riders,[10] and the extremities of

11
figures which overlap the frames.

The two remaining hydriai illustrate the application
of white-ground to the shoulder area. Even without slip,
the example in Leningrad would deserve special attention.
It appears unusual on account of the sharp contours, the
great width at the handles, and the rectangular but rather
low panel. The reason lies in the shoulder which is broad
and articulated into two rather flat degrees. The lower
degree forms a zone whose width corresponds to the thickness
of the vertical handle and whose decoration consists of a
net pattern. Set off by a chamfered edge, the upper degree
is divided into two sections by parallel vertical lines and
rows of dots. One part, which overlies the chariot scene on
the body, depicts two groups of three youths watching a cock
fight. The other part, at the back, displays a white slip
and a symmetrical composition of palmettes and lotus flowers.
In its subdivision and decoration, the shoulder of the
Leningrad hydria clearly depends on bronze counterparts
where the neck and body were first hammered separately, then
12
welded together at the shoulder.   As mentioned previously,
added white in conjunction with black-figure could serve
to identify metal objects like shields or helmets. On the
Lykomedes Painter's work, the white-ground supplements
three-dimensional details in evoking corresponding vessels
of bronze. Fulfilling more than an esthetic purpose, it
seems to have a specific meaning.

The hydriai with white-ground form a generally homogenous
group owing to the limited time span within which they occur
and the standard of quality which most of them maintain. It
seems that those with slip at the lip or in a band at the
neck show no further major peculiarities. The pieces with
larger areas of slip tend to present other unusual features
in shape or decoration. A direct interrelation between shape
and slip may thus exist in some cases and the potter may
prove to be the agent responsible.

B. Kalpides

1. Theseus Painter. Madrid 10930. ABL 252,73. Apollo and
   three Muses. WG: panel. CV pl. 29,3.

*2. Cape Town Class; Painter of Vatican G. 49. Louvre F 374.
    ABV 536,42; Para. 268. Horseman at fountain. WG: body
    and shoulder panels. [VII,1].

3. Cape Town Class; Painter of Vatican G. 49. Bartenstein,
   Roese, from Melos. ABV 536,43; Para. 268. Satyrs at mound.
   WG: body and shoulder panels. AA (1909), 31.

4. Cape Town Class; Painter of Vatican G. 49. Tarquinia RC
   1626, from Tarquinia. ABV 536,44; Para. 268. Herakles and
   Amazon. WG: body and shoulder panels. CV pl. 31,1.

5. Cape Town Class; Painter of Vatican G. 49. Maplewood,
   Noble. ABV 536,45; Para. 268. Theseus and Minotaur. WG:
   body and shoulder panels. Hesp. Art Bull. 10 (1959), 237.

6. Cape Town Class; Painter of Vatican G. 49. Cape Town 4.
   ABV 536,46; Para. 268. Fluting satyr, dancing goats.
   WG: body and shoulder panels. Boardman and Pope pl. 3,4.

7. Cape Town Class; Painter of Vatican G. 49. New York
   market (Eisenberg). ABV 536,47; Para. 268. Satyr between
   goats. WG: body and shoulder panels. Sotheby 13 June 1966,
   no. 138.

8. Painter of Vatican G. 49, possibly. Munich 1731, from
   Sicily. ABV 536-537. Apollo and goddess. WG: body and
   shoulder panels.

9. Painter of Vatican G. 49, possibly. Ancona. ABV 537 top.
   Unexplained subject: man with spear pursuing winged man.
   WG: body and shoulder panels.

10. Philadelphia market (Hesperia Art). Satyrs leading biga.
    WG: body and shoulder panels. Hesp. Art Bull. 39 (1967),
    A 12.

The kalpides represent a sequel to the preceding hydriai;
not only did their shape develop from the hydria proper,
but these vases are also rather small and carelessly executed.
They seem not to have been mass-produced since relatively
few exist. The example attributed to the Theseus Painter
is the odd work in the series, due to its greater size and
full complement of figures and ornament. The remaining
kalpides belong to one group, as indicated by the form and
the decorative schema: a panel on the body framed by two
rows of dots between vertical lines, palmettes on the
shoulder between horizontal rows of dots or rightward meander.
While the vases vary in the type and number of palmettes and
in the number of figures, they still show a certain correlation between picture and the ornament above. Moreover, in
subject, they suggest a predilection for scenes with satyrs.

The presence of white-ground sets these kalpides apart,
but it accompanies no unusual effects as we have seen on
the hydriai. Being applied over the whole available surface,
the slip serves as a light but neutral background rather than
as a means of selective emphasis. According to Beazley,
these pieces belong to the workshop of the Athena Painter,
the colleague of the Theseus Painter.[13] The workshop made
considerable use of white-ground for lekythoi as well as for

oinochoai, some of which were decorated by the Painter of
Vatican G. 49 and resemble the kalpides.[14]   Like the Light-
make neck-amphorae or the Athena workshop oinochoai, the Cape
Town Class ends a succession of white-ground vases whose
highpoint occurred in the late sixth century. During the latter
first quarter of the fifth century when the Class was produced,
red-figure monopolized creative artistic efforts and black-
figure supplied quantitative rather than qualitative demands.
Indeed, the kalpides demonstrate that the application of
white-ground did not depend on the quality of a vase or of
its decoration.

C. Neck-amphorae

1. Eye-siren Group. London B 215, from Vulci. ABV 286,1.
   Between eye-sirens, A, Peleus and Thetis; B, Apollo.
   Under handles, Artemis and Hermes. Below, goat between
   lion and panther; panthers and goats. Shoulder, lions
   and goats. WG: neck. CV pl. 52,1.

2. Eye-siren Group. Villa Giulia 1203, from Falerii. ABV 286,9.
   A, Herakles and Amazons. B, Warriors and women. WG: neck.
   CV pl. 7, 1-2.

3. Class of Cabinet des Médailles 218. Florence 3873. ABV
   319,2 below; Para. 140,D2. A, Apollo ?; B, Herakles ?
   WG: body.

4. Class of Cabinet des Médailles 218. Louvre F 115. ABV
   319,4; Para. 140,D6. A, Herakles and Geryon. B, Chariot.
   Neck, A, Dionysos; B, satyr. WG: body. CV pl. 37, 10-11,
   14-15.

*5. Class of Cabinet des Médailles 218. Vienna 3607, from
    Cervetri. ABV 319,10; Para. 140,D7. A, Ajax with body
    Achilles. B, Citharode. WG: body (and neck?). Jacobsthal
    O. pl. 49,a. [VII,2].

6. Class of Cabinet des Médailles 218. Oberlin 70.11. A,
   Chariot departing. B, Satyrs and maenad. Neck, A, Dionysos
   and satyr; B, the like. WG: neck, body. Allen Memorial
   Art Museum Bulletin, (Fall 1971), 60,63,65. [Bothmer].

7. Group of Faina 75. Boston 01.17. ABV 319,2 above; Para.

144 (ABV 327,4 quater). A, Dionysos with following; B, satyrs and maenads. WG: body. Richter and Milne fig. 33.

8. Group of Faina 75. London market (Christie). ABV 327,4[5]; Para. 144. A, Dionysos with following. B, Departure of warrior. WG: neck and body. Christie 23 Feb. 1965, no. 186.

9. Painter of Villa Giulia M. 482, compared with. Tarquinia, from Tarquinia. ABV 590,3 below. A, Ajax with body Achilles. B, Man with horse leaving home. WG: body. N.Sc. 1930, pl. 6.

*10. Light-make Class; Pescia Painter. Maplewood, Noble. A, boxers; B, the like. Under one handle, dog. WG: neck, body. [VII,3].

11. Light-make Class; Pescia Painter. Florence 71002, from Pescia Romana. ABV 593,1. A, Symposium with Dionysos. B, Fight. At handles, vine. WG: neck, body. EAA VI, 90, fig. 102.

12. Light-make Class; Pescia Painter. Goluchow, Czartoryski 214. ABV 594,5. A, Youths, with donkey; B, youth with satyrs. WG: neck, body. CV pl. 47,4.

13. Light-make Class; Pescia Painter. Würzburg 236. ABV 594,16. A, Dionysos (?), Ariadne (?), Athena. B, Komos. WG: neck, body. Langlotz W. pl. 63.

14. Light-make Class; Pescia Painter. Lucern market (A.A.). ABV 594,29; Para. 298. A, Women in orchard. B, Fight. WG: neck,body. A.A. II (1960), no. 144.

15. Light-make Class; Pescia Painter, probably. Naples RC 194, from Cumae. ABV 594,2. A, Theseus and Minotaur. B, Satyr, and youth on donkey. WG: neck, body. Mon. Ant. 22 (1913), pl. 62,3.

16. Light-make Class; Mariani Painter. Liverpool 56.19.34. ABV 595,4. A, Boxers; B, the like. Under one handle, dog. WG: neck, body.

17. Light-make Class; Mariani Painter. London B 615, from Vulci. ABV 595,6. A, Symposium; B, the like. Under handles, sphinx. WG: neck, body.

18. Light-make Class; Painter of Elaious 1. Berkeley 8.2161. ABV 596,VII. A, Komos; B, the like. WG: neck, body.

19. Light-make Class; Group X. Boston 13.79. ABV 597,7. A, Dionysos with following; B, satyr and goat. WG: neck, body.

20. Light-make Class; Group XI. Tübingen D 13. ABV 599,5.
    A, Horseman; B, the like. WG: neck, body. Watzinger pl. 7.

21. Aachen, Ludwig. A, Dionysos with following. B, Hoplites
    fighting over oriental archer. WG: neck, body. Lullies
    Ludwig 64, pl. 27.

22. Brussels R 322 ter. A, Hoplite between scythian archers;
    B, chariot with Athena ? WG: neck, body. CV pl. 1,19.

23. Karlsruhe B 298, from Vulci. A, Chariot departing; B,
    warriors departing. WG: body (and neck?)·. CV pl. 8, 5-6.

24. Villa Giulia inv. 911, from Civita Castellana. A, Aeneas
    and Anchises. B, Chariot. WG: neck. CV pl. 13, 1-3.

25. Como inv. C 23. A, Apollo and Athena; B,.the like, with
    vine branch. WG: body. CV pl. 1,2.

26. Greifswald 148,188,194, frr. A, Herakles in Amazonomachy;
    B, Herakles and Antaios. WG: body. (Peters Greifswald 26).

The application of white-ground to hydriai and neck-
amphorae produced markedly different results. The latter
vases display less variety and experimentation, and they come
exclusively from workshops where white-ground was already
known. The Eye-siren Group represents one of several styles
dependent on the Antimenes Painter, and it was the only one
to adopt the slip. Predictably, the two preserved examples
have white-ground underlying the neck ornament. London B 215
is noteworthy also for the rounded topside of the mouth and
the decoration with its three figured zones, the disposition
of the main subject around the whole body, and the two pairs
of eye-sirens; for its time, the piece shows much added white.

The Class of Cabinet des Médailles 218, which Beazley
has now subdivided,[15] is an offshoot of .the large class of
Nicosthenic neck-amphorae. For reasons of shape as well as

technique, the four white-ground examples do not fit into
Beazley's main categories. Louvre F 115 resembles the latter
most closely, apart from the slip which begins below the
neck and covers the remaining surface. Although it recalls
Louvre F 115, Oberlin 70.11 differs in the presence of slip
on the neck as well as the body, in the yet unparalleled
rightward meander above the zone of lotus buds, and in
compositional details. Florence 3873 is unique for its
unembellished, black-glazed neck, and it shows other unusual
features like the projections where the handles meet the
lip[16] and the decoration reduced to one figure on each side.
In the Louvre and Florence pieces, white-ground emphasizes
the main part of the vase and the primary decoration. In
Vienna 3607, it covers the entire reserved area; moreover,
the overlying ornament is particularly noteworthy. A
lotus-palmette band, taken from standard neck-amphorae,
circles the neck and a ring of linked palmettes, alternately
up and down, occurs on the topside of the mouth; the presence
of decoration on the topside is a recurrent feature in the
Class of Cabinet des Médailles 218[17] and it also recalls the
Leagran hydria Louvre CA 4716. Beneath each handle fits a
complex of circumscribed palmettes from which issue lotus
flowers and among which fly small swallow-like birds. Finally,
the kitharode on side B presents one of the rare occurrences
of "second white," the superposition of added white over
the slip.

The Group of Faina 75 depends, stylistically, on the

Euphiletos Painter; through two of its members,[18] it is
also connected with the Class of Cabinet des Médailles 218.
Of the two white-ground works in the Group of Faina 75,
Boston 01.17 displays a special elaboration of the Nicosthenic
handle form and the same black neck as Florence 3873. The
second neck-amphora is a very average example of the standard
type.

The vases discussed so far represent the main group of
post-Antimenean neck-amphorae that still fall within the
sixth century and that maintain a certain level of quality.
More striking than their small number is their derivation
from artists and workshops already familiar with white-ground
and the failure of the technique to acquire a wider following.
At the same time, this material contributes to the potter-
painter problem. Such works as London B 215, Florence 3873,
Vienna 3607, Boston 01.17 reveal other peculiarities besides
the white ground; they thus suggest that a design existed
before the application of either the decoration or perhaps
even of the slip and glaze. In other words, the appearance
of a vase may have been determined while in the hands of
the potter. Furthermore, the four neck-amphorae that are
most closely related in shape, those of the Class of Cabinet
des Médailles 218, also make similar use of the slip; it
tends to be present on the body and absent from the neck.

The remaining attributed neck-amphorae belong to the
Light-make Class, datable c. 490 B.C.; only a selection

appears in our catalogue, for the Class comprises fifty-six white-ground examples at present. Generally small in size, the vases are characterized by a lotus-palmette chain or three linked up-and-down palmettes at the neck, a row of strokes at the shoulder, a scene on each side delimited below by a groundline, a band of black glaze beneath, and rays radiating from the foot. The subjects are limited to Dionysos and his followers, symposia, komoi, boxers, and fights, with virtually no mythological episodes; the same subject may appear twice on one vase and an animal occasionally fills the space under the handles. Articulated with incision and added red, the decoration overlies a white ground which covers both the neck and body. According to Beazley, a number of artists painted neck-amphorae of the Light-make Class, though only two worked on slip to any extent. The Pescia Painter has been credited with thirty-one white-ground works, the Mariani Painter with twelve, and the Painter of Elaious 1, together with several anonymous hands, are responsible for the remaining thirteen.

In the development of neck-amphorae, the Light-make Class corresponds to the Cape Town Class of hydriai; the Light-makes occur in some quantity and represent the shape in its most reduced form. Though set apart as a group by their slip, the white-ground examples show no more inventiveness than their standard black-figure counterparts. They were the speciality of two hacks and a very few imitators, and it is noteworthy

that stylistic affinities, if any, exist with lekythoi;
Beazley associated the Pescia Painter with the Painter
of Athens 581,[19] the Painter of Elaious 1 with the
Haimon Group.[20] Finally, this material did not cater
exclusively to a Greek home market; although information
on provenience is very scant, fourteen white-ground pieces
came to light in Italy.[21]

The unattributed neck-amphorae add nothing to the existing
picture. The Ludwig vase must belong to the years c. 510;
however, Lullies' attribution to the Leagros Group[22] seems
questionable in view e.g. of the three-link chain within
each lotus-palmette unit and the rare rightward meander above
the lotus-buds. The neck-amphora in Brussels presents a
minor peculiarity in the continuation of slip over the
inner surface of the handles. The example in Como poses a
problem of condition. With its exaggerated downward taper
and clumsy foot, the vase suggests poor restoration incorporating one or more alien parts. Despite the worn surface
and mediocre hand, it also shows an improbably precise band
of tongues around the neck.

On the basis of existing evidence, the accomodation of
white-ground to the neck-amphora appears to have been
limited. Not only is the amount of good material small, but
the slip tends to underlie well-defined zones of decoration
rather than emphasize structural units; only with the Light-
make Class does it consistently cover the entire surface.
In the somewhat programmatic use of the slip and in the

concomitant lack of experimentation, the neck-amphorae differ from the hydriai. Since artists like the Antimenes and Euphiletos Painters can be associated with both vase types, the reasons for this divergency would seem to lie elsewhere. In our opinion, the handling of white-ground was affected by the conventions governing the decoration of each shape; moreover, it produced special effects in the ceramic hydriai because of influences from their metal counterparts.

D. Oinochoai and olpai

The black-figure oinochoai and olpai form the largest body of material in this and the following chapters. The works fall into two categories, those loosely related to Nikosthenes and those produced as a more or less important sideline by artists specializing in lekythoi. Accordingly, our catalogue and discussion will consist of two parts.

1. Ring-collar Class. Athens, Akropolis old no. 974, fr., from Athens. ABV 419 middle. Wedded pair in chariot. WG: body.

*2. Charinos (potter). London B 631. ABV 423 middle. Vine. WG: collar, body. +ΑΡΙΝΟϟ:ΕΓΟΙΕϟ; +ϟΕΝΟΔΟ[Κ]Ε...ΓΑ...ΚΑΛΕ . EAA II, 535, fig. 738; Jacobsthal O. pl. 31,a. [VIII,1].

*3. Class and Group of London B 632. London B 632, from Vulci. ABV 425,1 above. Patterns. WG: whole shoulder, rays at foot. Jacobsthal O. pl. 47,a. [VIII,2].

4. Class and Group of London B 632. Villa Giulia (M. 535), fr. ABV 425,2. Patterns. WG: shoulder. Mingazzini pl. 80,2.

5. Class and Group of London B 632. Vatican, ex Astarita, fr. ABV 697. (Patterns). WG: shoulder.

6. Class and Group of London B 632. Vatican, ex Astarita, fr. ABV 697. Heads of two youths. Shoulder, patterns. WG: shoulder.

7. Class and Group of London B 632, related. Munich 2447, from Vulci. ABV 425 middle. Patterns and palmettes with inscription. WG: whole shoulder. ΚΑΛΟΣ ΝΙΚΟΛΑ ΔΟΡΟΘΕΟΣΚΑΛΟΣ ΚΑΜΟΙΔΟ- ΚΕΙΝΑΙ ΤΑΤΕΡΟΣ ΓΑΙΣΚΑΛΟΣ ΜΕΜΝΟΝ ΚΑΜΟΙ ΚΑΛΟΣ ΘΙΛΟΣ. Cornelius 45, fig. 33.

8. Class of Vatican G. 47. Frankfurt, Städel inv. V4, from Vulci. ABV 430,23. Symposium: Dionysos, Herakles, satyrs. WG: ivy band, body. CV pl. 46, 1-3.

*9. Class of Vatican G. 47. Havana, Lagunillas. ABV 430,26. Satyrs and maenad. WG: body (and collar?). AJA 60 (1956), pl. 112,43. [VIII,3].

10. Briachos Class. Once Kiev, Khanenko. ABV 432,7; Para. 186. Amazonomachy. WG: body. Sobr. Khanenko 6 (1907), pl. 15, 929.

11. Class and Painter of London B 620. London B 620, from Vulci. ABV 434,1. Achilles brought to Chiron. WG: collar, body. Strong Melchett 43, fig. 21.

12. Class and Painter of London B 620. London B 621, from Vulci. ABV 434,2 below. Herakles and the Lion. WG: collar, body. Jacobsthal O. pl. 29.

*13. Class and Painter of London B 620. New York 46.11.7, from Vulci. ABV 434,3 below. Peleus up the tree. WG: collar, body, protomes. BMMA (June 1947), 256,257,259. [IX,1].

14. Class and Painter of London B 620. Brussels, Biblio- thèque Royale 5, from Vulci. ABV 434,4 below. Lion attacking boar; cow suckling calf. WG: collar, body, protomes. Feytmans pl. 10-14.

*15. Class and Painter of London B 620. Leipzig T 411, frr., from Orvieto. ABV 434,5. Wolf, goats. WG: body. Strong Melchett 44. [IX,2].

16. Class and Painter of London B 620. Vatican, ex Astarita, frr. ABV 434, 6-8; 697. Parts of patterns. WG: collar, body.

*17. Kevorkian Oinochoe. Berlin 1969.3, from Vulci. ABV 435 top. Maenads. WG: body, (topside of lip?). Sotheby 17-18 Oct. 1949, no. 221. [IX,3].

18. Kevorkian Oinochoe, compared with. Vatican 436, from Vulci. ABV 435 above. Man mounting chariot. WG: body. Albizzati pl. 61.

19. Painter of Louvre F 118. Munich 1828, from Vulci. ABV 440,1 middle. Athena and Dionysos with Herakles and Apollo. WG: body (and collar?). Richter and Milne fig. 127.

20. Painter of Louvre F 118. Louvre F 118, from South Italy. ABV 440, 2 middle. Aeneas and Anchises. WG: body. Jacobsthal O. pl. 30,a.

21. Kuhn Class. Florence 94328. ABV 442,C,3. Three warriors (Amazons). WG: body. (Bothmer Am. 55, no. 169).

22. Kuhn Class. Munich, ex Schoen. ABV 442,C,3 bis. Fight with wheeling chariot. WG: body, collar. Exhib. Kassel, 27/V-27/IX 1964, no. 45.

23. Flat-mouthed oinochoe: type C. Naples 86372 (RC 200), from Cumae. ABV 443,12. Herakles and bull. WG: shoulder, body. Fiorelli pl. 7,1. Modern copy: Harvard 2260 (CV pl. 21,9).

24. Flat-mouthed oinochoe: type C. Truro 1926.63. ABV 443,13. Dionysos and maenad. WG: body (and shoulder?).

The white-ground oinochoai in this section are primarily trefoil and they show several recurrent details of shape and decoration; these details include a collar at the neck enclosing a row of patternwork, a predilection for vegetation and ornament generally, a tendency towards affectation in the figure style. These features do not appear everywhere nor are they always equally pronounced; however, they present an alternative: influence of one artist or interrelation between several. The oinochoe London B 631 has a reserved and slipped zone covering the upper two-thirds of the body; it shows a grapevine growing from the groundline over the front, a lotus-palmette tendril spreading from the handle at the rear. Furthermore, it introduces the potter's signature and a further inscription beneath the [23] lower tier of vines. Charinos signed at least six vases, two of which are head vases with the bowl chequered on [24] on white-ground. Although the representations differ in

character and quality, Tarquinia 6845 shares with London
B 631 a noteworthy appreciation of pure vegetation or
patternwork as decoration; moreover, both works were painted
in silhouette, with neither incision nor added color.

The Class and Group of London B 632 is distinguished
by relief snakes which develop where the vertical handle
meets the mouth and by the ornament which is restricted to
the shoulder. The oinochoai show a white-slipped zone with
horizontally paired and circumscribed palmettes set between
tongues and a ribbon motif. On the related piece in Munich,
individual palmettes within outline "hearts" are set up-
and-down while around them runs an inscription, a conversa-
tion between youths about their favorites. This vase differs
from the two preceding ones in the band of dotted reticulation surrounding the tongues and in the absence of relief
snakes, but it shares with B 632 the rare detail of birds
flying among the leaves. Through the applied snakes,[25] the
consistent use of tongues,[26] the ribbon motif,[27] the zones
separated by multiple lines "imitating metalware,"[28] and
other details, the Class and Group of London B 632 recalls
the production of Nikosthenes.

The white-ground works in the Class of Vatican G. 47
represent the squatter shape II and one of them has a
framed scene; otherwise, they resemble B 631 in the ratio
of picture to glazed area on the body, in the collar on the
neck, in the simple strokes just below, in the importance
of the grapevines, and as Beazley pointed out,[29] in the

drawing of the vines. These works may again recall Nikosthenes, for the subject matter smacks of kyathoi and Städel V 4 shows the rather large heart-shaped ivy repeatedly used in that workshop.[30]

The groups of oinochoai considered so far may be divided into London B 631 and the Class of Vatican G. 47 where decoration fills a zone on the body, and the Class of London B 632 where it keeps to the shoulder; the Nicosthenic element seems discernible in the latter works, conjectural in the others. With the Class of London B 620, slip and decoration cover the entire body, and the influence of Nikosthenes is evident. The four complete pieces which form the core of the Class prove remarkably similar.[31] In shape, they are virtual replicas, showing a long ovoid silhouette, a collar at the neck, an echinus foot, and a handle embellished with two serpents and two female protomes. In the distribution of decoration, they present a variation of London B 631. While the collar motif is broader and tongues replace the strokes, the picture area again covers about two-thirds of the body and displays a symmetrical picture at the front, a lotus-palmette tendril at the back, and a double ground-line. Where London B 631 was glazed black, these oinochoai have outline rays above the foot and either blank white space or a row of ornament. They produce a particularly successful over-all effect, owing not only to the careful execution but also to the subordination of the patternwork and the ample space within the scene.

The vases in the Class of London B 620 have been
related to Nikosthenes on several occasions,[32] and we
need not reopen the arguments. However, in publishing
Bibliothèque Royale 5, D. Feytmans-Kallipolitis raised an
interesting point; while accepting the Class, she disassociated
it from Nikosthenes in favor of Psiax.[33] Works of comparable
quality produced by these two artists often reveal many and
close similarities. As Mrs. Kallipolitis suggests, the
oinochoai may well be compared with Petit Palais 310, and yet
their figural decoration is more stylized and mannered than
that of Psiax, except on a few of his small vases. The
Kevorkian oinochoe adds to this matter. It is clearly
a variant of the Class of London B 620. At the same time,
it corresponds to Nikosthenes' signed oinochoai in the
restriction of slip to the body, in the dotted lotus below
the scene, and in the elaborate, almost aggressive, handle
ornament. Although the Kevorkian piece may recall the Jameson
lekythos, Psiax endows his figures with grace and poise
just as he gives palmettes and tendrils a logical size and
place when they appear.

The oinochoai that remain to be considered represent
shapes other than the basic trefoil, yet they relate directly
to the groups of works just discussed. The beaked examples
by the Painter of Louvre F 118 belong near London B 631
and the Class of Vatican G. 47; they show the now familiar

ratio of decorated to glazed surface, the echinus foot,
the net-filled collar, the convex handles with rotelles
at the upper point of attachment. Unlike London B 620, the
female protome occurs only at the mouth and without snakes.
The newly created Kuhn Class is connected with the Class of
Vatican G. 47 in _Paralipomena_;[34] through the absence of a
panel, the two white-ground examples stand closer to the
Lagunillas piece, but the basic similarities extend beyond
form. The oinochoai that conclude this portion of our list
resemble one another[35] but represent a different shape and
approach to decoration; Naples 86372 also reflects a different
standard of quality and, in the treatment of the shoulder,
points forward to the next section.

A good many of the oinochoai discussed have already
been associated with Nikosthenes and have been studied
systematically by Beazley and Jacobsthal. Our interest has
focused only on the interrelation between certain specific
groups and on the importance of the Nicosthenic element. We
have proceded mainly in terms of shape, ornament, and the
distribution of decoration, arriving at the following
conclusions. Except for Naples 86372 and Truro 1926.63,
most of the oinochoai seem to present adaptations of one
pattern: collar with ornament at the neck, tongues or strokes
on the shoulder, a white-ground zone for decoration occupying
about two-thirds of the body and the entire circumference,
a wiry lotus and palmette tendril developing symmetrically
from the handle, a predisposition for relief details, and

an echinus foot. Owing to variables like shape and purpose,
each class or group shows a different combination of parts
in addition to a different style of painting. It would seem
that the Kevorkian oinochoe and the Class of London B
620 stand closest together, also chronologically. London
B 631, the Class of Vatican G. 47, the works by the Painter
of Louvre F 118 are somewhat farther removed, the Kuhn and
Briachos Classes even more so. While these oinochoai indicate one tendency, the Class of London B 632 represents another
it probably dates closer to 520 than 510, as indicated by
the kalos names on Munich 2447,[36] and we should take the
Kevorkian piece to be about contemporary.

If we apply the foregoing observations to personalities,
Nikosthenes should perhaps be credited with formulating
"the pattern" and providing the repertoire of ornament with
which potters like Charinos and painters worked. On the
basis of these hypotheses, Nikosthenes begins to acquire
a more definite place in the history of early white-ground
than had emerged in Chapter I. He, and his colleagues,
may have developed the white-ground oinochoe. In fact, they
may initially have catered to a specific purpose or clientele,
for the earlier pieces show an unusually high level of
quality; moreover, these are also the vases with technical
novelties, like the snakes decorated in red-figure and the
vine painted in pure silhouette.

Our list and discussion continues with the oinochoai
by painters of lekythoi.

25. Gela Painter. Louvre F 162. ABL 214,183. Palaestra. WG: body. ABL pl. 25,7.

26. Gela Painter. Compiègne no no. ABL 214,189. Dionysos with following. WG: body. CV pl. 12,15.

27. Gela Painter. Sorrento, from Sorrento? ABV 474,17 bis. Dionysos mounting chariot, with Apollo. WG: body.

28. Gela Painter. Athens, Agora P 8799, fr., from Athens. ABV 474,19. (Man with lyre, back of another's head). WG: picture surface.

29. Gela Painter. Ruvo, Jatta, from Ruvo. ABV 474,21. Harnessing chariot. WG: body. Iapigia 3 (1932), 17, fig. 12.

30. Gela Painter. Zürich, private. Para. 216. Dionysos with following. WG: body. M.M. 22 (1961), no. 148.

31. Gela Painter. Amsterdam. Para. 216. Satyrs at grape harvest. WG: body. M.M. 22 (1961), no. 149.

*32. Gela Painter. Villa Giulia, from Cervetri. ABL 215,198. Palaestra. WG: mouth, neck, body. Stud. Etr. I (1927), pl. 32,b,1. [IX,4].

33. Gela Painter. Louvre F 371. ABL 215,199. Hoplites. WG: body and ?

34. Gela Painter. Karlsruhe B 31, from Nola. ABL 215,201. Chariot, and fawn. WG: mouth, neck, body. CV pl. 10,1.

35. Gela Painter. Villa Giulia 47466, from Cervetri. ABV 475,28. Warriors leading horses. WG: body and ?

36. Theseus Painter. Paris, Petit Palais 313. ABV 519,6. Theseus and bull. WG: body. CV pl. 10, 5-6.

37. Theseus Painter. Adolphseck, Landgraf Philipp von Hessen 13. Para. 256. Two youths with drawn swords: masquerade. WG: body. CV pl. 14, 1&4; pl. 16, 3-4.

38. Sèvres Class; Athena Painter. Boston 98.924. ABV 524,1 below. Herakles leading monster. WG: body.

39. Sèvres Class; Athena Painter, workshop. Sèvres 2035, from Vulci. ABV 525,6. Warrior pursuing woman, snake at right. WG: body. CV pl. 22, 4-6.

*40. Sèvres Class; Athena Painter, workshop. Brussels, Bibliothèque Royale 6, from Capua. ABV 525,7. Odysseus escaping from Polyphemos. WG: body. Feytmans pls. 15-16. [X,1].

41. Sèvres Class; Athena Painter, workshop. Rome, Conservatori 51. ABV 525,10. Horseman, herm behind. WG: body. CV pl. 44, I-2.

42. Sèvres Class; Athena Painter, probably. Dunedin E 29.7. ABV 525,12. Centaur. WG: body. Anderson pl. 8,a.

43. Sèvres Class; Athena Painter, workshop. Rome, Conservatori 53. Para. 263. Fight. WG: body. CV pl. 44,3.

44. Sèvres Class; Athena Painter, workshop. Basle market (M.M.). Para. 263. Dionysos on donkey. WG: body. M.M., A.S.V. (1964), no. 77.

45. Class of London B 630; Athena Painter, workshop. London B 630, from Kameiros. ABV 525,1. Horseman. WG: body. Vos pl. 14,b.

46. R.S. Class; Athena Painter. Cambridge 37.8. ABV 526,1 above. Judgement of Paris. WG: collar, body. CV R.S. pl. 2,3.

47. R.S. Class; Athena Painter, workshop. Goluchow, Czartoryski 29, from Nola. ABV 526,2 above. Peleus and Thetis. WG: collar, body. CV pl. 42,1.

48. R.S. Class; Athena Painter, workshop. Once Cambridge, Seltman. ABV 526,3 above. Two mounted warriors. WG: collar, body.

*49. R.S. Class; Athena Painter. Basle market (M.M.). ABV 526,4 above; Para. 263. Achilles and Memnon. WG: body (and collar?). M.M. 22 (1961), no. 150. [X,2].

50. Class IV; Athena Painter, not far from. Copenhagen, Ny Carlsberg 2673. ABV 526,1 below. Dionysos and satyrs. WG: body, collar (?). Poulsen VG fig. 24.

51. Class IV; Athena Painter, workshop. Capua 149, from Capua. ABV 527,12. Satyr and maenads. WG: body, collar. CV pl. 8, 6-7.

52. Class IV; Athena Painter. Oxford 226, fr., from Capua. ABV 527,25. Dolon. WG: body, collar. Gardner 14, fig. 19.

53. Class IV; Athena Painter, workshop. Frankfurt, Museum für Vor-und Frühgeschichte β 307. ABV 528,46. Centauromachy: Kaineus. WG: body, collar. CV pl. 39,3-4.

*54. Class IV; Athena Painter, near. Harvárd 1927.154. ABV 528,47. Hermes and giant. WG: body, collar. CV pl. 21,7. [X,3].

55. Class IV; Athena Painter, workshop. Ferrara T 867, from Spina. <u>ABV</u> 529,65. Warrior leading horse, and warrior (Amazons). WG: body, collar. Aurigemma [1]87,3([2]93,3).

56. Class IV; Athena Painter. Thebes R 46.83, from Rhitsona. ABV 530,70. Ship and Nike. WG: body, collar. <u>Eph</u>. 1912, <u>102</u> and pl. 6,1.

57. Class IV; Athena Painter. Frankfurt, Museum für Vor- und Frühgeschichte β 306. <u>ABV</u> 530,72. Women at herm. WG: body, collar. <u>CV</u> pl. 39, 1-2.

58. Class IV; Athena Painter, workshop. Munich market, from Attica. ABV 530,74. Komast. WG: body, collar. <u>Helbing,</u> <u>27 June 1910</u>, no. 82.

59. Class IV; Athena Painter, by or near. Paris, Musée Rodin 232. ABV 530,85. Procession to an altar. WG: body. <u>CV</u> pl. 19, 1-4.

60. Athena Painter workshop, resembling. Louvre F 372 bis. <u>Para</u>. 265. Camel carrying a pointed amphora. WG: body, collar. <u>Bonner Jahrbücher</u> 155-156 (1955-1956), pl. 2, fig. 1.

61. Class V; Athena Painter. Louvre F 372. <u>ABV</u> 531,1 middle. Daughters of Pelias. WG: body. Pottier pl. 86.

62. Class of Copenhagen 68; Athena Painter. Berlin 4003, from Attica. <u>ABV</u> 532,1 above. Head of Hermes. WG: body. <u>ABL</u> pl. 45,1.

63. Class of Vatican G. 49; Athena Painter, workshop. Newark 28.202. <u>ABV</u> 533,12. Fight. WG: body, collar.

64. Painter of Vatican G. 49, by or near. Gotha Ahv. 44, from Caere. ABV 537, bottom. Herakles as splanchnopt. WG: mouth, neck, body. <u>CV</u> pl. 40,5.

*65. Seattle Group. Osnabrück. <u>Para</u>. 268,3. Maenads and silens dancing. WG: bands on neck and body. <u>M.M. 22 (1961),</u> no. 151. [X,4].

66. Basle market (M.M.). Quadriga in race. WG: collar, body. <u>M.M., A.S.V. (1964)</u>, no. 13.

67. Como, inv. C 25, fr. Palm tree, deer, between two figures. WG: body. <u>CV</u> pl. 5,2.

68. Philadelphia market (Hesperia Art). Athlete and trainer. WG: body. <u>Hesp. Art Bull.</u> 45/46 (Jan. 1969), A 17.

69. Basle market (M.M.). Quadriga and vines. WG: body. <u>M.M.,</u>

A.S.V. (1964), no. 76.

70. Villa Giulia 20839-40, from Cervetri. ABV 673. Citharode mounting platform. WG: body.

71. Vienna (S.K. 194, 58). Mounted amazon against crouching warrior. WG: body. LaBorde I, pl. 95.

72. Parma C 17, fr. Satyr, hindquarters of quadruped, maenad. WG: body. CV pl. 9,2.

73. Dresden ZV. 1608. Warrior, and woman offering. WG: body. Jacobsthal O. pl. 49,b.

74. Brussels R 293. Herakles and the Kerkopes. WG: mouth, neck, body. CV pl. 1,18.

75. Basle market (M.M.). Eos and Memnon. WG: mouth, neck, body.

76. Turin inv. 5768. Two women. WG: mouth. CV pl. 14,3.

77. Copenhagen ABc 979. Woman at fountain. WG: mouth. CV pl. 124,1.

During the early phase of their black-figure history, white-ground oinochoai seem to have issued mainly from one workshop and among their number appear works of artistic significance. During the second phase, which lasted some-what over three decades, they decline to the mediocre level of the lekythos workshops which produced them, but they again come from one main source. After the period of activity c. 520-510 and a brief lag thereafter, white-ground oinochoai and, for the first time, olpai reappear in associa-tion with the Gela Painter. The oinochoai are all trefoil and, in the treatment of the body proper, recall the Class of Vatican G. 47. As with the latter, the predominance of scenes with Dionysos relates directly to the function of the shape; moreover, although our information is incomplete, at least three examples [37] also have the picture enclosed

within a panel. The oinochoai of the Gela Painter differ
from those of the Class in the form of the mouth and handle
as well as in the drawing style.

Although we again know only the published examples,
the Gela Painter's white-ground olpai prove more informative,
due to the several rows of ornament. The piece in the Villa
Giulia shows the ivy current with Psiax, Nikosthenes, and
early red-figure painters[38] and the horizontal circumscribed
palmette that occurs with the Pioneer Group;[39] Karlsruhe
B 31 includes the dotted up-and-down palmette used e.g.
by Phintias.[40] The chequer pattern covering the mouth of
both olpai has appeared on Naples 86372, and it recurs on
other white-ground works dating to the end of the sixth
century.[41] Finally, the juxtaposition of several pattern
bands may appear unusual, but the Gela Painter must have
favored the effect, for he repeated it on lekythoi.[42] In
the use of white-ground, the trefoil oinochoai generally follow
existing conventions; the olpai present a new principle of
decoration through the subdivision of the vase into three
sections, with slip covering the upper two and the ornamented
crowning member contrasting with the black-glazed portion
below.

The Theseus Painter decorated a wider range of shapes
than usual for painters of lekythoi. His two white-ground
oinochoai represent the flat-mouthed and trefoil varieties,
and over their elongated bodies, they show a particularly
high ratio of slipped to glazed surface. The Adolphseck

example illustrates a singular subject; it suggests a
dance or performance, for two youths advance in unison
with swords drawn, scabbards extended, and caps on their
heads that support a female protome. While few later black-
figure artists worked on white-ground oinochoai, neither
the Gela nor the Theseus Painter developed this type of
vase to any degree. By contrast, the latter artist's colleague,
the Athena Painter, produced white-ground oinochoai in almost
as great a number as white-ground lekythoi.

The Athena workshop oinochoai have been classified by
Beazley, upon the groundwork laid by Miss Haspels; from
the total of ninety-six pieces, we give a selection that
includes every major subdivision.[43] The Sèvres Class is
characterized by the trefoil mouth, rounded handle, torus
foot, and squat, almost cylindrical body. It has a white-
slipped, unframed[44] picture area delimited by a red line
below and by strokes around the neck. Concentrated on the
front of the vessel, the representations consist of two
figures among long dot-leaved branches, although a single
figure or a symmetrical group of three occur as well.
Compared e.g. with the Class of Vatican G. 47, the subject
matter occupies more space; not only does it overlap the
neck ornament but the white field also extends farther
towards the foot. The Class of London B 630 contains about
a third of the white-ground pieces in the preceding class
and resembles the latter in general shape and in the continued absence of a panel. Since only one example has been

published with illustrations, we depend on Beazley for
these indications.

The R.S. Class consists of four white-ground oinochoai
which represent a more ambitious variant of the trefoil
through their larger size, the collared neck, and the
foot in two degrees. Of the three zones with decoration,
the body tends to have a mythological scene enclosed by a
panel, the shoulder has a row of strokes surrounded by
groups of three dotted palmettes alternately up and down,
and the collar contains a double net pattern. Displaying
perhaps the most careful execution among white-ground
oinochoai of the Athena workshop, these pieces make selective
use of the white ground; the latter appears on the body and
collar but is absent from the shoulder, thus producing an
alternation of slip and reserve between the extremities
that are covered with glossy black glaze.

Beazley's Sèvres Class and Class of London B 630 are
generally characterized by their compact form and by the
absence of a panel. The large Class IV contains trefoils
that are taller and that have a band of ornament and a framed
subject only on the front of the vase. While the preceding
works still included a residual motif around the handle,
the present ones have become even more stereotyped, with a
Dionysiac scene or a combat almost invariably accompanied
by a double net as the subsidiary pattern. The white ground
sets off the decoration more effectively than a reserved
surface but creates no special effects.

The three following subdivisions of oinochoai represent
further variations of the basic types which we have considered. Class V stands part way between the panelled
and panelless vases. The Class of Copenhagen 68 consists
of miniatures measuring c. 10 cm., somewhat under half
the average height for the workshop. The Group of Vatican
G. 49 brings us to a follower of the Athena Painter who painted
the Cape Town Class of kalpides[45] and a few olpai similar in
design to those of the Gela Painter. Concluding the attributed
list, the Seattle Group, like the R.S. Class, points to an
artist who tried something different. The novelty lies in
disposing the subject within a narrow white-ground zone
that circles the middle of the body; in one case,[46] the
subject occupies a panel on the shoulder, and in the Osnabrück example, an additional band of slip with dotted ivy
occurs on the neck. These four works, therefore, provide
welcome, but rare, exceptions to the mechanical treatment
of shape, decoration, and white ground that generally
characterize oinochoai from the Athena Painter workshop.

Within the larger framework of white-ground oinochoai,
the unattributed examples fall into place quite readily.
Thus, for instance, the first piece in the Basle market
shows a short neck-band, low picture zone, and simplified
motif that make the published date c. 520 seem at least
a decade too early.[47] In subject and execution, Como inv.
C 25 recalls a lekythos attributed to the Gela Painter[48]
and could well join his inferior oinochoai. The piece in

the Philadelphia market displays the basic features of the
Sèvres Class so that it probably issues from the Athena
Painter workshop. The second oinochoe in Basle shows several
peculiarities, e.g. the tall neck rising above a squat body,
the pronounced lateral extensions of the upper end of the
handle, the mass of circumscribed palmettes that press toward
an already crowded scene; in terms of lekythoi, such an
emphasis on and application of palmettes might point to the
wider circle of the Diosphos Painter. Despite appreciable
differences in style, Dresden ZV. 1608 corresponds to the
preceding vase in the treatment of the handle area; Jacobsthal's
date in the 460's[49] may be somewhat too advanced, yet it
brings out the red-figure, very late archaic character of
the ornament.

The olpe Brussels R 293 resembles the attributed examples
above in over-all design and in the application of slip to
each zone; it is probably the work of yet another hand, but
belongs to the same level of quality and development. The
olpe in Basle introduces a band of ivy, instead of chequers,
on the mouth; stylistically, it suggests the Athena Painter
workshop, possibly near the Painter of Vatican G. 49. The
pieces in Turin and Copenhagen present a variation insofar
as white-ground occurs only on the mouth; they now belong
to a group attributed by Lo Porto, to the "Pittore dei Mon-
cherini" and dated, too early in our opinion, 500-490.[50]

As other vases with white-ground, the oinochoai were
produced by few artists within a small number of establish-

ments. Those in our second group make particularly evident
the "industrial" nature of the lekythos workshops; the
latter are characterized not only by the article in which
they specialized but also by a prevailing style, type of
subject matter, and level of quality. The use made of
white-ground is a further significant variable. As we
have tried to bring out, each variety of shape shows a
rather restricted range of ornament and a rather consistent
localization of the slip. Where mediocre vases are produced
in quantity even the representation becomes stereotyped,
yet the essential point is that form, surface, and patternwork seem to vary less in terms of one another than the
decoration. Applying this idea, if it is tenable, to the
process of pottery production, we would associate the first
three features with the potter, the figure-work and actual
drawing with the painter.

Slipped oinochoai with black-figure came to an end with
the Athena Painter workshop.[51] They had begun in the earliest
period of white-ground c. 520 and continued until c. 460.
Apart from some isolated works, they, together with the
hydriai and neck-amphorae, represent the larger shapes to
which the slip was applied; though no less interesting
or significant, most of the remaining material in this
chapter consists of lesser shapes.

E. Column-kraters

*1. Sappho Painter. Karlsruhe B 32, from Locri. ABL 228,57.
  A, Amazons with chariot setting out. B, Odysseus under

ram. WG: side of mouth, body. <u>CV</u> pl. 9; Jacobsthal <u>O</u>.
pl. 50. [XI,1].

*2. Theseus Painter. Once Swiss market. Symposium. WG: side of
mouth, picture surface. [H. Cahn]. [XI,2].

The white-ground kraters may find a place here because
theirs is one of the more important and unusual shapes
decorated by painters of lekythoi. Karlsruhe B 32 is notable
not only for the technique, but also for its relatively
small size,[52] the ornament beneath the handles, and the extended representation of Odysseus' escape from Polyphemus.
Moreover, a purposeful use of white-ground sets off the
grandiose scenes and contemporary red-figure ornament. Of
the latter, the ivy on the mouth is already familiar. The
palmettes find counterparts in Beazley's Class III of eye-
cups[53] and, as Jacobsthal points out,[54] in the white-ground
neck-amphora Vienna 3607 as well as in the Euphronios calyx-
krater Berlin 2180. According to these black-figure and
red-figure parallels, the Karlsruhe krater can be dated
c. 510-500. The Sappho Painter may have relied on lekythoi
as the mainstay of his workshop; however, possibly through
some relation with Psiax,[55] he also experimented with white-
ground and Six's technique on shapes of various sizes. Indeed, the column-krater, as the kalpis in Goluchow, strongly
suggests a display-piece.

The krater by the Theseus Painter is just as much of a
rarity, but in design and execution, it falls short of the
preceding piece. The two prove quite similar in shape; moreover, they correspond in the allocation of ornament and bands

of slip or glaze from the side of the mouth to the rays of the foot. However, the second krater differs decisively in the main scene which forms a continuous frieze around the body; the subject fails to respect the shape and thus its presentation lacks clarity. The work probably belongs to the latter part of the Theseus Painter's career and post-dates the Karlsruhe example by at least a decade.

F. Kyathoi

1. Psiax, near. Oxford 1927.4074 c, fr. ABV 295,3. Maenad running. WG: picture surface.

2. Psiax, near. Oxford, fr. ABV 295,4. Between eyes, maenad running. WG: picture surface.

3. Psiax, near. Vatican, fr. ABV 295,5. Between eyes, maenad moving right. WG: body.

4. Psiax, near. Oxford 1927.4074 a, fr. Amazon. WG: picture surface. (Bothmer Am. 71, no. 25).

5. Group of Berlin 2095. Berlin 2095. ABV 610,1 top. Between eyes, maenad riding phallos-bird. WG: body. Licht III, 76.

*6. Painter of London B 620, related? Leningrad, ex Botkin, from Tarquinia. ABV 697. Between eyes, Dionysos and satyrs. WG: body. Trésors d'art en Russie (1902), 50,1. [XII,1].

7. Painter of London B 620, related? Heidelberg 263, fr. ABV 697. Between eyes, lost. At handle, cock. WG: body. CV pl. 40,8.

8. Group of Vatican G. 57. Vatican G. 57, from Vulci. ABV 611,1. Between eyes, Dionysos seated, satyr. At handle, sphinxes. WG: body. Beazley RG pl. 21.

9. Group of Vatican G. 57. Würzburg 437. ABV 611,2. Between eyes, Dionysos seated, satyr. At handle, sphinxes. WG: body, protome. Langlotz W. pl. 118.

10. Group of Vatican G. 57. Cambridge 9.37. ABV 611,5. Between eyes, Dionysos seated, satyr. At handle, sphinxes. WG: body, protome. CV R.S. pl. 3,1.

11. Group of Vatican G. 57. Philadelphia 4863.22, fr. ABV

611,9. (Part of left eye, satyr). WG: body.

12. Group of Vatican G. 57. Cambridge 10.37. ABV 611,15.
Between eyes, Dionysos reclining; beyond eyes, satyr.
WG: body. CV R.S. pl. 3,2.

13. Group of Vatican G. 57. Munich 1985, from Vulci. ABV 611,
16. Between eyes, Dionysos reclining; beyond eyes, satyr.
WG: body.

14. Group of Vatican G. 57. Hillsborough, Mrs. R. Hearst,
from Orvieto. ABV 611,18. Between eyes, Dionysos reclining,
with satyr beneath couch. At handle, panthers. WG: body,
protome (?). Raubitschek no. 11.

15. Group of Vatican G. 57. Sèvres 2036, from Vulci. ABV
611,19. Between eyes, Dionysos on donkey with satyrs.
WG: body. CV pl. 22, 1-3.

16. Group of Vatican G. 57. Sydney. ABV 612,21. Between eyes,
Dionysos on donkey. At handle, sphinxes. WG: body.

17. Group of Vatican G. 57. Compiègne 1074, from Vulci. ABV
612,22. Between eyes, Dionysos on donkey. At handle, lions.
WG: body, protome (?). CV pl. 7, 4 & 9.

18. Group of Vatican G. 57. Brussels R 270. ABV 612,28. Between
eyes, satyr and maenad. At handle, pegasoi. WG: body.
CV pl. 2,1.

19. Group of Vatican G. 57. Laon 37.1007. ABV 612,35 bis.
Between eyes, maenad on donkey. At handle, sphinxes.
WG: body. CV pl. 23, 7 & 8.

20. Group of Vatican G. 57. Vatican 479. ABV 612,40. Between
eyes, komos. At handle, sphinxes. WG: body. Albizzati
pls. 60, 67.

21. Group of Vatican G. 57. Munich 1988, from Vulci. ABV
613,41. Between eyes, Theseus and Minotaur. At handle,
sphinxes. WG: body.

22. Group of Vatican G. 57, of or near. Munich 1987, from
Vulci. ABV 613,4. Between eyes, satyr and maenad. At
handle, sphinxes. WG: body. Frel Sborník pl. 1,4.

*23. Group of Vatican G. 57, of or near. Munich 1986. ABV
613,4 bis; Para. 305. Between eyes, satyr and maenad.
At handle, lions. WG: body, protome (?). Frel Sborník
pl. 1,2. [XII,2].

24. Group of Vatican G. 57, of or near. Lugano, private.
ABV 613,7 (?); Para. 305. Between eyes, Dionysos seated

between dancing maenads. At handle, doves. WG: body.
M.M. 22 (1961), no. 144.

25. Group of Vatican G. 57. Greifswald 271, fr. Silen. WG:
body. Peters Greifswald pl. 21. [Peters].

26. Theseus Painter. Erlangen I 522, fr. ABV 519,17. Komos.
WG: body. Grünhagen pl. 13.

27. Greenwich, Bareiss 124. Perseus and Gorgon. WG: body.
Schauenburg Festschrift Lücken pl. 45.

28. Harvard 1969.15. Between eyes, Dionysos. At handle, cocks.
WG: body. Fogg Newsletter 6,4 (1969), 5.

29. Basle private. Between eyes, silen and goat. At handle,
sphinxes. WG: body. M.M. 34 (1967), no. 133.

30. New York 41.162.115. Between eyes, two horsemen. At
handle, panthers. WG: body. CV Gallatin pl. 45, 3 a-b.

31. Brussels 344. Between eyes, woman. At handle, peltasts.
WG: body. CV pl. 2,3.

32. Vienna 4679. Theseus or Herakles and Bull. WG: body.
(Masner no. 298).

33. Athens, Agora A-P 1513 a-b & 2501 c,fr., from Athens.
Rim: ivy. WG: ornament. Hesp. 9 (1940), 212, no. 179.

34. Athens, Agora A-P 1656 a-b, fr., from Athens. Rim:
crenelation. WG: ornament. Hesp. 9 (1940), 212, no. 178.

The white-ground kyathoi listed here follow upon Würzburg 436 and present a test of our conjecture that Psiax
collaborated with Nikosthenes.[56] The first four pieces were
placed near Psiax by Beazley; the Vatican and first Oxford
examples indicate the stylistic proximity quite clearly.
While, in each case the fragments are small, at least two
show the subject between eyes, and all lack the lip ornament of Würzburg 436. The Group of Berlin 2095 again belongs
near Psiax and the white-ground namepiece reflects its source
in the face of the maenad and in the form of the ivy branches.

The Group of Vatican G. 57 represents the largest concentration of white-ground kyathoi both near Psiax [57] and generally. While they do not form a class, these works are related by a number of features; not only are they all eye-kyathoi, but at least thirteen have an unornamented lip, and at least eight a pair of sphinxes flanking the handle; with at least six, a protome marks its upper join with the bowl. The vases correspond further in the extensive use of white. Besides the zone of slip which extends from the lip to slightly beneath the lower handle attachment, they show added white for a ring of the apotropaic eye and, [58] occasionally, for a relief protome or part of a figure. It is noteworthy that every one of these decorative details also occurs on Würzburg 436.

As indicated by the designation "group," the present kya-thoi were painted by several artists stylistically dependent upon Psiax. While they were probably made by more than one potter, they may well issue from a single workshop, that of Nikosthenes which apparently initiated and dominated pro-duction of the shape. Thus, the white-ground kyathos seems to have been a joint venture between associates of Psiax and Nikosthenes. If our hypothesis holds, Nikosthenes led in the use of white-ground on these vases as well as on oinochoai. Moreover, the two groups of material are linked by the kya-thoi in Leningrad and Heidelberg. As Beazley pointed out, the latter display a five-dotted crenelle which recurs, with four dots, on Leipzig T 428. The execution varies slightly in each case, for the motif on the kyathoi corresponds more closely to the simple light-on-dark crenelation used by Psiax. Nonetheless, the basic similarity is evident and significant, for it connects white-ground works which, on other grounds, could already be referred to the same potter's establishment. Furthermore, this correspondence between kyathos and oinochoe again illustrates the interrelation of a technique like white-ground with shape on the one hand, ornament on the other.

The last attributed work represents an artist whose production of kyathoi was greater than the lone example suggests. The Theseus Painter followed prevailing conventions for design and the use of slip, so that his importance to us lies in the evidence of connections between lekythoi and other shapes. Although his chronology seems a bit rigid, Michael Eisman is certainly correct in placing the Theseus Painter's kyathoi late in the sixth century and early in the artist's career,[59] around the time of his association with the White Heron workshop.[60]

The unattributed kyathos in the Bareiss collection is an ambitious vase which Eisman now assigns to a follower of the Theseus Painter. Harvard 1969.15 has become Eisman's namepiece of the Hanfmann Painter; the cock with its two tail sickles and a lotus bud before the tail recurs on the above mentioned fragment Heidelberg 263.[61] The Harvard piece antedates the Theseus Painter, but despite its sub-Nicosthenic style, it differs markedly from Leipzig T 428

by the Painter of London B 620. Two kyathoi from the Agora
exist only in diminutive fragments, yet they allow at
least preliminary classification. They are unusual for the
ornament on white-ground at the rim and the area of black
glaze below; the latter could serve as an intermediary
zone or as the surface for decoration in Six's technique,
perhaps even red-figure. On A-P 1513, the ivy between
parallel lines immediately points towards Psiax and/or
Nikosthenes. On A-P 1656, the crenelation filled with stars
and squares seems a variation of the dotted crenelation
considered above. Since patternwork on the rim occurs
mainly with earlier kyathoi, we would associate the fragments tentatively with Psiax and the kind of decoration
that occurs on his two white-ground alabastra.

G. Mastos

*Munich 2003. ABL 105. A, Herakles and stag; B, the like.
WG: body. Jacobsthal O. pl. 33. [XII,3].

This mastos is the only white-ground example known to
me. Presenting the basic stylistic associations, Jacobsthal [62]
groups it with the Nicosthenic oinochoai and Miss Haspels [63]
cites it with kyathoi now attributed to Psiax and his circle.
Two minor observations may be added. The drawing appears
careful, though not distinguished, in the figures, hasty
and perhaps more natural in the pattern borders. Thus,
while it may give the impression of a rather early date,
the mastos is more likely to be a good work by an average
artist active c. 510-500. Furthermore, from available photo-

graphs, the handles seem to have glaze outside, reserve

inside, as in cups. This detail may provide a further lead

both for dating and for identifying the hand.

H. Mastoids

1. Haimon Painter, manner. Munich 1998. ABV 558,473. A, Women seated at fruit tree; B, the like. WG: picture zone. Lau pl. 19,6.

2. Haimon Painter. Goluchow, Czartoryski 31. ABV 558,485. Herakles and bull, twice. WG: picture zone. CV pl. 42,4.

3. Haimon Painter, manner. Florence 4216. ABV 559,498. Dionysos with following, twice. WG: picture zone. Inghirami pl. 266.

4. Haimon Painter. Capua, from Capua. ABV 559,506 bis. Symposium, twice; and komast. WG: picture zone. CV pl. 12, 7-9.

*5. Haimon Group. Frankfurt, Museum für Vor- und Frühgeschichte β 316. A, Herakles and lion; B, the like. WG: body. CV pl. 51, 5-6. [XIII,1].

6. Leafless Group. Bern inv. 12321. ABV 649,243. Man (Dionysos?) reclining with satyrs and goats. WG: picture zone. I. Jucker Bern no. 43.

7. Leafless Group. Harvard 1927.145. Silen and goat, twice. WG: picture zone. CV Fogg pl. 21,5. [I. Jucker].

8. Bologna 125, from Bologna. Between eyes, A, Dionysos seated; B, the like. WG: picture zone. CV pl. 2, 2-3.

9. Bologna inv. C. 268, from Bologna. A, Maenad between two satyrs; B, the like. WG: picture zone. CV pl. 2, 4-5.

10. Philadelphia market (Hesperia Art). Hoplite race, twice. WG: picture zone. Hesp. Art Bull. 39 (1967), no. A 10.

The white-ground mastoids are few in number, negligible

in quality, and all but two of the attributed examples belong

to the workshop of the Haimon Painter; our selection of

Haimonian pieces was made from a total of sixteen. While

these vases occur with or without a pair of diagonal handles, they follow one design, with a slipped band for decoration on the upper half of the body, a glazed zone beneath, and frequently, one vertical ivy leaf under the handles. Frankfurt V.F. β 316 is atypical, for it illustrates the scheme of Lindos Group skyphoi [64] applied to a mastoid. Throughout, the white-ground seems nothing more than a novelty for greater contrast with the figurework.

If the Haimonian works date ca. 480, several unattributed mastoids may be slightly earlier. Bologna 125 represents a different variety owing to the eyes and the absence of reserved lines below the scene. Bologna C 268 shares the latter feature, but has a taller form. The piece in the Philadelphia market could belong to the Haimon Group. In shape as in subject, the mastoids strongly suggest debased successors of the kyathoi. Moreover, within the Haimon workshop, they constitute a sideline related to both the white-ground skyphoi and pyxides.

I. Skyphoi

1. Group of Rhodes 11941. Athens 639. Para. 88,39. A, Theseus and Minotaur. WG: picture zone.

2. Group of Rhodes 11941. Nauplion. Para. 88,40. A, Herakles and lion. WG: picture zone.

*3. Pistias Class M. London B 681. Para. 309. A, Apollo; B, Hermes. WG: body. Jacobsthal O. pl. 32. [XIII,2].

4. Pistias Class M. Athens 1726, from Athens. ABV 627,1 above. A, Hermes, Nike, youth running.. B, Komos. WG: body.

5. Pistias Class M. Thebes R. 82.37, from Rhitsona. ABV 627,7. A, Man reclining, woman seated; B, woman dancing. WG: body. Ure Sixth pl. 22.

6. Pistias Class M; Caylus Painter. Bologna 147, from
   Bologna. ABV 627,9. A, Horseman and hoplites; B, horse-
   man and archers. Under handles, ivy leaf. WG: body.
   CV pl. 2,1 & 6.

7. Pistias Class N; Haimon Painter, manner. Athens 18809.
   ABV 628,11. A, Athena seated, helmeted; B, Athena seated,
   helmet in hand. WG: body. AM 77 (1962), pl. 30,2.

*8. Pistias Class N. Copenhagen, Ny Carlsberg inv. 2759.
   ABV 628,16. A, Frontal male head in outline; B, the like.
   WG: body.ΓΙ΄ΤΙΑ΄. Bruhn, From the Colls. II, 125, fig. 10.
   [XIII,3].

9. Lańcut Group. Brussels R 430 G. ABV 577,19. A, Youth and
   goat; B, the like. WG: picture zone. CV pl. 2,5.

10. Haimonian. Basle market (M.M.). A, Warrior fighting
    griffin; B, the like. WG: picture zone. Sotheby 4 May 1970,
    no. 135.

11. Lindos Group. Copenhagen 184, from Greece. ABV 582,9. A,
    Seated figure; B, the like. WG: picture zone. CV pl. 119,6.

12. Lindos Group. Rhodes 12899, from Kameiros. ABV 582,18.
    A, Satyr ?; B, satyr ? WG: picture zone. Cl. Rh. 4, 276,
    fig. 304,2.

13. Lindos Group. Bonn 814, from Athens. ABV 583,31. A, Satyr;
    B, the like. Six's technique. CV pl. 39,3.

14. Lindos Group. Matera ?, from Banzi. Para. 291. A, Hydria.
    WG: picture zone. N. Sc. 1936, 435, fig. 9.

*15. Once Geneva market. A, Fluting satyr; B, maenad
    with krotala. WG: body (?). [XIII,4].

16. Athens, Akropolis 1332, fr., from Athens. Sphinx (?)
    and woman. WG: picture surface. Graef pl. 77.

17. Athens, Akropolis 1333, from Athens. A, Sphinx and figures.
    B, Herakles and lion. WG: picture zone. Graef pl. 78.

18. Athens, Agora A-P 1892 a-d, frr., from Athens. A, Dionysos
    WG: picture zone. Hesp. 9 (1940), 189, no. 99.

19. Oslo, Museum of Applied Art, fr. Two women. WG: picture
    zone. CV pl. 15,5.

20. Greenwich, Bareiss 247. A, Flute player and women dancing;
    B, the like. WG: picture zone.

21. Athens, Akropolis 1330 a-d, frr., from Athens. Herakles
and Apollo: struggle for the tripod. WG: picture zone ?

22. Athens, Akropolis 1331, fr., from Athens. Hare, hanging.
WG: picture zone ?

The white-ground skyphoi are problematical; while similarities in shape and design unify the series, the interrelations
producing this continuity are not always evident.[65] Neither
white-ground example in the Group of Rhodes 11941 has been
published, yet the Group derives from the Little-master cup
tradition and frequently retains the pair of upright handle
palmettes; the works probably date to the later third quarter
of the sixth century.

The Pistias Class M consists mainly of slipped skyphoi
which Beazley has characterized as "footed mastoi."[66] Having
lost its foot, London B 681 makes the relation to mastoi
particularly clear. Moreover, it points to the milieu where
this type may have originated. In her publication of the
black-figure Pistias skyphos Kerameikos 1676, Elena Karydi[67]
attributes the piece to the circle of the Amasis Painter
and cites London B 681 as its closest counterpart. Even without
this welcome parallel, the white-ground work displays several
Amasean features. It resembles the cup Oxford 1939.118[68]
in the drawing style as well as in the placement of a single
figure between lotus-bud tendrils and against a plain background. With the cup-skyphos Louvre A 479,[69] it shares the
similar disposition of ornament above the foot and a particularly deep, though less sagging, bowl. Furthermore, through
their ties with the Little Masters,[70] Amasis and his painter

have points of contact with the Hermogenean tradition
to which the Group of Rhodes 11941 belongs. Within Class M,
London B 681 is the most informative, and isolated, piece.
The remaining white-ground skyphoi are at least a decade
later, and so coarse that only the shape and ornament
indicate their derivation. They may have some connection
with the Leafless Group since Bologna 147 was decorated by
the Caylus Painter; otherwise, the Amasean element has all
but disappeared.

The Pistias Class N contains miniature skyphoi that
resemble the preceding ones in shape, but show a stereotyped design of two tall palmettes flanking a single motif;
the latter rests on alternating reserved and glaze lines,
with an occasional pattern between. As before, white slip
covers the bowl, but now the drawing is frequently in pure
silhouette. Class N stands near the Haimon Painter, and
since P.N. Ure is right in stressing the affinities,[71]
Class M may have been a slightly earlier product of the same
workshop. Ny Carlsberg 2759 adds ambiguous evidence to the
whole problem, for whether Pistias was a potter[72] or just
the butt of a joke we cannot know; in any event, the piece
exceptionally combines an outline face with a name.

The lowest, if not the latest, variety of white-ground
skyphos occurs with the miniature vases of the Lindos Group,
which again issues from the Haimon workshop. While their
heavy fabric contributes to the effect, these vases resemble
standard black-figure skyphoi more closely than the Pistias

Classes; they have squatter proportions and a picture zone limited to a band between the handles. As with Pistias Class N, the picture on the slipped ground consists of a figure or animal between two palmettes that develop from each handle. Bonn 814, painted in Six's technique, is the only noteworthy piece among our total of forty-five.

Between the mass of later material and our earliest, isolated skyphos, a gap exists which the vase once in Geneva may help to lessen; if it is white-ground, as photographs suggest, the added female flesh deserves note. Two features of ornament are important here. One is the light-on-dark crenelation above a series of alternately light and dark lines. The other is the arrangement of the handle palmettes. From each handle grows a reverse-S tendril ending in a vertical palmette; this scheme is standard on Little-master cups and continues on the Haimonian skyphoi discussed above. In a separate, lower row, two further palmettes develop from the line circumscribing a third which fits between the roots of the handle. This circumscribed handle palmette set above two "eyes" occurs on various red-figure vases dating c. 510,[73] notably the Brachas cup.[74] The latter is a problem in itself, for it cannot stand far from the Pioneer Group, but as Beazley indicates, it also resembles Psiax. Thus, the Geneva skyphos postdates London B 681, but reveals certain links with it, with Psiax, and with the progressive red-figure painters.

The skyphos Bareiss 247 is our only example of a normal-

sized skyphos with a white figure zone; it probably belongs
to the CHC Group.

This discussion of white-ground skyphoi has once again
brought in Psiax, and it has added evidence to several
other aspects of our subject. London B 681 provides us with
a white-ground vase near the Amasis Painter, whom we had
associated with the emergence of outline in black-figure
and with equivalent white-ground effects. Furthermore, it
is interesting that the potters around this.artist experimented not only with "footed mastoi" but also with other
types of deep cups;^{75} the Haimon workshop illustrates a
comparable development of mastoids and skyphoi. Regarding
technique, the Pistias Class N and the Lindos Group introduce the first extensive, though not the earliest, use of
silhouette. As long as silhouette was one of the newer
alternatives to standard black-figure, artists like the
painter of the Charinos oinochoe must have appreciated its
visual effect; about three decades later, the Haimon Group
exploited the facility of using glaze without incision or
added color. Finally, the works in this section reveal a
geographical distribution out of all proportion to their
substandard quality. Considering only the Lindos Group,
a large number came to light on Rhodes - in Kameiros, Ialysos,
Lindos, whence their name; further examples were found in
Olynthos, Athens, Corinth, Apollonia, and as far west as
Emporion. Altogether, therefore, these small slipped skyphoi
seem to have been turned out according to a formula and to

have reached Greek outposts widely scattered around the
Mediterranean.

J. Alabastra

1. Edinburgh Painter, related to. Athens 478, from Athens.
   ABL 221,5 above. Dionysos between satyrs and maenads
   dancing. WG: body. Couve-Coll. pl. 38, 1080.

2. Sappho Painter. Madrid 19493. ABL 228,51. Four women.
   WG: body. CV pl. 29,4.

3. Sappho Painter. Berlin inv. 4982.10. ABL 228,52. Four
   women. WG: picture surface.

4. Diosphos Painter. Amsterdam 318, from Attica. ABL 237,103.
   Peleus and Thetis. WG: body. CV pl. 1,1.

5. Diosphos Painter. Berlin 2032, from Chiusi. ABL 237,108.
   Zeus and Ganymede. WG: body. ABL pl. 37,1.

6. Diosphos Painter. Louvre CA 1706. ABL 237,109. Four gods.
   WG: body. ABL pl. 37,4.

7. Diosphos Painter. Naples RC 209. ABL 237,114. Zone of
   riders between zones of patterns. WG: body. Mon. Ant. 22
   (1913), pl. 63,6.

*8. Diosphos Painter. Once Barcelona, Montaner, from Emporion.
   ABL 237,115. Zone of riders between zones of patterns.
   WG: body. Anuari 1908, 224-225, figs. 45-46, no. 135.
   [XIV,1].

9. Diosphos Painter. Cagliari, from Nora. ABL 237,116. Palmettes.
   WG: body. Mon. Ant. 14 (1904), 205, fig. 30.

*10. Diosphos Painter. Gerona 9, from Emporion. ABL 237,117.
   Palmettes. WG: body. Anuari 1908, 224, fig. 44, no. 133.
   [XIV,2].

11. Diosphos Painter. New York, Bastis. ABV 510,21. A, Poseidon
   and Amphitrite (?); B, Herakles and Athena. Under one
   handle, eagle, snake, two lions. WG: body. Bothmer A.A.N.Y.
   pl. 76,217 and pl. 79.

12. Diosphos Painter. Chicago 07.11. ABV 510,22. A, Amazons; B, Amazon
   in chariot. WG: picture zone. Bothmer Am. pl. 64,3.

13. Diosphos Painter. Athens E 1576. ABV 510,24. Dionysos and
   Athena. WG: picture surface.

14. Diosphos Painter. Brauron, from Brauron. <u>Para</u>. 249.
    Courting. WG: body. <u>A.K. Beiheft</u> I, pl. 4, 1&2.

15. Painter of Würzburg 557. Würzburg 557, from Eretria. ARV^2
    304,1. Women washing. WG: body. Langlotz <u>W</u>. pl. 207.

*16. Theseus Painter. Havana, Lagunillas, from Greece. ABV
    518,5. Prothesis. Above, hunting a fawn. WG: body. [XIV,3].

17. Haimon Painter. Athens 12768. ABV 555,423. Above, Peleus
    and Thetis. Below, Gigantomachy. WG: picture zones. <u>ABL</u>
    pl. 41,3.

18. Haimon Painter. Harvard 1920.44.54. Above, Dionysos and
    following. Below, Athena in Gigantomachy. WG: picture zones.

19. Haimon Painter, manner. Bologna 100, from Bologna. ABV
    555,426. Palmettes. WG: body. Zannoni pl. 66, 12 & 15.

20. Emporion Painter. Barcelona 383, from Emporion. ABL 263,1.
    Two barbarians and a dog. Below, net pattern. WG: body.
    <u>Anuari</u> 1908, 221, fig. 38, no. 123.

21. Emporion Painter. Rhodes 12149, from Kameiros. ABL 263,11.
    Woman seated, two men. Below, net pattern. WG: body.
    <u>CV</u> pl. 1, 2&4.

22. Emporion Painter. Cabinet des Médailles 310. <u>ABL</u> 263,18.
    Net pattern. WG: body. <u>CV</u> pl. 87,14.

*23. Emporion Painter. Gerona 806, from Emporion. ABV 584,3.
    Net patterns etc. One zone, satyrs capering with animals.
    WG: picture zone. <u>Anuari</u> 1908, 221, fig. 37. [XIV,4].

24. Emporion Painter, manner of. Basle, private. <u>Para</u>. 292.
    Komos with silen. WG: body. <u>M.M</u>. 22 (1961), no. 152.

25. Beldam Class; Beldam-Python Group. London market (Sotheby).
    <u>Para</u>. 294. Two women, man, musician. WG: body. <u>Sotheby</u>
    23 Oct. 1961, no. 121,1.

*26. London B 669. Four maenads. WG: body. Walters <u>B.M. II</u>
    pl. 7. [XIV,5].

27. New York, Wagstaff. Amazon leading horse. WG: body.
    (Bothmer <u>Am</u>. 99, no. 100).

28. Athens, Agora A-P 1897, from Athens. Net pattern. WG:
    body. HE ΓΑΙϟ ΧΑΙ[ΡΕΤ]Ο . <u>Hesp</u>. 9 (1940.), 217, no. 192.

29. Leningrad 181 a. <u>ABV</u> 666. Warriors and chariot. WG:
    picture surface. (Εὐφαμίδας καλός) . (Waldhauer <u>KO</u>. 59).

White-ground alabastra decorated with black-figure seem
to begin with Psiax, but thereafter they come only from lekythos workshops.[76] Athens 478 has been related to the Edinburgh Painter, whom Miss Haspels considers the first to have
specialized in white-ground lekythoi.[77] The alabastron is
striking for its similarity in design to Leningrad 381 by
Psiax[78] and for the stylization of the maenad's nebris;
the latter represents a stage beyond the example near Psiax
in the Vatican.[79] Since a connection between Psiax and the
Edinburgh Painter is plausible, Athens 478 provides one possible
link.

The Sappho Painter has ties with both artists,[80] but unlike
their alabastra, Madrid 19493 shows a noteworthy reduction
of ornament in favor of picture space. The Diosphos Painter
worked concurrently with the Sappho Painter and reveals the
same stylistic affinities;[81] the first artist differs, however,
in his larger output of white-ground alabastra and in his
predisposition for patternwork. His pieces exhibit one basic
design: tongues, a broad zone of chequers, a leftward meander
above the scene, two reserved lines flanking a black band
below the scene, and black glaze over the bottom. Naples RC
209 and once-Barcelona are particularly elaborate variants,
for they have two primary zones of decoration; the upper one
contains a frieze of horsemen, the lower one palmettes. What-
ever the arrangement of motifs, slip covers all of the reserved
surfaces. Indeed, it heightens the contrast between the top

of the vessel which is densely patterned and the unarticulated
black base.

Most of the vases illustrate mythological subjects or the
everyday life of men and women. However, those in Cagliari
and Gerona represent a sub-group where rows of interlocked
palmettes replace figures. These alabastra belong near the
Diosphos Painter's palmette lekythoi[82] and the workshop's
Side-palmette lekythoi.[83] Furthermore, they are exact counterparts of the Pasiades alabastra whose decoration consists
exclusively of "bilingual" palmettes.[84] Here, as with the Side-
palmette lekythoi which are drawn in outline, the Diosphos
Painter adopts the procedures of red-figure. Though he seems
never to have used the latter, he has left a large oeuvre in
two contemporary alternatives: white-ground and Six's technique.

The Painter of Würzburg 557 is one of several artists related
to the Sappho and Diosphos Painters. Like the former, he
emphasizes figures in the decoration. Like the Diosphos Painter,
he draws heavily on red-figure, but for subject matter[85]
as well as for the outline technique.

The Theseus Painter has left two white-ground alabastra,
and he again exploits the tall field for purposes of representation. Between the lugs of the Lagunillas example, he introduces a subordinate frieze painted in silhouette and he juxtaposes it with the main scene in incised black-figure; as
ornament, he adds a cyma[86] as well as an almost Dourian
stopped meander with crosses. Slip underlies the entire
decoration.

The Haimon Painter seems to follow the Diosphos Painter's
lead. In three pieces,[87] he separates two picture bands on
white-ground by reserve and glaze chequers while Bologna 100
presents an altogether mechanical series of palmettes.

Except for a single example from the Beldam workshop,
the Emporion Painter is the last and largest producer of
white-ground alabastra. He makes almost equal use of the two
principles of design which we have distinguished. Thus, in
one group he devotes most of the cylindrical.surface to the
slipped picture area and frames it with strokes, horizontal
lines, and an occasional pattern. In the second, somewhat
less hackneyed group, he manipulates zones of cross-hatching,
combining one zone with a scene or separating two zones by
a narrow row of ornament or a frieze; the slip changes in
effect from one part to the next, and especially beneath
the dense reticulation.

The white-ground alabastra form a continuous succession
from Psiax to the Emporion Painter; however, an unattributed
example raises the recurrent possibility of collaboration
between Psiax and Nikosthenes. On London B 669, the ornament
includes a light-on-dark crenelation and a smaller version of
the same with four dots in the interstices. As will be
recalled, the second motif occurs in dark-on-light on the
fragmentary oinochoe Leipzig T 411 by the Painter of London
B 620 and it reappears, with five dots, on the kyathoi in
Leningrad and Heidelberg.[88] In style, the London alabastron
points to a lesser hand near Psiax, for the maenads suggest

dishevelled, somewhat degenerate descendents of Psiax's
ladies on the Jameson lekythos, the Leningrad alabastron,
and the Basle plate. Other unattributed alabastra, especially
of poor quality, exist in some number; the Agora and Leningrad examples are among the few with inscriptions.

The white-ground alabastra with black-figure offer some
compensation for their general lack of artistic merit. They
are not invariable concomitants of lekythoi, for they were
not produced by all workshops; instead, they form a continuity
of their own extending from the beginnings of white-ground
to the virtual end of black-figure. The alabastra bring us
particularly close to aspects of red-figure, whether in
subject matter, technique, or ornament. Thus, they differ
from e.g. the kyathoi, mastoids, and skyphoi whose stylistic
reference was mainly to the past, black-figure tradition
rather than to recent, progressive developments.

K. Pyxides

1. Rycroft Painter, near. Athens, Akropolis 2082, fr., from
   Athens. ABV 338,4. (Dionysos seated, with maenads). WG:
   picture zone. Graef pl. 95.

2. Sappho Painter. London B 677. ABL 228,55. Chariot race.
   WG: picture zone on lid.

3. Diosphos Painter. Athens, Akropolis 2083, fr. ABL 237,119.
   Chariot race. WG: picture zone on lid.

4. Haimon Painter, manner. Louvre CA 2588, from Athens. Para.
   284. Perseus and Gorgons. WG: picture zone on lid. Merlin
   Mélanges Glotz pl. 1.

5. Haimon Painter, manner. Basle market (M.M.). Para. 284.
   Maenads. WG: picture zone on lid. M.M. A.S.V. (1964), no. 4ら

6. Haimon Painter, manner. Bremen, Focke Museum. Para. 284.

Four bulls and woman. WG: picture zone on lid. Schaal Brem. pl. 9.

*7. Haimon Painter, manner. Maplewood, Noble. Para. 284. Four bulls. WG: picture zone on lid. [XV,1].

8. Haimon Painter, manner. Athens, Agora P 23132, from Athens. Para. 284. Youth leading ram to altar, and woman; horseman approaching altar, and Hermes. WG: picture zone on lid.

9. Haimon Painter, manner. Paris market (Segredakis). Para. 284. Chariot race. WG: picture zone on lid?

10. Haimon Painter, manner. Brussels A 1907. Para. 284. Chariot race. WG: picture zone on lid. CV pl. 2,2.

11. Haimon Painter, manner. Athens, Akropolis.2111, fr., from Athens. Para. 284. Chariot race. WG: picture zone on lid?

12. Haimon Painter, manner. Syracuse. Para. 284. Symposion; one mounting chariot. WG: picture zone on lid ?

13. Basle market (M.M.),fr.Chariot race. WG: picture zone on lid. M.M. A.S.V. (1964), no. 50.

White-ground pyxides are rarer in black-figure than in red-figure, but they engaged the same artists as have concerned us before. Beazley identified our first example as a late work near the Rycroft Painter, whom he relates both to the Priam Painter and Psiax.[89] Neither the Sappho Painter nor the Diosphos Painter favored pyxides, yet each has left one white-ground piece.

The only concentration of material comes from the workshop of the Haimon Painter. The standard form consists of a rather deep black-glazed bowl surmounted by a knobbed lid. The lids, which are sometimes all that we have, show a broad band of slip decorated with a circular or processional composition; the painting is in black-figure or silhouette and is bounded by black glaze on the outside and a series of concentric

black rings around the knob. The unattributed fragment
in the Basle market should be included in the group. This
small class probably occupied no more than one potter
collaborating with one or two painters, and its quality is
average for the establishment. However, it belongs with
the various bowl-shaped vases which join lekythoi and
alabastra as specialities of the Haimon workshop. In both
major categories of material, white-ground occurs at least
as frequently as normal black-figure.

L. Kalathoi

*1. Louvre no no. Palmettes. WG: decorated surface. [XV,2].

2. Swiss private. Black stripes. WG: decorated surface.

3. Swiss private. No decoration. WG: exterior of bowl.

4. Geneva market (Koutoulakis). Youths and riders. WG:
   picture surface.

The first three kalathoi are stemmed, but the appearance of only one is known to me. The pieces may not form
a class, but they appear together for the time being on
account of their rarity. On the exterior of the bowl, the
Louvre example has a white ground and two subordinate
bands of ornament framing large circumscribed palmettes.
Though less carefully executed, the palmettes resemble
those of the Diosphos Painter's alabastra; the work may
therefore be related to this workshop. The pieces in
Switzerland show a comparable use of slip. One includes
black stripes just below the lip and near the base of
the bowl; the other is apparently undecorated. The Koutou-

lakis kalathos is decorated with a scene of eight figures
beneath a rightward meander. According to Dr. von Bothmer,
the style is Haimonian.

M. Other shapes

1. Psykter. Munich, ex Schoen. A, Two riders. B, Athena
   in Gigantomachy. WG: picture zone. Lullies Schoen no. 54.

2. Plate. Athens, Agora P 2766, from Athens. Herakles and
   Amazons. WG: picture surface. Hesp. 15 (1946), pls.
   56 & 64, no. 186.

3. Plate. Brussels A 1962. Woman at fountain. WG: whole
   obverse. CV pl. 1,4.

*4. Phiale. London B 678, from Capua. Around omphalos, spirals
    with crosses, hare hunt, animals. WG: ornament and
    pictures. AZ 1881, pl. 5. [XV,3].

5. Edinburgh Painter. Lekanis lid. Palermo, fr., from
   Selinus. ABL 219,62. Dionysos seated, dancing maenad.
   WG: picture zone.

6. Open vessel. Braunschweig AT 524, fr. Heads of two horses.
   WG: picture zone. CV pl. 10,10.

7. Aischines (potter). Base ? Athens, Akropolis 2692, frr.,
   from Athens. ABV 351. (Chariot). WG: body.ΛΙϟΤΙΝΕϟ retro.
   ΕΓΟΕϟΕΝ. Graef pl. 113.

   The present section consists of isolated works, all
but one of which are unattributed. The Munich psykter
is unique for its combination of small size[90] and slip
over the paunch. While the decoration and potting appear
equally undistinguished, the style suggests a date
c. 490 B.C.; the horses do not yet display the
thin, elongated bodies and spindly legs prevalent at the
very end of black-figure.

   Plates have already concerned us in discussing Psiax,
and the Agora example provides an informative contrast. It

shows a composition which respects the tondo far more
than did Psiax and an allocation of slip and glaze which
recalls early red-figure cups with lip offset. The incision,
however, points to a black-figure artist. The Brussels
piece is slight, though tolerably composed; it may belong
to a lekythos workshop.[91] The phiale London B 678 came to
light in Capua and by assigning it to the "Nicosthenic
period,"[92] Beazley provided leads for further investigation.
The piece reveals important ties to the Nicosthenic workshop in its shape,[93] its technique, and more loosely, in
the composition[94] and the spiral motif.[95] It thus shares
various features with the attractive ceramic novelties
created for export by Nikosthenes.[96]

Of the three remaining items, two allow little comment.
The lekanis lid in Palermo remains unpublished but is the
only white-ground example among several by the Edinburgh
Painter. The Braunschweig fragment may belong to a drinking
vessel rather than to a larger shouldered shape. The third
piece, Akropolis 2692, is a white-ground object of a different kind. The main part preserves the signature of a potter,
and thus again associates potter and slip. More important,
the work itself seems not to have been a vase but a base
so that it is the terra-cotta equivalent of an object
generally made of stone. Recalling works like the marble
capital from Lamptrai,[97] it suggests that a slip was deliberately applied to simulate another material; on certain hydriai

the white ground referred to metal, on alabastra to

alabaster, on this base to stone. Since it comes from the

Akropolis, the base was originally a dedication, and as

various scholars have observed,[98] it may be related to the

agalma which one Aischines offered to Athena.

N. Plaques

1. Skythes. Athens, Akropolis 2586, frr., from Athens.
   ABV 352,2. Athena mounting chariot. WG: obverse.
   ΣΚVΟΕ𝈀ΕΛD[ΑΦΣΕΝ]   . Graef pl. 110.

*2. Paseas. Athens, North Slope A-P 2073 a-ç & 1774 d, frr.,
   from Athens. ABV 399; ARV² 164. Athena and woman. WG:
   obverse. Hesp. 9 (1940), 235, fig. 46. [XV,4].

3. Paseas. Athens, Akropolis 2583, frr., from Athens. ABV
   352 bottom; ARV² 164,3. Athena and worshipper. WG:
   obverse.…Ν ΓΑ𝈀ΕΟːΛΡΑΜΑΤΟΝ retro.   JHS 75 (1955), 154, fig. 1 a&b.

4. Paseas. Athens, Akropolis 2584 & A-P 2360, frr., from
   Athens. ABV 399,1 middle; ARV² 164. Athena and giant.
   WG: obverse. Hesp. 9 (1940), 160, fig. 12.

5. Paseas. Athens, Akropolis 2585, fr., from Athens. ABV
   399,1 below; ARV² 164. Athena. WG: obverse. Graef pl. 109.

6. Paseas. Athens, Akropolis 2587, fr., from Athens. ABV
   399,2 below; ARV² 164. Athena. WG: obverse. Graef pl. 109.

7. Paseas. Athens, Akropolis 2588, fr., from Athens. ARV²
   164,1. Athena and giant. WG: obverse. Graef pl. 109.

8. Paseas. Athens, Akropolis 2589, fr., from Athens. ARV²
   164,2. Athena. WG: obverse. JHS 75 (1955), 154, fig. 1,c.

9. Paseas. Athens, Akropolis 2591, frr., from Athens. ABV
   400,3 top; ARV² 164. Herakles and Iolaos in chariot,
   with Athena. WG: obverse. Graef pl. 110.

10. Euthymides, related to ? Athens, Akropolis "BF" 2590 &
    Oxford 1927.4602, frr., from Athens. ARV² 1598 bottom.
    Athena. WG: obverse.ΓΟΜΙΑ𝈀ΑΝΕΘΕΚΕ.   JHS 76 (1956), pl. II,1.

11. Euthymides, related to. Athens, Akropolis 1037, from
    Athens. ARV² 1598,5. Warrior. WG: obverse. ΜΕΛΛ[Κ]ΙˌΙLΕ]𝈀,later
    ΛΛΑV[Κ]V[Τ]ΙΕ𝈀 ΚΛLΟ𝈀 . Langlotz pl. 80; Robertson 94.

12. Group of Athens 581. Athens, Akropolis 2499, fr., from

Athens. ABV 506. A, Owl between olive sprigs. B, Four
rows of figures. WG: side A. Graef pl. 102.

Just as bilingual vases provide a graphic, though not
entirely accurate, [99] symbol of the transition from black-
figure to red-figure, so the present series of plaques
illustrates the change as it affects white-ground. Certain
examples would more properly belong in the next chapter, but
the group has been kept together and, at this point in our
study, it may serve as both a conclusion and a preface.

The painter Skythes has left his signature on two
black-figure plaques, one with a reserved ground, one with
slip. Despite the elaborate incision, Athens 2586 displays
the white-ground technique as we have hitherto seen it. Furthermore, it makes particularly clear the "unrealness" of dark
flesh against a light background. While its execution may
appear typically black-figure, a problem exists with the
identity of the artist. An early red-figure painter of the
same name has signed at least four cups, and although Beazley
doubted that one hand painted both groups of works, [100]
the question does remain. For instance, besides their chronological proximity, the oeuvres of both Skythes reveal a
similar technical inventiveness; the one includes white-
ground, the other coral red. These considerations have a
direct bearing on Akropolis 2586, though not on the technique
as it occurs there.

The group of plaques now attributed to Paseas [101] are
of first importance because they seem to document a pro-

gression that begins where Skythes left off; one should
note that their order in our discussion need not have been
the order of production. Paseas was a red-figure painter
best known today for a series of nine plates; as mentioned
earlier, [102] he stands particularly close to Psiax, and if
he learned about white-ground from the latter, he evidently
found the technique most appropriate for plaques. Like
Akropolis 2589 and Skythes' work, Akropolis 2587 makes use
of standard black-figure; however, the incision has the
fluency of red-figure drawing.

Akropolis 2584 and 2588 introduce two developments,
for not only does a second white mark the flesh areas but
a black line also traces their contours and articulates the
ear. Thus, Paseas here rejects the "black flesh convention";
similarly, and more important, he treats at least some of
the forms in terms of outline rather than mass. Akropolis
2073 shows yet a further stage, for the face and feet of
the subordinate figure are drawn in pure outline on the
slipped surface. Second white occurs extremely rarely with
black-figure; as Akropolis 2073 and 2591 suggest, it may
represent a means of distinguishing Athena. Nonetheless, its
absence from the Athena in Akropolis 2587 and its presence
elsewhere still point to a change of procedure, if not of
outlook; the possibility remains that the white has disappeared
where it once overlay glaze, but the published descriptions
mention none of the usual telltale traces. The Paseas plaques
illustrate a red-figure artist's accomodation to black-figure.

Insofar as outline is a hallmark of red-figure, they present
one of its earliest appearances on white-ground. At the
same time, they incorporate features of black-figure and
thus they admirably demonstrate a basic difference between
the material in our present and succeeding chapters.

The plaque Akropolis 2590 is a development beyond
Akropolis 2073, and again it shows the use of a second white.
Its essential features have been discussed by Boardman[103]
who, in the process, virtually attributes the piece to
Euthymides and associates it, stylistically, with Akropolis
1037, the famous Megakles plaque. The latter is probably
most noteworthy for its combination of matte brown for
the warrior's skin, glaze for the garment, and outline
for the helmet and shield. Though perhaps more striking,
Akropolis 1037 is actually a straightforward counterpart
to Akropolis 2590. When considered together, the two plaques
show figures drawn in the red-figure manner but filled in
with color; quite logically, the flesh of Athena is light
and that of the warrior dark lest it have the tonality of
slip. The procedure recalls black-figure because the subjects
are painted onto the background, but the present solution
could only have occurred with red-figure. It is particularly
unusual in the Megakles plaque and may depend as much on
terms of the commission or dedication as on the artist.
Despite these and other possible considerations based on
vase-painting, the work brings to a head the issue of
contemporary Grossmalerei. We are neither able nor prepared

to take up the subject here; however, for the archaic period,
Boardman provides a recent and particularly well-reasoned
discussion.[104]

The final plaque in our series comes from the workshop
to which the Marathon Painter belonged. On the obverse, it
shows the subject in outline against a slipped background,
on the reverse, it displays the same kind of drawing as the
establishment's usual lekythoi; parenthetically, its iconography suggests a thought-out program which might warrant
investigation. Since black-figure lekythos workshops produced
most of the vases which we have been considering, Akropolis
2499 may serve as yet another reminder that this material
dates after the invention of red-figure and borrows more
or less freely from it.

Between our discussions of Andokides, Psiax, the Antimenes
Painter on the one hand, and the plaque painters on the
other, we have covered much ground, but relatively little
time -- hardly more than two generations. Nonetheless,
we have considered two-thirds of the basic picture of
white-ground. One third may be said to concern the invention
and establishment of the technique; the second third covers
the black-figure series whose earlier phases present a few
noteworthy vases and solutions before the use of white-
ground became widespread. The final third consists of the
red-figure or outline series which displays a comparable,
and partly parallel, development. These three aspects constitute the foundation for an understanding of our subject which

the chapters on white-ground cups and lekythoi will help
to fill out.

CHAPTER II: Footnotes

1 The only other instance known to me: hydria once Adrian Hope (Spink, Greek and Roman Antiquities (1923), no. 57); the neck-zone probably not white-ground.

2 CVA: Petit Palais (France 15), 1941, 68.

3 Pp. 35 ff.

4 The hydria has disappeared; besides the Langlotz publication, the only other documentation consists of photographs in the German Institute, Rome (nos. 70.241-70.249). However, Dr. von Bothmer saw that four fragments in the Love collection belong to the vase. The time at which the vase and Love fragments became separated is not known, yet this must have occurred before restoration of the hydria and the Heyl sale in 1930.

5 P. 40, nos. 2&3.

6 Beazley Antimenes 91.

7 Dr. von Bothmer pointed out that the incorporation of animals within foliate or geometric ornament is an East Greek feature. As examples, he cites the amphora Munich 586 (CV pls. 297-298) and the oinochoe ex-Kevorkian (Sotheby 18 June 1968, no. 85), now in Hamburg.

8 There is no reason to attribute the decoration on the body and on the neck to different hands. The neck and predella palmettes correspond e.g. in the presence of seven fronds, in the separation of palmette from volute-calyx, and in the uncertain drawing of the circumscribing line.

9 E.g. London B 310 (ABV 361,12); Copenhagen, Thorvaldsen 56 (ABV 363,40); London B 309 (ABV 364,56).

10 E.g. Lucern market (A.A.) (ABV 362,25 bis; Para. 164).

11 Cf. the examples in the two preceding footnotes.

12 Cf. D. von Bothmer, Review of Die Hydria by E. Diehl (Mainz, 1964) in Gnomon 37 (1965), 605-606. Bothmer also attributed the Bareiss hydria to the Lykomedes Painter.

13 ABL 141 ff.

14 E.g. London 99.2-18.68 (ABV 535,22).

15 Para. 140.

16   Other examples e.g. Brussels R 390 (ABV 319,1 below);
      Vienna 3607 (ABV 319,10).

17   Vienna 3722 (ABV 320,11); Villa Giulia 50560 (ABV 320,12);
      Louvre G 2 (ARV² 53,2); Louvre G 3 (ARV² 53,1); Leipzig
      T 4817 (ABV 319,3); Aachen, Ludwig (Para. 140,D,4).

18   Cabinet des Médailles 218 (ABV 319,1 top; 319,5); Geneva
      market (Koutoulakis (ABV 319,4 ter)); Para. 143-144.

19   ABV 593 below.

20   ABV 574.

21   Pescia Painter: Pescia Romana, Tarquinia, Vulci, Cumae;
      Mariani Painter: Castel Campanile, Capua, Vulci;
      Group X: Locri, Cervetri. No proveniences in Greece
      have yet been recorded.

22   R. Lullies, Griechische Kunstwerke: Sammlung Ludwig,
      Aachen (Aachener Kunstblätter 37 (1968)), 64.

23   ARV² 1531-1532.

24   Cf. p.147.

25   Louvre F 99 (ABV 228 above).

26   E.g. Cabinet des Médailles 334 (ABV 234,3); Florence
      76931 (ABV 229,VII); London B 364 (ABV 229, VI); Boston
      60.1 (ABV 226,7 bis; Para. 107); London B 295 (ABV
      226,1) etc.

27   E.g. Boston 60.1 (ABV 226,7 bis; Para. 107); Providence
      23.303 (ABV 220,34); Baltimore, Archaeological Society
      (ABV 220,36); Montauban NP 7 (ABV 223,59 bis; Para. 104).

28   E.g. Florence 76931 (ABV 229,VII); Louvre F 99 (ABV
      228 above); London B 295 (ABV 226,1).

29   ABV 697.

30   Copenhagen inv. 13809 (ABV 216,4 bis; Para. 105);
      London B 297 (ABV 218,16); Louvre no no.

31   Dr. von Bothmer has established that New York 46.11.7
      and Bibliothèque Royale 5 form a pair. They appear
      as nos. 195 and 196 in the Canino sale of 1837 and
      were not separated until 1848 at the sale of the W.W.
      Hope vases (nos. 49 and 50; cf. AZ 1849 col. 100).
      London B 620 also belonged to Canino (sale no. 136).
      London B 621 was no. 268 in the Durand sale of 1836,

probably once Canino as well. Thus three of these four vases certainly belong together.

32 E.g. E.N. Gardiner, "Wrestling," JHS 25 (1905), 273 n. 40 citing H.B. Walters; E. Pottier, Vases Antiques du Louvre, III (Paris, 1906), 882 and cited by P. Baur, Centaurs in Ancient Art (Berlin, 1912), 102; Pfuhl MuZ, I, 282; E. Strong, Catalogue of the Antiquities of Lord Melchett (Oxford, 1928), 44; ABV 425.

33 D. Feytmans-Kallipolitis, Les vases grecs de la Bibliothèque Royale de Belgique (Brussels, 1948), 34-36.

34 Para. 192.

35 Para. 191-192.

36 ABV 425.

37 Compiègne (ABL 214,189); Zurich private (Para. 216); Amsterdam (Para. 216).

38 E.g. Louvre G 30 (ARV^2 15,9); Turin 4123 (ARV^2 28,11); London E 437 (ARV^2 54,5); Villa Giulia (ARV^2 77,90).

39 It occurs frequently with Euthymides, for instance, except that the tear-shaped filler is placed vertically. E.g. Orvieto, Faina 68 (ARV^2 28,16); also Hypsis Munich 2423 (ARV^2 30,1); Rome, Torlonia 73 (ARV^2 30,2).

40 E.g. Louvre G 42 (ARV^2 23,1); Tarquinia RC 6843 (ARV^2 23,2); Munich 2421 (ARV^2 23,7); Munich 2422 (ARV^2 24,8); London E 159 (ARV^2 24,9).

41 Chequers in black and white, as opposed to reserve, occur e.g. on two plaques associated with Euthymides (p.105 nos. 10-11), three plates by or near Euthymides (p.119, nos. 1-3), two head vases by Charinos (p.147 nos. 3-4). Dr. von Bothmer had already related the Euthymidean plates with the Charinos vases, cf. ARV^2 9 top. The alternation of larger black and white squares occurs in the Class of London B 620 (p.64 , nos. 11 & 14).

42 Boston 93.99 (ABL 206,5); Boston 93.100 (ABL 207,42); Basle market (M.M.) (Para. 215).

43 Our total number of oinochoai in each subdivision:

I Sèvres Class - 17
II Class of London B 630 - 6
III R.S. Class - 4

IV Class A - 45
V Class C - 8
VI Class of Copenhagen 65 - 5
Class and Group of Vatican G. 49 - 7
Seattle Group - 4

44   The only exception: Dunedin E 29.7 (ABV 525,12).

45   Pp. 55-56.

46   Antwerp, Museum Vleeshuis (Para. 268,4).

47   Cahn in M.M. A.S.V. (1964), no. 13. The subject is
interesting, for it seems adapted from Panathenaic
amphorae. Cf. the small neck-amphora New York 52.11.17,
also for the ivy band.

48   Agora P 2569 (ABL 210,101). Dr. von Bothmer has suggested
that Como C. 25 might rather belong to a Light-make
neck-amphora.

49   O. 77.

50   CVA: Turin 2 (Italy 40), 1969, 7.

51   One single later example is known to me: Haimon Painter,
manner. Boulogne (ABV 555,430).

52   It measures 0.34 m. in height.

53   ARV^2 40; cf., for example, Swiss private (ARV^2 172,4).
The Karlsrune palmettes, however, have red hearts
which do not occur in palmette-eye cups.

54   O. 70,81.

55   ABL 77,106.

56   P. 37.

57   ARV^1 948 centre.

58   E.g. Dionysos' himation on Vatican G. 57, wings of the
handle sphinxes Cambridge 9.37. Interesting also is the
white kylix held by Dionysos on Cambridge 10.37.

59   M. Eisman, "The Theseus Painter, the Marathon Tumulus,
and Chronology," AJA 75 (1971), 200.

60   A.D. Ure, "Krokotos and White Heron," JHS 75 (1955), 90 ff.

61   For these new attributions, I thank Dr. von Bothmer who

allowed me access to his correspondence with Mr. Eisman.

62 O. 53.

63 ABL 105-106.

64 P. 92.

65 Our total number of skyphoi in each subdivision:

Group of Rhodes 11941 - 2
Pistias Class M - 8
Pistias Class N - 10
Lindos Group - 45

66 ABV 627.

67 E. Karydi, "Ein Skyphos aus dem Kerameikos," AM 77 (1962), 105 ff.

68 ABV 157,89.

69 ABV 156,80.

70 Cf. Beazley Dev., Chapter V, especially 56 ff.

71 Ure Sixth 71.

72 A. Bruhn, "Greek Vases in the Ny Carlsberg Glyptothek," From the Collections 2 (1939), 124.

73 E.g. Euphronios, Louvre G 103 (ARV^2 14,2); Chelis Painter, Munich 2589 (ARV^2 112,1 top); Oltos, London E 437 (ARV^2 54,5).

74 Victoria and Albert Museum 275.64 (ARV^2 9 top).

75 ABV 156.

76 Our total number of alabastra in each subdivision:

Edinburgh Painter, related - 1
Sappho Painter - 2
Diosphos Painter - 24
Painter of Würzburg 557 - 2
Theseus Painter - 2
Haimon workshop - 6
Emporion workshop - 25
Beldam workshop - 1

77 ABL 86-87.

78 P.35, no. 2.

79 P.82, no. 3.

80 ABL 77,101.

81 ABL 77, 94, 101, 104.

82 E.g. Athens 2213 (ABL 233,36); Syracuse 43.051 (ABL 233,37).

83 ARV^2 301 ff.

84 ARV^2 99, 3-6; cf. ABL pp. 101-102.

85 Palermo (ABL 113; ARV^2 304,2); cf. e.g. Louvre G 2
    (ARV^2 53,2); London E 44 (ARV^2 318,2). Würzburg 557
    (ARV^2 304,1): London E 34 (ARV^2 110,8); Brussels A 889
    (ARV^2 329,130).

86 Cf. Select Exhibition of Beazley Gifts to the Ashmolean
    Museum (London, 1967), no. 162. Infra, e.g. pp.163,
    nos. 12-13, 181, no. 63.

87 Also Barcelona 3829 (ABV 555,422).

88 Pp. 85-86.

89 ABV 335.

90 It measures 10.5 cm. The closest parallel in black-figure
    is Brussels inv. A 1312, CV pl. 27,4.

91 For the treatment of the hair and gesture, cf. Leyden
    XVII^a 20 (ABL 241,5); for the hydria, once Halle, Ross
    (ABL 242,24); for the drapery ends, Louvre CA 2588
    (Para. 284).

92 J.L. Caskey and J.D. Beazley, Attic Vase Paintings in
    the Museum of Fine Arts, Boston I (Oxford, 1931), 55.

93 ABV 234,XII.

94 Cf. the cups Berlin 1805 (ABV 223,65); Berlin 1806
    (ABV 223,66).

95 E.g. Louvre F 104 (ABV 222,58); London B 364 (ABV 229,VI).

96 The phiale recalls the hydria Louvre CA 4716 in two
    respects: the treatment of the birds and a sense of whimsy
    that seems to underly the combination of motifs. This
    observation implies no direct connection.

97 G.M.A. Richter, The Archaic Gravestones of Attica
    (London, 1961), no. 20, figs. 66-69.

98   B. Graef, Die antiken Vasen von der Akropolis zu Athen
     I (Berlin, 1925), 259; J.D. Beazley, Potter and Painter
     in Ancient Athens (1949), 23; A.Raubitschek, Dedications
     from the Athenian Akropolis (Cambridge, 1949), 50.

99   Bilingual vases may occur later in an artist's career
     than purely red-figure examples. The Andokides Painter
     provides a well studied instance: Bothmer Andokides 212.

100 ARV^2 82; ABV 352.

101 See especially ARV^2 164; J. Boardman, "A Name for the
     Cerberus Painter," JHS 75 (1955), 154-155.

102 P. 38.

103 J. Boardman, "Some Attic Fragments: Pot, Plaque, and
     Dithyramb," JHS 76 (1956), 20-22.

104 Boardman Votive Plaques 186 ff., especially 189-190.

CHAPTER III: THE WHITE-GROUND VASES DECORATED WITH OUTLINE

The vases in this chapter were decorated by artists trained in the red-figure technique. They show a special form of red-figure in which outline serves for the drawing but the glaze background is absent. As indicated previously, this procedure had begun to develop in the second quarter of the sixth century and it came into its own c. 530 B.C. with the inventions of Andokides and the Andokides Painter. In the hands of red-figure artists, white-ground undergoes several technical changes,[1] most notably the introduction of larger surfaces of color for the representation of garments; this feature adds weight to the figures and contrast to their light flesh. The material to be discussed reveals a shift in subject matter that also deserves mention. The scenes on white-ground vases now increasingly concern women, whether drawn from mythology, like maenads and Amazons, or from everyday life. They by no means replace heroic encounters, the palaistra, and other such themes, but they gradually outnumber them. This development has already appeared, e.g. on black-figure alabastra, and it forms part of the larger evolution from the archaic to the classic; it might also have a technical reason, insofar as outline and slip may have seemed better suited to women and youths. Thus the present chapter will include new shapes, techniques, and subjects. It contains the material not covered by the two preceding chapters and it completes the sequence of all shapes except cups and lekythoi.

A. Plates

*1. Euthymides. Adria Bc 64.10, frr., from Adria. ARV^2
28,18. Warrior. WG: rim. ΕΥΘΥΜΙ[ΔΕ϶] ΕΛΡΑΘΕ. CV pl. 2,7;
Hoppin Rf I 438. [XVI,1].

2. Euthymides, manner. Boston 00.325, from Tarquinia. ARV^2
30 top. Nereid. WG: rim. Caskey-Beazley I pl. 2,3 & p.
3, fig. 3.

3. Euthymides, manner ? Villa Giulia, fr., from Veii. ARV^2
30 top. WG: rim.

*4. Berlin Painter. Athens, Akropolis 427, frr., from Athens.
ARV^2 214,244. Athena. WG: tondo. Langlotz A. pl. 32.
[XVI,2].

5. Berlin Painter, like. Athens, Akropolis 428, fr., from
Athens. ARV^2 214;1635. Maenad. WG: picture surface.
Langlotz A. pl. 32.

6. Group of the Negro Alabastra. Taranto inv. 61, from
Taranto. ARV^2 268,34. Negro. WG: picture surface. EAA
I 972, fig. 1224.

7. Group of the Negro Alabastra. Tübingen E 47, fr. ARV^2
268,35. Negro. WG: tondo. Watzinger pl. 16.

8. Painter of New York 21.131. Athens, Akropolis 425, from
Athens. ARV^2 269 bottom. Amazon. WG: tondo. Langlotz
A. pl. 32.

9. Athens, Akropolis 426, from Athens. Iris or Nike. WG:
picture surface. Langlotz A. pl. 32.

10. Amsterdam, Scheurleer inv. 4558. (Drawing modern). WG: tondo.

11. New York 41.162.148. (Drawing modern). WG: tondo.

Although they represent a small shape that would
normally appear later in our discussion, the plates occur
first because of their early date and direct relation to
the plaques. The first three examples are connected by
the pattern of small black chequers on white-ground covering
the rim; they share this rare motif with the plaques

Akropolis 2590 and 1037. Euthymides is best known as one
of the "pioneers" of the new figure drawing made possible
by red-figure.[2] His technical versatility tends to be over-
looked, yet it appears in the two cups with coral red[3]
as well as in the plates and plaques with their white
ground and flat surfaces. On the basis of signatures
hitherto available, Euthymides seems to have specialized
as a painter; an as yet unpublished vase now also documents his activity as potter.[4] For our subject alone, the
discovery proves of first importance, for it may help to
establish that this major artist prepared the coral red
and white-ground himself; however, rather than draw on
these surfaces, he preferred to use them as frames for
red-figure subjects.

The plate Boston 00.325 is interesting for its earlier
attributions. It was once assigned to the late Psiax by
Beazley[5] and to Euthymides by Hoppin.[6] It thus calls to
mind the Brachas cup which is stylistically reminiscent
and which occupies a similar, intermediate position between
Psiax and the Pioneer Group; however, the plate stands
closer to the latter, the Brachas cup to Psiax.

Two white-ground plates have been associated with the
Berlin Painter, a follower, if not a pupil, of Euthymides.[7]
Though very incompletely preserved, they reverse the
Euthymidean design because slip here underlies the picture,
and Akropolis 427 includes a framing cyma within the
plain glazed rim. Like the examples by Psiax and Euthymides,

they depict a single figure rather than a narrative subject, as Paseas tended to do.

The last three attributed plates are datable at least a decade later; they represent one of two shapes which occasionally use the iconography of the Negro Alabastra.[8] Corresponding to the latter in technique, style, and quality, they again show figures drawn upon a white ground in outline and silhouette; this procedure creates curious details like the blacks' light hair. Akropolis 425 is the earliest example, with ties in execution to the Paidikos Alabastra;[9] the helmet recalls those of Athena and the warrior on the Euthymidean plaques.[10]

The unattributed plate, Akropolis 426, points to a late archaic hand, but close parallels are lacking for the treatment of the wings. The present state of Scheurleer 4558 and New York 41.162.148 resembles that of several white-ground cups. The objects themselves are ancient, but the decoration was added in modern times, probably during the later nineteenth century. The New York example preserves traces of a lotus pattern on its border; according to Dr. von Bothmer, it may therefore be dated to the mid-sixth century B.C.

When considered as a group, the white-ground plates prove to be few in number and restricted to a period of c. thirty years, extending from Psiax roughly to the time of the Berlin Painter. The main pieces were decorated by painters of large shapes rather than of cups, as one might have expected; concerning the potters, virtually no evidence

exists as yet. Finally, their generally high quality, the

three different uses of the white ground, and their

distribution [11] suggest that these works were specially

made, if not specially ordered.

B. Kraters

1. Calyx-krater. Pioneer Group. Taranto, frr., from Taranto. ARV² 33,7. (Satyr, maenad, and third). WG: picture surface.

2. Calyx-krater. Pioneer Group. Oxford 1934,354, fr. ARV² 33,7. Ivy pattern. WG: ornament.

*3. Column-krater. Goettingen Painter, by or manner. New York 91.1.462. ARV² 234,1. A, Herakles and (Kyknos ?). B, Komos. Neck, A, hunters and hounds. WG: neck zone of A. Richter and Milne fig. 46. [XVI,3].

4. Calyx-krater. Villa Giulia Painter. Reggio, frr., from Locri. ARV² 619,11 bis. Athena; woman holding sleeping child. WG: picture surface.

5. Calyx-krater. Villa Giulia Painter. Lausanne 3700, fr., from Tarsus. ARV² 619,12. (Upper part of woman, led to right). WG: picture surface.

*6. Calyx-krater. Methyse Painter, probably. Cincinnati, Art Museum 1962.388, frr. ARV² 634,5. Paris and Helen. WG: picture surface. Ghali-Kahil H. pl. 10. [XVII].

7. Volute-krater. Methyse Painter. Ancona, frr., from Septempeda, San Severino. Return of Hephaistos. Neck, A, Amazonomachy; B, Judgement of Paris. WG: neck. (Bothmer Am. 144, no. 32.)

8. Calyx-krater. Phiale Painter. Agrigento, from Agrigento. ARV² 1017,53. A, Perseus and Andromeda. B, Two women, one with sceptre. WG: picture surface. ΕΥΑΙΩΝ ΚΑΛΟΣ ΑΙΣ+ΥΛΟ. EAA VI, 68, fig. 76

9. Calyx-krater. Phiale Painter. Vatican, from Vulci. ARV² 1017,54. A, Hermes bringing infant Dionysos to old Silenos. B, Three muses. WG: picture surface. Arias and Hirmer pls. XLIII-XLIV.

The krater was a red-figure addition to the repertoire

of shapes with white-ground; due probably to the extensive
picture surface, it attracted a few early classic and
classic pot painters. The first two examples date to the
last decade of the sixth century and may belong to the
same calyx-krater. The Taranto fragments have slip over
their entire surfaces and the maenad, who is most complete,
makes clear the competent, though somewhat wooden, drawing
style. The Oxford fragment preserves some of a black-glazed
rim and a length of leftward ivy alternating with a bud motif;
the latter seems exceedingly rare.

Besides the black-figure examples by the Sappho and
Theseus Painters, New York 91.1.462 is the only other
column-krater. On the neck of side A, it has a slipped
frieze that consists of a hunting scene painted in silhouette. The vase reveals a carefully planned program, for
the two main subjects are in red-figure, the subsidiary
zone in silhouette on white-ground; as often, the ornament
framing the panels and covering both side and topside of
the mouth is in silhouette on reserve. Through the treatment
of the neck, Beazley related this work to the Leagros
Group;[12] however, it does represent a distinct tendency,
and should be dated within the earlier first quarter of the
fifth century.

After a gap of c. three decades, three white-ground
calyx-kraters and one volute-krater occur in the circle
of the Villa Giulia Painter. They now comprise only iso-

lated fragments, remnants of the magnificent pictures
which the large shapes made possible. Informative nonetheless, the Lausanne and Reggio pieces preserve female
figures, with flesh in added white; the first also shows
a red-figure palmette ornament above the scene.

The three calyx-krater fragments now in Cincinnati
belong to a follower of the Villa Giulia Painter and within
our study they mark an important point. They are the first
pieces to demonstrate the coloristic and tonal gradations,
the heightened expressiveness which could only be achieved
on a white ground. For the first time, they present us
not only with drawing but also with painting. The technique
resembles traditional outline in the glaze and dilute that
delineate the contours, the pleated chitons, the facial
features, the hair, etc. New, however, are the purple
mantles and headbands, the golden brown chlamys with its
purple border, or the golden stephane with white and
purple dot rosettes. With its lack of drama, its rather
vacuous figures, and its easy accomodation of color and
line, the present vase provides a fitting introduction
to many that appear in subsequent sections.

The volute-krater in Ancona has been attributed to
the Methyse Painter by Dr. von Bothmer.[13] More completely
preserved than the foregoing work, it shows the main subject
in red-figure on the body and a subsidiary motif on each
side of the slipped neck. This differentiation of parts

by technique is noteworthy on such a large shape, yet it
involves the same principle as, for instance, New York
63.11.6 by Andokides. Furthermore, the decoration of the
neck seems deliberately subordinated, for it consists of
figures drawn in outline with little added color to de-
tract from the scene below. Indeed, with both this krater
and the Goettingen Painter's, the presence of a crowning
frieze on white-ground creates a strongly architectonic,
if not architectural, effect.

Concluding our series are the two complete calyx-kraters
by the Phiale Painter; since the calyx-krater predominates
among the white-ground examples, these works may compensate
for our otherwise fragmentary evidence. In both, the slipped
picture surface is framed above by a red-figure foliate
motif, below by one or two rows of ornament that include
a stopped meander interrupted by crosses. The scenes include
details of setting drawn with dilute, garments in ochre and
purple, and features like the women's flesh and the old
silen's hair in added white. For their conception and
execution, the vases may well depend upon monumental
painting, [14] but even without its influence, they will have
offered unprecedented possibilities to an ambitious Attic
painter of the mid-fifth century.

The existing kraters represent two phases in the use
of white-ground by red-figure artists. The one or two
examples of the Pioneer Group belong to the experimental

period and such pieces will have influenced the Sappho
Painter's column-krater. The works of the Villa Giulia
and Phiale Painters, especially, belong to the time of
greatest white-ground activity; they were produced by
artists who also decorated lekythoi and who exploited the
technique for its pictorial and coloristic effects. While
the latter appear most commonly on cups, the kraters give
their subjects a scale which more satisfactorily approxi-
mates our idealized visions of classical painting.

C. Oinochoai

1. Epeleios Painter, connected with. Palermo, from Selinus.
   ARV^2 152,1 below. Komos. WG: picture surface (only ?).

*2. Foundry Painter. London D 13, from Locri ? ARV^2 403,38.
   Woman spinning. WG: body. Bieber Entw. pl. 1,2. [XVIII,1].

3. Ikaros Painter. Oxford 1927.4467. ARV^2 700,84. Nike,
   flying with sash. WG: body. Van Hoorn Choes fig. 150.

*4. Painter of London D 14. London D 14, from Vulci. ARV^2
   1213,2 above. Herakles and Athena. WG: body. Murray
   W.A.V. pl. 21,b. [XVIII,2].

5. Naples 2439, from Nola. ARV^2 1561,4. Mistress and maid.
   WG: body. ΛΛΚΙΜΑ+ΟC ΚΛΛΟΣ   . Eph. 1905, 36, fig. 1.

6. Athens 2186, from Athens. ARV^2 1562 top. Woman seated.
   WG: body. CC pl. 50, 1846.

7. Athens, Akropolis 701, fr., from Athens. Youth. WG:
   picture surface. Langlotz A. pl. 54.

8. Geneva 20300. Nike and warrior. WG: body. A.K. 8,2 (1965)
   advt. p. II.

9. Athens, Akropolis 705, fr., from Athens. (Komast).
   WG: band within neck. (Langlotz A. pl. 54).

As indicated above, white-ground oinochoai with black-
figure form a sequence that begins with the workshop of
Nikosthenes and ends with that of the Athena Painter.

Their decline marks the virtual disappearance of white-
ground oinochoai, for the outline examples are isolated
and represent various forms. The most important works
are London D 13 and D 14. The first belongs to the circle
of the Brygos Painter which produced a few white-ground
lekythoi and alabastra in addition to the well-known cups.
Attributed to the Foundry Painter, London D 13 displays a
completely slipped body with a single figure standing on
a ground line; sparse ornament in glaze with added red
occurs around the neck and below the handle. The piece
reveals particular skill in the presentation of the subject
and, at the same time, it illustrates a handling of glaze,
dilute, and color typical of late archaic red-figure artists.
D 14, the   namepiece of the Painter of London D 14, has
been dated by Beazley c. 430.[15] Its main distinction lies
in the impressed lotus motif that occurs on the shoulder
and the row of impressed eggs above and below the scene.
Some red-figure works show a metal vessel, a piece of
military equipment, a piece of jewelry, or an anklet in
raised clay, but such details were originally gilt.[16]
The London oinochoe proves exceptional not only for the
use of impression but also for its application to all of
the subsidiary ornament;[17] the latter will have been done
in the potter's workshop before the vase received its slip
and painting.

Among other attributed works, the piece in Palermo

resembles the type of mug associated with the Painter
of Berlin 2268.[18]   Oxford 1927.4467 is a chous by a lesser
painter of lekythoi. Naples 2439 and Athens 2186 show an
elongated variety of Shape I and have been related stylistically by Beazley.[19]   By their subject matter, the added
matte colors, and the kalos name on Naples 2439, they point
to early classic workshops which might have specialized
in Nolan amphorae or lekythoi.

Of the unattributed oinochoai, the first Akropolis fragment seems to have had slip over much of the body; the
figure recalls certain youths of the Colmar Painter[20]
and may at least be contemporary with them. Geneva 20300
suggests a painter of the mid-fifth century who, again,
transferred a subject common on Nolans and lekythoi to a
white-ground oinochoe. Finally Akropolis 705 has been
included here because it presents the rare feature of a
broad white band inside of the neck.

The outline oinochoai give the impression of incidental
works produced by artists who were familiar with white-
ground from other shapes. They suggest that an appreciable
change of taste occurred after the black-figure series ceased
and that their own continued existence depended on two
factors: the interest of a novelty and the influence of
contemporary lekythoi and cups.

D. Alabastra

*1. Group of the Paidikos Alabastra (a); Pasiades Painter.
London B 668, from Marion. ARV² 98,1. Woman with phiale,

woman (maenad ?) running with sprigs. On bottom, rf
palmette. WG: body.ΓΑϟΙΑΔΕϟΙΕΓΟΙΕϟΕΝ.ΗΟΓΑΙϟΚΑϟΟϟ: Mon. Piot
26 (1923), 86, fig. 9; Thimme figs. 11-12. [XVIII,3].

2. Group of the Paidikos Alabastra (a); Pasiades Painter.
Athens 15002, from Delphi. ARV² 98,2. A, Maenad. B,
Amazon. On bottom, rf palmette. WG: body.ΓΕΑϟΙΑΔΕϟΙϟ ΕΓΟΕΙΕϟΕΝΙ.
Mon. Piot 26 (1923), pl. 3 & p. 70, fig. 3; Thimme fig. 10.

*3. Group of the Paidikos Alabastra (b). Louvre CA 1920. ARV²
99,3. Palmettes; on bottom, rf palmette. WG: body.
ΓΑϟΙΑΔΕϟΕΓΟΙΕϟΕΝ: Mon. Piot 26 (1923), 87-88, figs. 10-12.
[XVIII,4].

4. Group of the Paidikos Alabastra (b). New York 21.80.
ARV² 99,5. Palmettes; on bottom, black palmette on
reserve. WG: body.ΗΙΓΓΑΡ+ΟϟΚΑϟΟϟΝΑΙ: Richter and Milne
fig. 109.

5. Group of the Paidikos Alabastra (c); Euergides Painter,
manner. Tübingen E 48. ARV² 100,28. A, Dancing girl;
B, youth. On bottom, rf palmette. WG: body.ΕΗΟΓΙΑΓΙΙϟΚΑΛΟΓϟΙ.ΓΡΟϟ
ΑΛΟΡΕΝΟ.ΓΕΡΙΟϟΕΑΛΙΟΡΕΝΟ. Watzinger pl. 21.

6. Group of the Paidikos Alabastra (c); Euergides Painter,
manner. Boston 00.358. ARV² 101,30. Woman dancing and
two women. On bottom, black komast (?) on reserve. WG:
body.ΓΡΟϟΑΛΟΡΕΝΟ.ΓΑΙϟΚΑϟΟϟ: . Smith Forman pl. 12,366.

7. Syriskos Painter. Swiss private. ARV² 264,59. Woman with
alabastron and mirror at altar. WG: body.

8. Syriskos Painter. Athens, from Attica. ARV² 264,61.
Woman. WG: body. Holmberg Stathatos III, pl. 24,82.

9. Syriskos Painter. Dunedin F 54.78. ARV² 264,63. Woman
with torches approaching altar. WG: body. Anderson pl. 12,84.

10. Group of the Negro Alabastra. Leningrad, from S. Russia ?
ARV² 268,8. Negro with axe and pelta. WG: body.

11. Group of the Negro Alabastra. Louvre CA 4193. ARV²
268,26 bis; Para. 352. Negro. WG: body. M.M. 26 (1963), no. 121.

12. Group of the Negro Alabastra. Leningrad. ARV² 268,26 ter.
Negro. WG: body.

13. Group of the Negro Alabastra. Where ?, from Megara.
ARV² 268,32. Two negroes. WG: body. AM 14 (1889), 45 & 41.

14. Group of the Negro Alabastra. London B 673, from Kameiros.
ARV² 268,33. Amazon. WG: body. Thimme fig. 8.

15. Painter of New York 21.131. Meggen, Käppeli. ARV^2 269,2. Amazon. Youth leaning on stick; heron. WG: body. Thimme figs. 3-4.

16. Painter of New York 21.131. Reggio 5347, from Locri. ARV^2 269,5. Amazon. WG: body. N.Sc. 1917, 138, fig. 45.

*17. Painter of New York 21.131, near. Berlin inv. 3382. ARV^2 269 below. Amazon; negro. WG: body. Thimme figs. 1-2. [XIX,1-2].

18. Group of the Cracow Alabastron. Cracow inv. 1292. ARV^2 270,1. Amazon. WG: body. CV pl. 13,7.

19. Triptolemos Painter. Louvre CA 2575. ARV^2 363,29. A, Woman with alabastron; B, woman with box. WG: picture surface.

20. Painter of London D 15. London D 15, from Greece. ARV^2 390,1. Youth with dog; acontist. WG: body.+ΑΙΡΙΡΡΟϟ ΚΑΛΟϟ,+ΑΙ-ΡΙΡΡΟϟΚΑΛΟϟ. Klein L. 151, fig. 37.

21. Painter of Munich 2676. Basle market (M.M.). ARV^2 394,51. Woman seated; woman with distaff at wool basket. WG: picture surface. M.M. 40 (1969), no. 110.

22. Painter of Munich 2676, near. Karlsruhe B 3056, from Alike. Zeus and Hera. WG: crowning meander. CV pl. 29,1-2. [Bothmer].

23. Foundry Painter, manner. Berlin 2258, from Tanagra. ARV^2 405 top. Nike; athlete. WG: body. Die Antike I (1925), pls. 28-29.

24. Villa Giulia Painter. Louvre MNC 627, from Greece. ARV^2 625,91. Youth and woman; youth and boy. WG: picture surface.

25. Villa Giulia Painter. Giessen. ARV^2 625,93. A, Woman spinning; B, woman with mirror. WG: picture surface, only? Angermeier pls. 1-4.

26. Ikaros Painter. Oxford 1947.113. ARV^2 700,82. Woman and girl. WG: picture surface.

27. Aischines Painter, connected with. Louvre CA 1856. ARV^2 722,3 above. A, Woman with oinochoe at altar; B, woman with phiale. WG: body. Perrot 10, 696, fig. 382.

28. Painter of Copenhagen 3830. Copenhagen inv. 3830, from Attica. ARV^2 723,1 below. Woman with hen and chaplet;

woman with wreath. WG: picture surface, ornament above.
CV pl. 174,1.

29. Painter of Palermo 1162. Palermo (1162). ARV^2 725,2 above.
Maenad; woman with oinochoe. WG: picture surface.

30. Painter of Taranto 2602. Warsaw 142456. ARV^2 725,6.
Woman with mirror, woman. WG: picture surface. CV
Czartoryski pl. 42,8.

31. Two-row Painter. Cambridge 143, from Athens. ARV^2
726,7. Above: A, woman; B, woman. Below: A, Nike;
B, woman seated. WG: picture surface and dividing
ornament. Gardner pl. 30,3; CV pl. 29,10.

32. Two-row Painter. Athens 16457. ARV^2 726,16. Woman with
mirror, woman with flower, girl with krotala. WG:
picture surface. CV pl. 19.

33. Two-row Painter. Berlin 2259, from Athens. ARV^2 727,20.
Judgement of Paris. WG: picture surface. Jacobsthal Mel. 84.

34. Athens 1725, related. Reggio, from Locri. ARV^2 728,2 centre.
Patternwork. WG: body. N.Sc. 1913 suppl., 38, fig. 48.

35. Athens 1725, related. Athens 12767, from Eretria. ARV^2
728 centre. Death of Aktaion. WG: body. AM 38 (1913),
pl. 17, 2-3.

36. New York 22.139.27. ARV^1 202,b. Two Amazons. WG: body.

37. Louvre CA 1682. ARV^1 202,a. Oriental warriors. WG: body.
BCH 87 (1963), 583, fig. 6.

38. Basle, Cahn. Two satyrs and baby. WG: body. Hesp. Art
Bull. 19 (1962), no. 120 (part).

39. Brussels A 2314. Seated helmet maker and Athena. WG:
picture surface, ornament above. CV pl. 5,8.

*40. Louvre CA 2515. Eos and Tithonos. WG: picture surface.
[XIX,3].

Outline alabastra are the most abundant shape in this
chapter; unlike the oinochoai, they run parallel to their
black-figure counterparts and outlive them by several decades.
The Group of the Paidikos Alabastra must follow very quickly
upon the white-ground pieces by Psiax.[21] Though related

stylistically to the Euergides Painter, the Group seems to
issue from a different potter's workshop, that of Pasiades
who may be identical with Paidikos.[22] The works fall into
three categories, two of which display the basic design:
a figured zone over the centre of the body, varying amounts
of blank space and ornament above and below, a tondo on
the bottom filled either with a red-figure palmette or
with a motif in silhouette. The drawing consists of outline
generously supplemented with dilute for the garments. The
third category is related to the others by the potter's
signature and by the treatment of the bottom, but the
decoration comprises circumscribed palmettes drawn in silhouette;
thus, these bilinguals anticipate the Diosphos Painter's
black-figure palmette alabastra by about a decade.[23]

Although the Syriskos Painter worked on large shapes
primarily, he exerted a particular influence on alabastra.
The eight examples attributed to his hand vary somewhat
in form; however, they correspond in the limitation of glazed
zones and ornament, in the female figure occupying most of
the vertical surface, and in a predisposition for unarticulated dark areas, as for clothing or elements of setting.
The pieces owned by a Swiss collector and once by Mme.
Stathatos lead directly to the Group of the Negro Alabastra;
they supplement stylistic connections with iconographic ones
like the palm tree, alabastron, heron, and altar.

The Negro Alabastra[24] per se constitute a distinct type

which must have been produced by one workshop containing
close followers of the Syriskos Painter and possibly the
artist himself. Numbering at least forty-five, their over-
all uniformity suggests that these works served a specific
and short-lived function. Virtually all of them have slip
covering the cylinder except for the bottom, the very top,
and an occasional narrow band above the figure. They show
a single Negro soldier whose dress, equipment, and setting
vary among certain fixed possibilities but who usually stands
frontally with head to left and feet to right. The drawing
consists of outline with some silhouette and exceptionally
diversified brushwork that substitutes for dilute or added
color. In fact, the bold dots and strokes produce the
harlequin-like effect of the figures. Finally, of the few
exceptions to the basic type, two are the plates with a
single Negro[25] and three are alabastra with a pair of Negroes
or a single Amazon.[26]

The Painter of New York 21.131 was distinguished by
Bothmer[27] within Beazley's larger Paidikos Group.[28] The
seven white-ground pieces resemble the latter in the iconography
of Amazons and youths, yet they stand even closer to the
Negro Alabastra in the rendering of costume and through
the inclusion of the palm tree, the diphros with helmet,
etc.[29] Peculiar to these works is the row of ornament both
above and below the subject; generally, however, they
suggest early derivatives of the Syriskos type occurring

between the Paidikos and Negro Alabastra. The Group of the
Cracow Alabastron is a second, perhaps somewhat later, offshoot. Among several distinctive features, the two examples
have added white.

The later archaic white-ground alabastra of c. 500-480
can be associated with three artistic circles, not to say
workshops, that of the Euergides Painter who favored cups,
that of the Syriskos Painter who favored larger shapes,
and that of the Brygos Painter who again specialized in
cups. Louvre CA 2575 is the sole, and unpublished, exception,
for the Triptolemos Painter stands near Douris. The two
works by the Painter of London D 15˙ show palaistra scenes
drawn in a dry, unembellished manner between zones of ornament.[30] The piece in the Basle market depicts a domestic
scene framed by stopped meanders. Berlin 2258, which depends
on the Foundry Painter, presents a figured zone restricted
by patternwork and a noteworthy use of glaze and dilute to
heighten the contrast between Nike and youth.

The greatest number of slipped alabastra, with black-
figure or outline, belong to the first two decades of the
fifth century; thereafter, their production declines and
virtually ceases by the classic period. Five examples are
associated with the Villa Giulia Painter, the only early
classic painter of large pots who also decorated alabastra;
they show the now prevalent themes of women either with
youths or in domestic situations. The piece in Giessen

illustrates another recurring feature: a vertical interrupted
meander separating the subjects on each side. The remaining
vases belong to artists who specialized in minor lekythoi
and alabastra. Those by the Ikaros and Aischines Painters
down to the Painter of Taranto 2602 have bands of glaze
or ornament and scenes drawn in outline with an occasional
animal in silhouette; on Louvre CA 1856, a vertical meander
begins at each lug. The only larger group of alabastra and
the last one in our series belongs to the Two-row Painter.
Thirteen of the twenty-two pieces contain two superimposed
figures on white-ground and a few include the vertical
meander; characteristic of all is the ornament on reserve
at the top and bottom, and the simple, rather stiff drawing
without color or dilute. The example from Reggio related to
Athens 1725 documents the persistence of pure pattern decoration.

The list of unattributed alabastra opens with two
whose closest ties are with the Negro-Amazon group. New
York 22.139.27 shows the same design as New York 21.131 and,
despite evident stylistic differences, might be loosely
related to it. Louvre CA 1682 is unusual for its intent,
rather savage warriors as well as for its peculiar dotted
square and crenelle patterns; the latter occurs in outline
on the Palermo alabastron [31] by the Painter of New York
21.131, but otherwise CA 1682 remains isolated. The piece

in the Cahn collection is noteworthy for its subject matter
as well as for its fine execution by an artist probably of
the late archaic period.[32]   Finally, Louvre CA 2515 is one
of the very rare Columbus alabastra with figured decoration
and the only example with white ground.[33]   It may come
from an early classic workshop that specialized in lekythoi,
alabastra, and other small vases.

The white-ground outline alabastra appear soon after
the technique itself and, in view of the Paidikos and Negro-
Amazon connection, they may initially have responded to a
specific demand. Throughout, they are associated with artists
specializing either in this shape or in lekythoi, as was
the case with the black-figure series. Besides the iconographical and technical features adopted from larger vases,
the present alabastra sometimes also introduce a second tier
of decoration or a row of vertical ornament to frame and
separate each subject. The disappearance of this white-ground
genre by c. 450 is puzzling, for the production of lekythoi
continued and the use of unguents and perfumes certainly
did also. The explanation must involve a combination of
factors, perhaps the unavailability of a particular cosmetic preparation, the partial assimilation of the alabastron's
function by small lekythoi, or an appreciable change in
fashion or custom.

E. Pyxides

*1. Hesiod Painter. Boston 98.887, from Eretria. <u>ARV</u>[2] 774,

1 top. Muses and neatherd (Hesiod?). WG: picture surface.
Caskey-Beazley I pl. 15,37. [XX,1].

2. Sotheby Painter. Baltimore, Walters 48.2019, from Greece.
ARV^2 774,1 bottom. Maenads. WG: picture surface. Journ.
Walt. 20 (1949), 66 right.

3. Sotheby Painter. Mississippi, from Greece. ARV^2 775,2
above. Fight. WG: picture surface. CV Robinson I pl. 47,2.

4. Sotheby Painter, perhaps connected with. Louvre MNB
1286, from Athens. ARV^2 775 centre. Perseus and Medusa.
WG: picture surface. Riv. Ist. N.S. 9 (1960), 186,
fig. 78.

5. Penthesilea Painter. New York 07.286.36, from Cumae.
ARV^2 890,173. Judgement of Paris. WG: picture surface.
Richter and Hall pl. 77.

6. Splanchnopt Painter. Ancona 3130, from Numana; lid:
New York, private collection. ARV^2 899,144. Birth of
Aphrodite. WG: picture surface and zone beneath. Riv.
Ist. 8 (1959), 46-52.

7. Splanchnopt Painter. Athens, Serpieri. ARV^2 899,145.
Women. WG: picture surface.

8. Splanchnopt Painter. London D 11, from Eretria. ARV^2
899,146. Wedding. WG: picture surface. W.A.V. pl. 20.

*9. Veii Painter. Berlin 2261, from Athens. ARV^2 906,116.
Women. WG: picture surface. CV pl. 136. [XX,2].

10. Painter of London D 12. Athens 2188. ARV^2 963,94. Women.
WG: picture surface. AA 1943, 114, fig. 3.

11. Painter of London D 12. Toledo Museum 63.29. ARV^2
963,94 bis; Para. 434. Women. WG: picture surface.
M.M. 26 (1963), no. 149.

12. Painter of London D 12. Athens, Goulandri. ARV^2 963,
94 ter. Women. WG: picture surface.

13. Painter of London D 12. Oxford 1929.754,fr., from Greece.
ARV^2 963,95. Women with lyres. WG: picture surface.

14. Painter of London D 12. London D 12. ARV^2 963,96. Women. WG:
picture surface. Smith B.M. III pl. 22.

15. Painter of London D 12. Boston 65.1166. Women. WG:
picture surface. ΛVΣΑΝΔΡΗΕΔΟΚΕVVΣΙΜΑ↓+ΟΙ. BMFA 67 (1969),
73-75, figs. 1-5.

16. Circle of the Penthesilea Painter. Meggen, Käppeli. Bridal procession arriving with gifts. WG: picture surface. A.A. V (1964), no. 134.

17. Painter of London D 14. New York 40.11.2, from Greece. ARV² 1213, 1 above. Nereids. WG: picture surface, zone beneath, topside of lid. AJA 44 (1940), 429-430, figs. 1-3.

*18. Dresden ZV. 54. Palmettes. WG: zone on body. Dresdener Kunstblätter 14,VI (1970), cover. [XX,3].

19. Brauron, from Myrrhinous. Nikai. WG: picture surface, ornament beneath. BCH 85 (1961), 631, fig. 10.

20. Brauron, lid fr., from Brauron. Panther, bovine. WG: picture surface. A.K. Beiheft 1 (1963), pl. 14,b.

21. Harvard 1927.152 a & b. Women, erotes, youth. WG: side, lower edge of body. CV pl. 20, 5a & b.

Although they were produced from the late sixth century on, white-ground pyxides represent yet another shape for which a demand arose and for which a decorative schema was formulated during the late archaic and early classic periods. Those of the Haimon workshop illustrate the most common black-figure solution. The outline examples begin with the Hesiod Painter. Boston 98.887 exemplifies the main type of outline pyxis; it is of shape A, it has a white-ground frieze on the body and zones of red-figure ornament on the topside of the lid; its decoration includes glaze and dilute supplemented by red and gilding. Furthermore, it illustrates one of the two favored kinds of subject matter, a mythological or festive situation with a string of figures in an outdoor setting. By allowing pictures to be developed laterally, such pyxides were the small-scale counterparts of the kraters.

Like the Hesiod Painter, the Sotheby Painter was active c. 460-450 B.C.[34] and has left a small number of works,

all white-ground. The pyxides of type A differ from the
preceding example in their somewhat more elongated form
and in the lid ornament consisting of an interrupted
meander and a zone of laurel instead of palmettes. The
piece now in Mississippi is of type C in which figure-
work occupies a band on the lid and red-figure palmettes
cover the projecting borders.

With one exception, the remaining attributed pieces
come from the workshop of the Penthesilea Painter. In
relation to its total production,[35] pyxides predominate not
only among non-cup shapes but also among all those with
white-ground. New York 07.286.36 is the best preserved
and most elaborate example, with a finely articulated pro-
file from foot to knob, a bud-like motif painted on the
knob, and a branch of laurel on the side of the lid; its
exquisite figured scene makes use of glaze and relief lines,
red and various concentrations of dilute for the garments,
added white for patterns and borders. The Ancona pyxis by
the Splanchnopt Painter has both laurel and palmette on
the lid, which is in New York; through the raised ground
line, the work also presents a different subdivision of
the body. Representing the shape type B, London D 11
retains the continuous frieze but lacks all subsidiary
ornament.

In the series of outline pyxides, Berlin 2261 holds
a transitional position; like the foregoing pieces, the

lid shows tongues and a meander framing a band of folia-
tion, but the scene now depicts an interior with women.
Over half of the Penthesilean pyxides were decorated by
the Painter of London D 12 and all show the domestic rather
than mythological iconography. They also reflect a decline
in quality, for profiling and ornament on the lids become
simplified, drawing becomes heavy and awkward.

The latest attributed pyxis belongs to the Painter of
London D 14 whose oinochoe with impressed decoration concerned us above. Dated c. 430,[36] New York 40.11.2 proves
particularly elaborate owing to the meander on white-
ground that occurs below the scene and the white slipped
lid which had a figured scene within the meander border.
Noteworthy also is the main frieze which seems to combine
the two types of subject so far used separately. Despite
its damaged condition, this piece greatly surpasses
the lesser Penthesilean examples in the use both of line
and color.

According to the attributed material, white-ground
pyxides by red-figure artists begin and flourish during
the early classic period. However, the unattributed work
in Dresden now provides an example of the late sixth
century. It is decorated with two rows of circumscribed
horizontal palmettes which best compare with the palmette
alabastra of Pasiades; owing to these stylistic similarities
and the existence of other pyxides from late archaic cup

workshops, Dresden ZV. 54 may be related to the Group of
the Paidikos Alabastra. The pyxis from Myrrhinous is datable
c. 460; the ornament, style, and use of second white set
it apart from the groups considered above. The lid fragment from Brauron reflects a particularly fine hand and,
indeed, recalls the shoulder of Leningrad TG 19 by the
Meidias Painter.[37] Finally, Harvard 1927.152 is an example
of type C from the end of the fifth century; here the slip
merely covers the side and projecting lower·border of the
box proper.

Although white-ground pyxides were produced over the
relatively long period of a century, they occur in two main
concentrations. The second, Penthesilean group together
with the remaining early classic examples present a unique
coincidence of purpose, iconography, and frequency. Thus,
at the time when white-ground pyxides are most common,
their function as women's cosmetic boxes seems to determine
their decoration. Furthermore, the entire series, both
black-figure and outline, maintains a standard of quality
which suggests that these works, like bobbins and kylikes,
may not have been ordinary articles of production.

F. Bobbins

1. Sotheby Painter. Athens 2350. ARV^2 775,3 above. A, Tondo:
   uncertain subject with chariot; surrounding zone: rape
   of Leukippides. B, Tondo: Europa; surrounding zone:
   unexplained subject (two youths, three women, waiting
   chariot). WG: picture surface. Eph. 1885, pl. 5,1.

*2. Penthesilea Painter. New York 28.167, from near Athens.

ARV^2 890,175. A, Zephyros and Hyakinthos. B, Nike and boy victor. WG: picture surface. Richter and Hall pls. 76 & 178,74. [XXI,1].

3. Penthesilea Painter. Athens, Kerameikos Museum, fr., from Athens. ARV^2 890,176. A, Ganymede. B, Zeus ? WG: picture surface. AA 1940, 335, fig. 15.

4. Athens, Agora P 5113, fr., from Athens. Helios in chariot. WG: picture surface. Hesp. 5 (1946), 334, fig. 1; Robertson 110.

Three bobbins are by artists who painted pyxides and all are of exceptional quality. Athens 2350 suggests a two-dimensional reduction of a pyxis, for each part contains a tondo surrounded by an evenly disposed narrative. While the decoration includes even more rocks and vegetation than the Sotheby Painter's other works, it reveals the same predominance of line over color. The Penthesilean examples have only one subject on each surface, and New York 28.167 displays a masterful adaptation of poses and attributes to the circular format. With the garments in various tonalities of red and brown, the patterned borders in yellow or white, the once gilded anklets and bracelets, the sensitive drawing in glaze and dilute, the New York bobbin marks a highpoint in polychrome painting on white-ground.[38] Belonging to the preceding artistic generation, Agora P 5113 shows more limited technical means but a similar conception and design.

The white-ground bobbins are puzzling because their exact function remains unclear. However, they share two features which may not be insignificant. While the proveniences of two are certain, all four probably came to light in the area of Athens. Moreover, like red-figure bobbins, the subjects include scenes of abduction and figures in actual or imminent motion, whether they have wings or other means of locomotion. These works therefore suggest a correlation between purpose and iconography and, in another medium, they call to mind the figural reper-toire of temple akroteria.[39]

G. Other shapes

*1. Loutrophoros. Louvre CA 4194, from Greece. Youth seated at tomb. Neck: A, woman; B, the like. Shoulder: A, panther; B, two panthers. WG: picture surfaces. A.K. Beiheft 4 (1967), pls. 51-52. [XXI,2].

*2. Round aryballos. Syriskos Painter. Taranto 4553, from Taranto. ARV² 264,57. A, Men and boy. B, Man leading horse. On bottom, wheel. WG: picture surface, shoulder. ΛΙΟΛΕΝΕΣ-ΚΑΛΟΣ retro.,ΚΑΛΟΣ retro.;ΛΙΟΛΕΝΕΣΚΑΛΟΣ;ΗΙ[ΓΓ]ΟΛΟ+ΟΣΚΑΛΟΣ; Riezler 54-56, figs. 1-6. [XXI,3].

3. Round aryballos. Painter of the Yale Lekythos. Athens, Vlasto, from Markopoulo. ARV² 661,77. A, Athlete; B, the like. WG: picture surface.

*4. Phiale. Painter of London D 12. Boston 65.908. Procession of women around altar. WG: picture surface. BMFA 67 (1969), 88-89, figs. 19-20. [XXI,4].

5. Skyphos. Painter of Athens 10464, near. Florence 9 B 17, frr. ARV² 981,1 below. A, Symposium; B, the like. WG: white band below scene. CV pl. 9, B 17.

6. Skyphos. Painter of Athens 10464, near. Tübingen E 108, frr. ARV² 981,2 below. A, Symposium; B, the like. WG: white band below scene. Watzinger pl. 29.

7. Open vessel. Athens, Akropolis 543, fr., from Athens. Back and mane of lion. WG: picture surface. Langlotz A. pl. 41.

Before concluding this chapter with white-ground plastic vases, we have collected the isolated works of various shapes. Louvre CA 4194 is the only known white-ground

loutrophoros. As H. Cahn first indicated,[40] it belongs
to the very end of the fifth century and to a stylistic
milieu like that of Group R. Leaving aside such peculiarities as its shape and shoulder panel with panthers, the
piece is most interesting for its technical and iconographical dependence on funerary lekythoi.

The Syriskos Painter, who proves so important for
alabastra, decorated one of two surviving aryballoi. On
Taranto 4553, white slip underlies both the main scene
and the shoulder ornament; the black band between these
parts contains a particularly prominent kalos inscription
and, as in the alabastra, a vertical interrupted meander
separates sides A and B.

Attributed to the Painter of London D 12, Boston 65.908
displays the same correspondence between shape and decoration that occurred on the pyxides. Although it is the
only white-ground phiale with outline, it resembles the
Sotadean mastoi and phialai in the alternately dark and
light ridges and furrows on the exterior.

Finally, during the middle and later fifth century,
slip occasionally occurs by itself without overlying
decoration. On the two skyphoi near the Painter of Athens
10464, it forms a narrow band separating the symposium
around the lip from the remainder of the body. The pyxis
Harvard 1927.152, the Sotadean pieces discussed below, and
a few cups illustrate other applications of the same

principle.

H. Sotades

1. Phiale. Sotades (potter). Boston 98.886, from Athens. ARV^2 772,d. I: white, black lip, black omphalos with plastic cicada. Outside: fluted, white, black, red, black lip.ʃΟ[ΤΑΔΕʃ] Ε[ΠΟΙΕ]　. Fröhner <u>Brant</u>. pl. 35.

*2. Phiale. Sotades (potter). London D 8, from Athens. ARV^2 772,e. I: white, black lip and omphalos. Outside: fluted, white, black, red, black lip.ʃΟΤΑΔΕʃ ΕΠΟΙΕ. Fröhner <u>Brant</u>. pl. 36; Jacobsthal <u>Pins</u> fig. 203. [XXII,1].

3. Mastos. Sotades (potter). London D 9, from Athens. ARV^2 773,1 above. I: white. Outside: fluted, black, red, white. Fröhner <u>Brant</u>. pl. 37.

4. Mastos. Sotades (potter). London D 10, from Athens. ARV^2 773,2 above. I: white. Outside: fluted, black, red, white.

5. Rhyton: sphinx. Sotades Painter. London E 788, from Capua. ARV^2 764,8. Kekrops and Nike, goddess and seated youth. Below: A, satyr as hunter; B, goddess. WG: body and wings of sphinx. <u>CV</u> pl. 40,1 & 42,1.

6. Rhyton: sphinx. Tarquinia Painter. London E 787, from Capua. ARV^2 870,89. Eos and Tithonos; Eos. WG: body and wings of sphinx. <u>CV</u> pl. 40,2.

*7. Rhyton: horse or horseman. Sotades (potter); Sotades Painter, possibly. Louvre SB 4138, SB 4151, frr., from Susa. ARV^2 773 centre. Below: A, (Amazon); B, (similar). WG: surface below. Bothmer <u>Am</u>. pl. 82,5. [XXII,2].

Plastic vases represent a special aspect of Attic ceramic production that combines the coroplast's art with the potter's. Most white-ground examples belong to groups for which the workshop or the potter is unknown. However, the pieces in this section are associated with Sotades, a potter who specialized in novel shapes that were widely exported[41] and who used coral red almost as often as white-ground; indeed, in some respects he seems a fifth-century counterpart to Nikosthenes.

The phialai have white-slipped interiors save for
the black glazed omphalos and offset lip; on the
exterior, below the lip, they are concentrically fluted
and painted with black, coral red, and white. Boston 98.886
differs from London D 8 in the sequence of colors and in
the plastic cicada on the omphalos, so that the two make
a pair without being replicas. The mastoi correspond
almost exactly to one another, and although they have no
signature, they form a group with the phialai. While their
function and the reasons for their production escape us,
these works are unique both in design and as a set. Moreover, they were produced by an artist known to us as a
potter; the incised rather than painted signature would
support this assumption[42] and it provides further evidence
that shape, glaze, and slips were the potter's responsi-
bility.

The Sotadean vases with figural representations consist
mainly of cups and rhyta; the former, with their fine
fabric and wishbone handles, will concern us in the next
chapter. Of the rhyta, London E 788 has slip over the body
and wings of the sphinx; although certain inner markings,
facial features, and other details were drawn on the slip,
the latter is really an overlay rather than a ground.[43]
By contrast, the Louvre example preserves part of two
Amazons painted in color on the white-ground surface
between the horse's legs. London E 787 gives one further

insight into the potter's activity. Though it was decorated by the Tarquinia Painter, of the Pistoxenos Painter's
circle, the object itself depends on London E 788 and may
well have come from the same mould. It differs from the
original in the plinth, the modelling, and the red-figure
scene on the mouth; nonetheless, the slip recurs as though
it were inseparable from the form.

The Sotadean vases deserve a special place within this
chapter. Their unusual shapes and techniques can be related
to a specific potter and they even prompted imitations,
e.g. the phiale by the Painter of London D 12 and the
Tarquinia Painter's sphinx rhyton. Furthermore, they
illustrate the two different uses of slip occurring concurrently, within one workshop. In certain contexts,
white-ground carries a reference or meaning,[44] but it also
serves as a means of emphasis, especially when applied
without decoration; the latter situation appears on cups
and related shapes as well as on plastic vases.

I. Head kantharoi

*1. Syriskos Painter. Boston 98.928, from Tanagra. $\underline{ARV^2}$
265,78. A, Woman with mirror. B, Negro. WG: picture
surface. JHS 49 (1929), 48, fig. 4 & pl. 5,2. [XXIII,1-2].

2. Group of the Cracow Alabastron. Oxford 1966.917, fr.
ARV^2 270,3. Amazon (fallen or sitting on ground). WG:
picture surface. Beazley Select. pl. 50,359.

3. Charinos Class. Villa Giulia, frr., from Vignanello.
ARV^2 1531,1 middle. Bowl: chequers on WG. [+]ΑΡΙΝΟϟ-
ΕΓΟΙΕϟΕΝ,…ΙΚΟϟΚΑΡΤΑΚΑⱢΟϟ. Hoppin Bf 73.

*4. Charinos Class. Tarquinia 6845, from Tarquinia. $\underline{ARV^2}$
1531,2 middle. Bowl: chequers on WG. +ΑΡΙΝΟϟ ΕΓΟΙΕϟΕ.
CV pl. 42 & p. 13. [XXIII,3].

5. London Class. Ferrara T. 682, from Spina. ARV^2 1533, 2. Bowl: black cushion pattern and palmettes on WG. Aurigemma[1] 101,8 (^{2}113,8).

6. London Class. New York market (E. Brummer). ARV^2 1533,3. Bowl: black textile pattern on WG. Perhaps identical with the next (Bothmer).

7. London Class. Geneva. ARV^2 1533, 4ter; Para. 502. Bowl: black textile pattern on WG. M.M. 34 (1967), no. 115.

*8. London Class. Leningrad. ARV^2 1533, 5 bis. Bowl: black pattern on WG. Trudy 7,32. [XXIII,4].

9. London Class. Berlin inv. 3357. ARV^2 1533,6. Bowl: black pattern on WG (?).

10. London Class. Boston 98.926. ARV^2 1534,9. Bowl: chequers, palmettes, inscription. WG: palmettes, inscription. ΗΟΡΑΙϟΚΑΛΟϟ; ΚΑΛΟϟΗΟΡΑΙϟ . JHS 49 (1929), 46. fig. 3.

11. London Class. Villa Giulia 50571, from Tarquinia. ARV^2 1534,10. Bowl: inscription, chequers, black band. WG: inscription, chequers. ΗΟΡΑΙϟΚΑΛΟϟΝΑΙ . Bartoccini & de Agostino pl. 33.

This section consists only of kantharoi where white-ground provides a background for decoration; it does not include the later head vases[45] with a light slip over the whole face or selected features. Earliest are the two examples signed by the potter Charinos. One takes the form of a Negro, the other of a woman, and both have chequers on white-ground covering the entire bowl.[46] Tarquinia 6845 warrants particular attention not only for its quality and for the inclusion of silhouette but also for possible stylistic affinities with the Pioneer Group and the Nicosthenic circle.[47] The two following pieces belong to another familiar milieu. Attributed to the Syriskos Painter, Boston 98.928 combines a woman's head with two motifs typical of

the Syriskos and Negro alabastra; indeed, it definitely
connects the two latter groups and, through the palmettes,
it also ties in the Paidikos alabastra. Perhaps because
its special shape required more elaborate decoration,
the work proves to be particularly informative. Oxford 1966.917
shows the Amazon of the Cracow Alabastra adapted to a
different format.

The largest number of white-ground kantharoi occur in
the London Class, with the janiform examples that join the
heads of two women or of a woman and negress; they vary
considerably both in the modelling and in the type of ornament on the bowl. Villa Giulia 50571 has a broad zone of
chequers framed below by a black band, above by a white
one with a kalos inscription on each side. Though it
recalls Tarquinia 6845, it makes relatively greater use
of plastic than painted articulation. Like the preceding
janiform, Boston 98.926 juxtaposes a black with a reserved
head and includes a kalos inscription painted over slip,
but the remaining ornament consists of chequers on reserve
and palmettes. Ferrara T. 682, which is more typical of the
London Class, combines a pair of female heads and a textile
pattern above a row of palmettes. The average product may
be exemplified by the pieces in Geneva and Leningrad with
their broadly modelled, scarcely differentiated faces and
the slipped bowl displaying one horizontal and one vertical
motif.

The application of white-ground decoration to a plastic
vase depended partly on the availability of a surface;
excepting virtuoso solutions as on the Sotadean rhyta,
few possibilities existed beside the head kantharoi. The
white-ground examples extend from c. 510 through the first
quarter of the fifth century; apart from Boston 98.926
and Oxford 1966.917, they correspond in the predominance
of foliate and geometric ornament and in the almost
exclusive use of silhouette without added color. Despite
these similarities, they were certainly the work of several
potters and painters, especially as concerns the London
Class. In succeeding categories of head vases, the type with
a trefoil mouth becomes at least as popular as the kantharos;
as a result, white-ground serves increasingly as a slip
rather than as a painting surface.

To conclude this chapter, the white-ground vases with
outline present a remarkably different picture from those
with black-figure. Not only are they fewer in number, but
the shapes common to both groups often differ in relative
frequency. Thus, outline oinochoai decrease sharply while
kraters, plates, and pyxides increase; alabastra seem to
change least. Several black-figure categories disappear
completely, either because the shape itself declined
(hydriai, standard neck-amphorae) or because the black-
figure versions remained canonical for white-ground (e.g.
mastoids, skyphoi). Within the outline series, therefore,

few shapes appear for the first time, but the greater
popularity of some compensates for the disappearance of others.
A more striking feature of the present chapter is
the relatively great decline in evidence concerning potters.
No signatures exist beside those of Charinos, Pasiades,
and Sotades and the material is too scanty for general-
izations about shape, design, and ornament. While certain
personalities recur, like the Syriskos and Penthesilea
Painters, essentially all but Sotades are painters. The
reasons for this development are unclear, yet they certainly
have to do with the rise of wall painting and the new values
and problems it introduced. Generally speaking, the white-
ground vases with outline seem to be even more specialized
and incidental than their black-figure counterparts. However, the succeeding chapter on cups will modify somewhat
the existing picture of the outline material.

CHAPTER III: Footnotes

1 Cf. p. 14.

2 Cf. J.D. Beazley, Attic Red-figured Vases in American Museums (Cambridge, 1918), 27-28.

3 Florence 7 B 2 (ARV^2 29,19); Athens, Akropolis 211
(ARV^2 29,20).

4 I owe this information to Dr. H. Cahn.

5 Beazley Vases in America 6.

6 J.C. Hoppin, Handbook of Attic Red-figured Vases
(Cambridge, 1919), I, 440.

7 ARV^2 196.

8 Pp. 132-133.

9 ARV^2 269 centre.

10· As Dr. von Bothmer points out, it also recalls the
helmets placed on diphroi in the Negro Alabastra.

11 Of the plates by Psiax, the white-ground example was
found in Vulci, as were the other two black-figure
ones with a known provenience. The three plates by
Euthymides also came to light in Italy, i.e. in
Tarquinia and Veii. Those decorated by the Berlin
Painter came from the Akropolis.

12 ARV^2 235 centre.

13 Bothmer Am. 144, no. 33 & p. 149.

14 Robertson 123-129.

15 "An Amphora by the Berlin Painter," A.K. 4 (1961), 57-58.

16 Dr. von Bothmer called my attention to the cup fragment Akropolis 247 (Langlotz A. pl. 14) where the
entire interior decoration is in relief.

17 Impressed decoration occurs on a fragmentary black-
figure oinochoe, Boston 41.58 (ABV 440 below). Dr.
von Bothmer pointed out a group of fourth century
Attic vases also with impressed decoration; cf. K.
Schauenburg, Perseus in der Kunst des Altertums
(Bonn, 1960), 46.

18　ARV^2 152.

19　ARV^2 1562 top.

20　E.g. Florence 3944 (ARV^2,353,4); Colmar 48 (ARV^2
　　353,9); Munich 2667 (ARV^2 353,11).

21　The catalogue includes only a selection. The three
　　subdivisions of Paidikos Alabastra contain the
　　following totals of white-ground pieces: a - 2, b - 4,
　　c - 6.

22　ARV^2 102 below.

23　Cf. p. 98.

24　A recent iconographical study is J. Thimme, "Griechische
　　Salbgefässe mit libyschen Motiven," Jahrbuch der
　　staatlichen Kunstsammlungen in Baden-Württemberg 7
　　(1970), 7 ff. Another important, but more wide-
　　ranging, work is F.M. Snowden, Jr.'s Blacks in
　　Antiquity (Cambridge, 1970).

25　Cf. p. 121.

26　The Amazon alabastron not included in the catalogue
　　is Karlsruhe inv. 69/34, published in Thimme figs. 5-6.

27　Bothmer Am. 158.

28　ARV^2 269.

29　The iconography in this group, as in the two related
　　ones, consists of conventionalized motifs variously
　　combined. Thus, Schefold's suggested interpretation
　　of Theseus and Antiope for the Käppeli example does
　　not seem necessary (cf. e.g. Meisterwerke griechischer
　　Kunst (Basle, 1960), 202 a).

30　The motif above the scene in BM D 15 is a chequer pattern.

31　Palermo no no., from Selinus (ARV^2 269,4).

32　Dr. von Bothmer augmented the Cahn fragments with a
　　piece offered by Hesperia Art.

33　Dr. von Bothmer has identified the piece as Vente
　　Hirsch (Paris, 1921), no. 182. It is mentioned by
　　Beazley, CVA: Oxford 1 (G.B. 3), 1927, text to pl. 47,14.

34　Caskey-Beazley I, 36.

35 I owe this information to Dr. von Bothmer's compila-
   tion of the relative frequency of shapes produced
   by the Penthesilea workshop.

36 G.M.A. Richter, "Four Notable Acquisitions of the
   Metropolitan Museum of Art," AJA 44 (1940), 431.

37 Cf. p. 212.

38 Talcott Agora Well 333-335.

39 Dr. von Bothmer brought to my attention both this
   parallel and M. Bieber's "Personification of Clouds,"
   Studies Presented to D.M. Robinson I (1951), 556 ff.

40 M.M. 26 (1963), 81-82.

41 In discussing the provenance of London E 788, Beazley
   discerned a particular interest in Attic plastic
   vases among the Capuans ("The Brygos Tomb at Capua,"
   AJA 49 (1945), 157). Such an observation is most
   important for forming a picture of pottery distribution, as is, e.g. the amount of Sotadean material
   found in Southern Russia, in Egypt, and in Persia.

42 Dr. von Bothmer notes that the potters Andokides and
   Hieron also incised their signatures on a black
   glazed part of a vase.

43 For this reason and owing to the omission of e.g.
   the donkey-head rhyta, London E 787 and E 788 should
   perhaps not have been included here. Nonetheless,
   they do appear because they help illustrate Sotades'
   different uses of slip and the reuse of terra-cotta
   moulds.

44 Cf. pp. 104-105.

45 E.g. London E 790 (ARV^2 1550,1); London E 791 (ARV^2
   1550,3); Rhodes inv. 12913 (CV pl. 1,1); Thasos (?),
   from Thasos (BCH 83 (1959), 778, fig. 5).

46 For the frequency of Negroes in plastic vases, cf.
   Beazley's appealing idea in "Charinos," JHS 49 (1929), 39.

47 Cf. pp. 65-66.

CHAPTER IV: THE WHITE-GROUND CUPS

Cups with white slip form a sufficiently large and distinct group to warrant discussion in a separate chapter. Taken together, as they are here, the black-figure and outline examples are contemporary with white-ground vases of other shapes; they also reintroduce artists familiar from previous contexts. Philippart's "Coupes attiques à fond blanc" provides a valuable introduction to this material; however, it describes pieces without ever considering the whole series, and it can now be supplemented with half again as many examples.

A. White-ground cups with black-figure decoration

1. Durand Painter. Louvre F 133. ABV 208,2 top. I, Gorgoneion. A, Between feminine eyes, Dionysos (?) on donkey, with following; B, the like; at each handle, vine. WG: tondo, ivy at lip. CV pl. 108, 4-5 & pl. 109,6.

2. Painter of Vatican G. 69, near. Louvre C 10330, fr. ABV 210,4 below. I, Gorgoneion. A, Between eyes, youth reclining. At handles, open palmettes. WG: exterior picture surface.

*3. Pamphaios (potter). New York, Jan Mitchell, from Orvieto. ABV 236,7. I, Horseman. A, Two panthers; B, the like. WG: interior, exterior picture zones, band below. ΓΑΝΦΑΙΟΣΕΓΟΙΕΣΝ . AJA 49 (1945), 478, fig. 9. [XXIV,1-2].

4. Kevorkian Oinochoe, compared with. Berlin F 2060, from Tarquinia. ABV 435, 1 above. I, Gorgoneion. A, Gods seated in Olympos. B, Athena mounting chariot, with Herakles. Under each handle, fawn. WG: exterior picture zone. Gerhard Trinksch. pls. 4-5.

5. Kevorkian Oinochoe, compared with. Athens, North Slope, A-P 402 & 418, frr., from Athens. ABV 435,2 above. A, Between eyes, woman running or dancing; beyond each eye, the like; B, the like. WG: exterior picture zone. Hesp. 4 (1935), 264, fig. 26.

6. Psiax, possibly. Athens, Akropolis 1742, frr., from Athens. ABV 674 above. I, White, with black lip. A, (Bird, will have been flying over horse or like). ϚΜΙΚΡΙΟΝ . Graef pl. 86.

7. Pittsburgh Painter, compared with. Louvre C 10380. ABV 630,1 centre. I, Floral. A, Between eyes, Dionysos and Ariadne; beyond each eye, Dionysos; B, between eyes, satyr on donkey; beyond each eye, Dionysos. Under each handle, swan. WG: exterior picture surface. CV pl. 110, 9 & pl. 111, 2, 8, 10.

*8. Pittsburgh Painter, recalling. Lucern market (A.A.). I, Gorgoneion. A, Between eyes, dancing maenad; beyond each eye, satyr; B, the like. Under each handle, swan. WG: exterior picture surface. A.A. II (1960), no. 143. [XXIV,3].

9. Painter of Louvre F 120. Louvre F 120. ABV 630,1 below. I, Gorgoneion. A, Between eyes, satyr; beyond each eye, maenad; B, the like. Under each handle, dolphin. WG: exterior picture surface. CV pl. 109, 3,4,7,12.

10. Painter of Louvre F 120. New York 12.234.4. ABV 630,2 below. I, Gorgoneion. A, Between eyes, Hephaistos on donkey; beyond each eye, satyr; B, between eyes, satyr; beyond each eye, satyr. Under each handle, dolphin. WG: exterior picture surface. CV pl. 32 & pl. 42, 49.

11. Munich 2081 (war loss). I, Gorgoneion. A, Between eyes, Dionysos on donkey; B, between eyes, Dionysos with silen. WG: ivy at lip. (Bloesch 18,1).

12. Karlsruhe B 777. I, Gorgoneion. A, Between eyes, two musicians under palm tree; B, the like. At each handle, vine. WG: exterior picture surface. CV pl. 10,6 & 11,2-3.

13. London B 680, from Vulci. I, Gorgoneion. A, Between eyes, Apollo, Leto, Artemis; B, the like. Under each handle, siren. WG: exterior picture surface.

*14. London B 679, from Vulci. I, Gorgoneion, surrounded by four ships. A, Symposion; B, the like. WG: exterior picture surface. Morrison and Williams pl. 21 d (part, before cleaning). [XXV,1-2].

15. London market (Spink). I, Gorgoneion (?). A, Satyr and maenad between two satyrs on donkeys; B, the like (?). WG: exterior picture surface.

16. Karlsruhe B 168, from Vulci. I, Gorgoneion. A, Between

eyes, Dionysos; B, the like; at each handle, vine. WG: handle zone. CV pl. 10,7 & 11,5.

17. Athens, North Slope, A-P 1618, fr., from Athens. A, Athena in fight. WG: picture surface. Hesp. 9 (1940), 193, fig. 28.

18. Athens, Akropolis 1656, fr., from Athens. A, Hoplite duel. WG: picture surface. Graef pl. 82.

*19. Athens 408, from Tanagra. Cover: tondo, love-making; around this, Herakles and Amazon, and combats. A, Between eyes, woman dancing before two youths; B, the like. WG: picture surfaces. CC. pl. 36. [XXV,3-4].

20. Cabinet des Médailles 182. Cover: tondo, gorgoneion; around this, chariot race and trumpeter. WG: picture surface. CV pl. 81,6.

21. Athens, North Slope, A-P 1667, fr., from Athens. A, Chariot with woman and Hermes. WG: picture surface. Hesp. 9 (1940), 193, fig. 28.

22. Braunschweig AT 514-16, frr. A, Chariot, satyr, et al. ·WG: picture surface. CV pl. 10, 4-6.

23. Athens, North Slope, A-P 2187 a-b, frr., from Athens. A, (Dionysos on donkey ?). WG: picture surface. Hesp. 9 (1940), 207, fig. 35.

24. Athens, Akropolis 1498, fr., from Athens. A, Horse and youth. WG: picture surface. Graef pl. 81.

25. Athens, Akropolis 1499, fr., from Athens. A, Scythian archer. WG: picture surface. Graef pl. 80.

26. Athens, Akropolis 1531, fr., from Athens. I, (Gorgoneion). A, B (Symposium). WG: exterior picture surface. (Graef 165).

27. Athens, Akropolis 1672, fr., from Athens. A, (Warrior). WG: picture surface. (Graef 176).

The black-figure cups are primarily of type A with slip underlying the exterior picture surfaces, and they date to the years c. 500. Louvre F 133 is an eye-cup with white-ground used, exceptionally, for the tondo and for the band of ivy circling the exterior of the lip. It comes from the

Krokotos workshop to the successor of which the Theseus
Painter belonged[1] early in his career. Since this artist
seems to have decorated kyathoi almost concurrently,[2]
the question arises of a link between the White Heron
and Nicosthenic workshops. With its somewhat higher date,
Louvre F 133 becomes important because Beazley has recognized its footplate as being Nicosthenic.[3] Louvre C 10330
represents a variant of type A known as a "topband" and it
resembles red-figure eye-cups in the palmettes by the
handles. It shows a considerable use of white, which
extends to the decoration; most notable is the kylix held
by the reclining youth. As Beazley suggests,[4] a red-
figure painter seems likely.

The next three works lead to the immediate vicinity of
Nikosthenes. The cup now owned by Jan Mitchell is a topband with a particularly unusual interior. The latter presents an uninterrupted field entirely covered with slip.
As Dr. von Bothmer discovered, it initially served as a
drawing surface, for it preserves sketches of three ships
and an anchor incised with a sharp point. The sketches were
so light that the horseman and the potter's signature were
subsequently painted on top in the standard technique.[5]
Pamphaios collaborated with black-figure and red-figure
artists on vases of various shapes[6] and, although Bloesch[7]
and Bothmer[8] characterize the relation differently, he does
emerge as "the junior partner of Nikosthenes."[9] In ABV,

Berlin F 2060 and Agora A-P 402 are compared for style with
the Kevorkian oinochoe. While both cups are of type A,
F 2060 has the more modern form[10] and slip which continues
within the handles; A-P 402 more closely resembles the drawing of the oinochoe.

Almost inevitably, Psiax enters the picture as well,
but he makes a weaker showing. The surely attributed
cups have decoration in red-figure, black-figure, and
coral red. Akropolis 1742 is a small fragment with white-
ground, tentatively attributed by Beazley on the basis of
the technique and the name Smikrion. The remaining evidence
consists of two pieces associated with the Pittsburgh
Painter; their more or less remote dependence on Psiax's
style stems from the former painter's ties with the Group
of Vatican G. 57. Apart from these considerations, Louvre
C 10380 deserves note only for the foliate motif within
its tondo.

The cups by the Painter of Louvre F 120 belong within
the wider Leafless circle but they show a distinct stylistic
orientation. Through the unusually low foot, they recall
cups of type C. Through the eye-palmette combination and
the form of the palmettes, they are also comparable to
Louvre C 10330 and to red-figure cups like those of the
Euergides Painter;[11] indeed, their resemblance to the
latter is increased by the dolphins beneath each handle.
Louvre F 120 illustrates one of the rare early occurrences

of added white, here used for the maenad's skin.

The first five works in the unattributed category are
of type A. Munich 2081 was an eye-cup dependent on red-figure
models;[12] while it resembled Louvre F 133 in the treatment
of the lip, Ure disassociated it from the Krokotos workshop.[13] Karlsruhe B 777, also an eye-cup, shows an unusual
subject of two musicians under a palm tree and, again,
second white for flesh. London B 679 stands apart as the
only black-figure cup with white-ground that has a representation around the tondo on the inside;[14] in addition
to the conventional gorgoneion, it displays four galleys
sailing counter-clockwise over the scalloped surface
of black-glazed sea. On each side of the slipped exterior,
without eyes, a symposium is set among vines which grow
from the handles; the patternwork below combines rays above
the stem with a ribbon motif between two rows of alternating dots. In shape, ornament, and figured decoration,
B 679 reveals a number of possibly Nicosthenic features.

Karlsruhe B 168 is an eye-cup of type C, and according
to Bloesch,[15] it reflects a deliberately archaizing tendency among late sixth century potters; thus, despite its
poor quality, it presents a noteworthy dichotomy between
the antiquated shape and the progressive white-ground
technique. Although their exact form cannot be determined,
the two following fragments seem to have formed part of
eyeless topbands. Agora A-P 1618 combines a developed

red-figure type of palmette with black-figure drawing that
still includes added red and rather careful incision. Akropolis 1656 is most interesting for its different applications of white, i.e. for the background, for the corslet
articulated with red, and for the shield device.

Within the white-ground series, covered cups represent
the rarest shape. [16] Those decorated with black-figure are
mainly of documentary value, for their quality falls
short of the outline examples. Athens 408 is an eye-cup
with a foot of type C but otherwise imprecise potting. On
each side, it shows a conventional scene of a woman dancing
before two seated youths; on the cover, it has a small
central tondo containing a symplegma, a surrounding zone
of combats, and a framing border of strokes. Of Cabinet
des Médailles 182 only the cover remains and it displays
a gorgoneion within a band of dots, then a chariot race
and a border of strokes. In both cases, the execution
is careless and it may possibly be by the same hand active
during the first quarter of the fifth century. The remaining
unattributed fragments most probably come from cups of
type A. Relatively early in date, Agora A-P 1667 shows
two instances of added white. Braunschweig AT 514-16
suggests a hand working at the level of Louvre C 10380.
The youth on Akropolis 1498 remotely recalls the cup in
the Lucern market.

Even without being compared to the outline examples,

the black-figure cups with white-ground prove undistinguished.
They appear derivative for two interrelated reasons: their
mediocre execution by artists of generally peripheral
importance and their recurrent incorporation of red-figure
features. The examples listed here span about four decades,
though most probably date between 520 and 490. They seem
to have prompted neither experiment nor innovation,
and they in no way rival the cups of the red-figure masters.

    B. White-ground cups with outline decoration

  This section contains ninety-two cups and fragments
with outline decoration. Following natural subdivisions
within the material, the catalogue and discussion fall
into three parts that treat the late archaic, early
classic, and unattributed pieces, respectively.

*1. Euphronios. Greenwich, Bareiss. I, Dionysos and satyr.
WG: picture surface. HSCP 76 (forthcoming). [XXVI,1].

*2. The Gotha Cup. Gotha 48, from Kolias. ARV^2 20 above.
I, Youth courting boy. A, Man reclining; B, the like.
WG: exterior picture band. NIC...JESE; ...ASIAAES retro.
CV pl. 42,1-2 & 43, 1-3. [XXVI,2-3].

3. Myson, probably, Cambridge, Museum of Classical Archaeology
UP 129, fr. ARV^2 242; Para. 349. A, (Warrior). WG:
picture surface.

4. Eleusis Painter. Eleusis 618, frr., from Eleusis.
ARV^2 314,3. I, Triton. WG: picture surface. ...OS;⊕...
Robertson 97.

5. Eleusis Painter. Eleusis 619, fr., from Eleusis.
ARV^2 315,4. I, Athena and Giant. WG: picture surface.
ʟ[EAAPOS]retro.,KA[ʟOS] . Delt. 9 (1924-1925), 16, fig. 14.

6. Onesimos. Cabinet des Médailles 604 & L 155 & L 40
& no no., frr. ARV^2 321,15. I, Archer; A-B, fight.
WG: zone around tondo. (Philippart 37).

*7. Onesimos. Florence PD 265, from Chiusi. $\underline{ARV^2}$ 322,29.
I, Naked boy running with tray. A-B, Athletes. WG: zone
around tondo.ᴄᴴᴼᴵᴾᴸᴬᴵ꒱ꜱ ᴷᴬᴸᴼ꒱,ᴱᴾᴼᴏᴇᴍᴵꜱ . $\underline{CV}$ pl. 92. [XXVII,1].

8. Onesimos. Vatican, Astarita 705. $\underline{ARV^2}$ 322,37 bis. I,
Man courting boy. A, Boy pancratiasts. B, Youths and
boys. WG: zone around tondo.

9. Onesimos. Berlin, Goethert, fr. $\underline{ARV}^2$ 327,103. I,
White ground or white zone. A, (Youth leaning on
stick). $\underline{AA}$ 1958, 14, fig. 2.

10. Onesimos, by or manner. Berlin inv. 3376, fr. $\underline{ARV^2}$
330,4. I, (Eros). A, Komos. WG: interior picture
surface. $\underline{CV}$ pl. 51, 5-7.

*11. Onesimos, manner. Athens, Akropolis 434 and a lost
piece, frr., from Athens. $\underline{ARV}^2$ 330,5. I, Athena.
A, Man invoking Zeus; B, male pouring libation. WG:
interior.ᴸᴱᴠᴼᴾᴼᴶᴺᴵᴸᴼᴵ꒱ᴱᴾᴼᴵᴱ꒱ᴱᴺ; ᴵᴱᴠ꒱ᴼᴛᴇᴾ ʳᵉᵗʳᵒ.ᴶᴵᴄᴠᴵ...;꒱ᴾᴱᴺᴬᴼᴛᴼᴵᴬᴬᴵᴹᴼᴺᴵᴛᴼᴵᴬᴬᴬᴏᴸᴼᴵᴵ
(all dipinti). Benndorf pl. 29,1; Langlotz $\underline{A}$. pls.
35,33. [XXVII,2].

*12. Onesimos, manner. Athens, Akropolis 432, frr., from
Athens. $\underline{ARV^2}$ 332,27. I, Herakles and Apollo: struggle
for the tripod. WG: picture surface. Langlotz $\underline{A}$. pl.
33. [XXVII,3].

13. Panaitios Painter, manner. Athens, Akropolis 433, frr.,
from Athens. $\underline{ARV^1}$ 216,10. I, Athena and boy (Erich-
thonios ?). WG: picture surface. Langlotz $\underline{A}$. pl. 34.

14. Onesimos, not remote from. Athens, Akropolis 441, fr.,
from Athens. $\underline{ARV^2}$ 333,a. I, (White). A, (Dionysos),
on white-ground.ꝓLanglotz $\underline{A}$. pl. 37.

15. Colmar Painter. Cabinet des Médailles 607, 2, fr.
$\underline{ARV^2}$ 356,55. I, (White zone). A, (Youth with stick,
running). Possibly belonging: Cab. Méd. 605, fr.,
I, leg of one in chiton with white zone around,...ᴏ꒱,
A, leg of male in chlamys; Cab. Méd. 607, 1, fr.,
A, leg of animal. (Philippart 55).

16. Brygos Painter. Munich 2645, from Vulci. $\underline{ARV^2}$ 371, 15.
I, Maenad; A-B, Dionysos with maenads and satyrs.
WG: tondo and zone at lip. Robertson 107; Lullies and
Hirmer pls. 64-69.

17. Brygos Painter. Vatican, from Vulci. $\underline{ARV^2}$ 375,68. I,
Plain white. A-B, Men, youths, boys. Cambitoglou pl. 6,1-2.

18. Brygos Painter, not unlike, Freiburg S 212, fr. $\underline{ARV^2}$

399 centre. I, (Obscure remains). A, (foot, chitons). WG: exterior picture surface. (Philippart 29).

19. Painter of London D 15, perhaps comparable to. Brauron, fr., from Brauron. ARV[2] 1701. I, Girl runner. WG: picture surface. A.K. Beiheft I pl. 10,1.

*20. Foundry Painter, near. Berlin inv. 3240, from Cervetri. ARV[2] 405 below. I, Youth and boy. A, Woman spinning, and youths; B, woman and males. WG: zone around tondo. CV pl. 71,1-7. [XXVIII,1].

*21. Briseis Painter. Ruvo, Jatta 1539, from Ruvo. ARV[2] 408,33. I, satyr. A, Women and youth; B, women. WG: interior. Sichtermann pl. 9. [XXVIII,2].

22. Briseis Painter, manner. Tübingen E 26, fr. ARV[2] 411,7. I, (White). A, (Youth, man). Watzinger pl. 20.

*23. Painter of the Paris Gigantomachy. Cabinet des Médailles 608, frr., from Tarquinia. ARV[2] 421,74. I, Maenad. A, (Shoe). WG: tondo. ...ΓΛ... (Philippart 17). [XXVIII,3].

24. Painter of the Paris Gigantomachy. Sèvres 2617.1-2, frr. ARV[2] 421,75. Probably belongs to last. I, (White band). A-B, Komos. CV pl. 18, 1-2.

25. Painter of the Paris Gigantomachy, recalling. Villa Giulia, fr. ARV[2] 424,a. I, (Maenad); A, (Toes, part of handle floral). WG: interior picture surface.

*26. Douris. Louvre G 276. ARV[2] 428,11. I, Youth and boy. A, Youth pursuing boy; B, male and seated woman. WG: zone around tondo. [ΗΟ]ΓΛΕ:]5Κ[Λ]Ι0Ε5];[ΗΟΓ]ΛΙ5ΚΛΕ05]. Pottier pl. 133. [XXIX,1].

*27. Douris. London D 1, frr., from Naukratis. ARV[2] 429,20. I, Europa. A, Herakles and Apollo: struggle over the tripod. B, Fight. WG: tondo and exterior picture zone. Philippart pl. 2. [XXIX,2-3].

28. Douris, manner. Cabinet des Médailles 603, frr., from Tarquinia. ARV[1] 295,1. I, Fight ?; around this, unexplained subject (male running with sword; males running). WG: picture zone around tondo. Hartwig 500, fig. 61.

White-ground vases by the Pioneer Group are as interesting as they are rare. Leaving aside the unattributed krater fragments,[17] the plates and plaque[18] discussed

above comprise the known white-ground works near Euthymides.
Two cups are what survives from the Euphronian circle.
The Bareiss cup has an unusual shape in that the bowl
presents a smooth curve on the exterior but an offset
lip within. While this feature does occur in works of
type B, it predominates among those of type C, particularly
within Bloesch's Eleusis and Euaion Classes.[19] Moreover,
it appears in two pieces associated by Bloesch with
Pamphaios.[20] The exterior of the Bareiss piece has only
black glaze, but the interior displays a white-slipped
field framed by the offset lip. The representation shows
a black satyr playing the flute before Dionysos who is
drawn in outline; it creates a far stronger effect than,
e.g. the Akropolis plaque, because here the techniques
are used separately as a means of characterization.

The Gotha Cup belongs within Euphronios' sphere of
influence, but its very damaged condition makes analysis
difficult. In shape, it is a variant of type B with the
lip offset and glazed on the inside and outside. The
exterior suggests something of a topband through the
white zone between areas of black and through the palmette
motifs at each handle; indeed, in design, though not in
figurework, it recalls the Mitchell cup signed by Pamphaios. On each side, it shows a symposiast drawn in
outline and provided with a dark mantle. The interior
contains a normal red-figure tondo. Although the Gotha

piece has no close counterparts, the palmettes as well
as the presence of slip on the outside relate it to the
black-figure rather than the outline cups with white-
ground.

As the more representative of the two examples, the
Bareiss cup brings out a frequently neglected aspect of
the Pioneer Group. It exemplifies the technical versatility of these artists who not only developed the new
drawing in red-figure[21] but who also combined it with
white-ground and coral red, primarily on cups; among
their successors, this shape is standard for the use of
coral red and it forms the largest white-ground series
of consistently high quality. The fragment Cambridge
UP 129 is an immediately relevant case in point, as Myson
may have been the pupil of Phintias.[22]

The main group of late archaic white-ground cups
occurs with Onesimos and his circle. This material directly
involves Euphronios, for when the latter turned to potting
later in his career, he collaborated with Onesimos on
several occasions. The two cups in Eleusis are by a
painter contemporary with and related to the earliest
phase of Onesimos' activity. They have white-slipped
interiors and undecorated black exteriors, as in the
Bareiss example. Eleusis 619 shows a further resemblance,
for the bowl was originally inside-lipped only. The four
pieces attributed with certainty to Onesimos illustrate

a distinct use of white-ground. All apparently had a
broad slipped zone around a red-figure tondo; the two
techniques remain separate, thus presenting the strongest
possible value contrast. The most complete piece, Florence
PD 265, has a kalos inscription on the white field as
well as a black band at the lip whose purpose corresponds
to a three-dimensional offset; Dr. von Bothmer has
tentatively associated a new fragment with the cup.
Berlin 3376, which is near Onesimos if not by him, combines
the more usual procedure of drawing on white-ground with
unusually delicate handling of line and dilute.[23]

Three cups in the style of Onesimos came to light on
the Akropolis. Unlike the painter's above mentioned
works, these are display pieces with white-slipped interiors
that figure Athena or Herakles and that twice include an
exergue. In addition to glaze, they make use of matte
color, added white, and relief details that were painted
or gilded. According to Beazley,[24] Akropolis 434 preserves
the signature of Euphronios, and one wonders whether he
did not also contribute to the other two works. The small
fragment Akropolis 441 has white-ground on both sides
and what remains of the exterior recalls the Bareiss cup
in subject as well as in the quality of execution. As
Beazley suggested, the drawing may be close to Onesimos,
but through its precise, somewhat mannered detail, it also
suggests a temperament like that of Phintias. In addition

to artistic considerations, the white-ground works of
Onesimos are noteworthy for two reasons: the possible
connection with Euphronios when he worked as potter and
the alternative use of white-ground. Florence PD 265,
for instance, leads directly to Cabinet des Médailles
607,2 and associated fragments. If the latter indeed
belong together, they would present a red-figure tondo
set within an inscribed white zone bordered, in turn,
by black glaze at the lip. The decoration is by the
Colmar Painter who seems to have acquired his training
near Euphronios and Onesimos.[25]

The second major group of late archaic white-ground
cups comes from the workshop of the Brygos Painter. The
Munich and Vatican examples are by the painter himself;
according to Bloesch, they were potted by Brygos who,
at various times, reveals the influence of Euphronios.[26]
While both pieces have red-figure exteriors, the interior
of Munich 2645 presents a broad white band below the lip
in addition to the famous tondo of a maenad running with
a thyrsos and panther cub; it thus displays another
original solution in the use of white-ground. The Vatican
Brygos apparently had nothing but slip on its interior
surface. While this exceptional feature may have been
intentional,[27] Dr. von Bothmer suggests that the cup
was fired in an unfinished state to save the shape and
the completed decoration. Freiburg S 212, not surely
attributed, preserves part of a slipped figure zone on

the exterior as well as a band of red-figure ornament.
In Berlin 3240, near the Foundry Painter, the meander
framing the tondo is an unusual, somewhat outdated
feature; replacing the normal glaze line, it creates a
very definite separation between the red-figure picture
and the area of slip which extends to the rim.

Of the two pieces associated with the Briseis Painter,
Jatta 1539 illustrates yet another variation in white-
ground cup design; its shape points to a potter near
Brygos.[28] Preceding cups with a black band at the lip
and a white framing zone had red-figure tondi in the
centre; here, however, slip covers virtually the whole
bowl. Indeed, as the direct opposite of Berlin 3240,
Jatta 1539 gives the impression that the glaze circle
hardly isolates the figure from its surrounding space.
The fragments by the Painter of the Paris Gigantomachy
apparently belong to one cup with a white band and to
two with a slipped tondo. Cabinet des Médailles 608,[29]
like Munich 2645 and the Bareiss piece, illustrates how
much the light background enhances the fine, resilient
line and the modulation of dilute that characterize the
best Brygan drawing. Stylistically, the group as a whole
runs parallel to Onesimos and produces its own innovations.
However, it may have points of contact with the Euphronian
tradition if Brygos was the potter.

The third late archaic workshop producing white-ground

cups was that of Douris. In his very early pieces,
Douris clearly reflects the influence of Onesimos
and he seems to have worked with the potter Euphronios;[30]
however, one should note that he collaborated with Python
from the beginning and that he also signed as potter
himself.[31] Louvre F 276 belongs among the earliest cups,
and it has a red-figure tondo within a broad white zone;
apart from the pronounced horizontal composition,[32]
it recalls Florence PD 265 by Onesimos. London D 1 is
of the same period, but considerably more ambitious.
Like the Bareiss cup and Eleusis 619, its shape is inside-
lipped only. On the white-slipped exterior, the better
preserved side A shows Herakles and Apollo disputing the
Delphic tripod; the representation suggests an adaptation
of Akropolis 432 varied, e.g. by the mirror reversal,
the inclusion of bystanders, and Herakles' dress, but
corresponding down to details like Apollo's sandals and
the pointed toes of the hero's left foot. Within the black-
glazed lip of the interior, the London cup has an entirely
slipped surface and an exergue of the type in Akropolis
432. It again shows a perfectly horizontal composition,
here consisting of Europa on the bull. In execution, it
lacks the embellishments of the Akropolis cups near
Onesimos, but it presents a mythological figure in the
same splendid isolation. Thus, through its shape, its
design, and style, London D 1 documents a point when

the young Douris stood particularly close to Euphronios
and Onesimos.

In ARV^1, Cabinet des Médailles 603 appears as an early
piece in the manner of Douris. Decorated inside only,
it contains a red-figure tondo surrounded by a white
band; the latter underlies a second representation.
Because of the slip, the present work is a rare variant
within an already small class.[33]   These three cups are
the only known white-ground examples by Douris; owing to
their consistently early date, they suggest an influence
which later ceased or changed. The evidence they provide
reinforces foregoing indications that Euphronios may
have initiated the white-ground outline cup tradition.
As we have seen, the innovation took firm root, and it
continued to flourish through the early classic period.

29. Hermonax. Brauron, fr., from Brauron. ARV^2 491,132.
    I, (Wing). A, (Woman). WG: interior. HEPMⳔOⳋNA+Ⳇ.
    A.K. Beiheft I, pl. 10, 5-6.

30. Pan Painter. Leipzig T 3365, frr., from Cervetri.
    ARV^2 559,151. I, (Remains of two figures). A-B,
    Infant Herakles and the snakes. WG: interior. Philippart pl. 7.

31. Villa Giulia Painter. Athens, Akropolis 443, fr., from
    Athens. ARV^2 625,100. I, (Foot with chiton hem). WG:
    picture surface. Langlotz A. pl. 37.

*32. Karlsruhe Painter, resembling. Boston 00.356, from
    Vari. ARV^2 741 below. I, Apollo and a muse. A, Woman
    running with tendrils in hands; B, the like. WG:
    tondo on cover. Caskey-Beazley I pl. 15 & p. 33. [XXX,1].

33. Karlsruhe Painter, compared with. Delphi, from Kirrha.
    ARV^2 741 bottom. Cover: tondo, (woman playing flute);
    around this, symposium. A, Dionysos and maenad; B,
    the like. WG: cover. BCH 62 (1938), pl. 53,C.

*34. Sotades; Sotades Painter. London D 6, fragmentary, from Athens. ARV² 763,1. I, Hesperides. WG: interior. [ςοτ]ΛΛΕ$ΕΡΟΙΕ$ΕΝ . Murray W.A.V. pl. 17. [XXX,2].

35. Sotades; Sotades Painter. London D 5, from Athens. ARV² 763,2. I, Polyidos and Glaukos. WG: interior. [$οτ]ΛΛΔΕ$. Murray W.A.V. pl. 16.

36. Sotades Painter. London D 7, fragmentary, from Athens. ARV² 763,3. I, Unexplained subject. WG: interior. Robertson 129.

37. Sotades Painter, workshop. Brussels A 890, from Athens. ARV² 771,1 centre. I, Mother and baby. WG: zone around tondo. CV pl. 1,1.

*38. Sotades Painter, workshop. Brussels A 891, from Athens. ARV² 771,2 centre. I, Woman spinning top. WG: tondo. ΕΓΕ$ΙΒΟΛΟ$ΕΡΟΙΕ$ΕΝ . CV pl. 1,2. [XXX,3].

39. Sotades Painter, workshop. Amsterdam, Six 8200, fr., from Athens. ARV² 771,5. I, (Feet). WG: picture surface.

40. Sotades, workshop. Boston 13.4503, from Athens. ARV² 771,1 below. Picture modern. WG: interior. Fröhner Tyszk. pl. 12,1.

41. Sotadean; Danaë Painter, recalling. Boston 00.357, from Vari. ARV² 772 above. I, Woman with hydria at fountain. WG: zone around tondo. Philippart pl. 33,b.

42. Hesiod Painter. Louvre CA 482, from Attica ? ARV² 774,2. I, Muse tuning kithara. WG: interior. Mon. Piot 2 (1895), pl. 5.

43. Hesiod Painter. Louvre CA 483, from Attica ? ARV² 774,3. I, Muse. WG: interior. Mon. Piot 2 (1895), pl. 6.

44. Hesiod Painter, compared with. Berlin inv. 3408, from Athens. ARV² 774 below. I, Woman at altar. WG: interior. CV pl. 108, 1-2.

45. Telephos Painter, recalling. Strasburg, Univ., 837, fr. ARV² 820 bottom. I, WG. A, (Sponge, strigil, aryballos, hip of naked male)....$.

46. Boot Painter. Nicosia V 414, from Vouni. ARV² 821,1. I, Woman; A, males and women; B, males and boy. WG: interior. Gjerstad S.C.E. III pl. 84.

*47. Stieglitz Painter. Brauron, from Brauron. ARV² 827,1.

I, Girl at fountain. A-B, Women. WG: interior.
A.K. Beiheft I pl. 9. [XXXI,1].

48. Stieglitz Painter. London 88.6-1.611, fr. ARV^2 827,2.
I, (RF wreath at lip; within, WG). A, (Woman).

49. Stieglitz Painter. Oxford 1962.350, from Aegina. I,
(Left hand, forearm of woman). A, (Handle palmette,
chair leg with end of a pelt). WG: interior picture
surface. Philippart pl. 21. [Bothmer].

*50. Lyandros Painter. Florence 75409, from Cesa. ARV^2
835,1 top. I, Aphrodite. A-B, Athletes. WG: interior.
[ΛΙVΑΝΔΡ[OS] . CV pl. 1. [XXXI,2].

51. Sabouroff Painter. Munich 2685, from Vulci. ARV^2
837,9. I, Hera. A-B, Triptolemos. WG: interior. Philippart pl. 31.

52. Sabouroff Painter. Prague, private, fr., from Greece.
ARV^2 838,21. I, (WG). A, (Women). Frel R.V. fig. 44.

53. Pistoxenos Painter. Berlin 2282, from Vulci. ARV^2
859,1. I, Youth seated and woman. A-B, Horse race. WG:
interior.[EV]ΘΡΟΝΙΟΣ:ΕΡΟΙΕΣΕΝ;ΛΙΑVΚΟΝ ΚΑ[ΙΟΣ];EVΘ.... CV pls. 102-103.

*54. Pistoxenos Painter. Athens, Akropolis 439, frr., from
Athens. ARV^2 860,2. I, Death of Orpheus. A-B, Cavalry-
men with horses. WG: interior and exterior.[EVΘΡΟΝΙΟS-
ΕΡ]ΟΙΕSΕΝ;ΓΛΙΑVΚ]ΟΝ . JHS 9 (1888), pl. 6; Langlotz
A. pl. 36 & 35,2. [XXXII,1-2].

55. Pistoxenos Painter. Taranto, from Locri. ARV^2 860,3.
I, Satyr and maenad. A, Males and women; B, (woman).
WG: interior.[EVΘΡΟΝΙΟSΕΡ]ΟΙΕSΕΝ;ΓΛΙΑVΚ]ΟΝ [ΚΑΙΟ]S . Arch.
Class. 3 (1951), pls. 1-3.

56. Pistoxenos Painter. Ancona 19515, from Pitino di
Sanseverino. ARV^2 860,4. I, Klytaimestra and Talthybios.
A-B, Youths with horses. WG: interior.ΗΕΡΛ...
(Fasti 4 (1949), no. 2357).

57. Pistoxenos Painter. London D 2, from Kameiros. ARV^2
862,22. I, Aphrodite on goose. WG: interior.ΛΙΑVΚΟΝ ΚΑΙΟS.
Robertson 113.

58. Pistoxenos Painter, probably. Reggio, fr., from Locri.
ARV^2 863 centre. I, (Drapery, bit of a figure).
A, (Shanks and feet of a woman, shanks of a male).
WG: interior.

59. Pistoxenos Painter, akin to. Samos, frr., from Samos.

ARV² 865,1 centre. I, Herakles. A, (Youths). WG:
interior.[?ΑΛΚΙϳΜΑϯΙΟ⁵. AM 54 (1929), pls. 5-6.

60. Pistoxenos Painter, akin to. Boston 03.847, from
    Attica. ARV² 865,2 centre. I, Diomedes and Odysseus.
    WG: interior. Arch. Class. 3 (1951), pl. 5,1.

*61. Tarquinia Painter. London D 4, from Nola. ARV²
     869,55. I, Anesidora. A, Youths, and horse; old
     man and woman; B, youths, and horse; man and woman.
     WG: interior. Philippart pl. 20 & 19,b. [XXXII,3].

*62. Splanchnopt Painter. Athens, Akropolis 589, fr.,
     from Athens. ARV² 898,136. I, Judgement of Paris.
     WG: picture surface. Langlotz A. pl. 45 [XXXIII,1].

The second phase of white-ground outline cups begins
with several by painters who specialized in large shapes
A fragment in Brauron preserves the name of Hermonax,
a pupil of the Berlin Painter whose white-ground plates
concerned us earlier.³⁴ Enough of the piece remains to
show that slip extended from the tondo into the surrounding
area and that added color was used for the figures.
While matte colors have already appeared in the Akropolis
cups near Onesimos, and e.g. in London D 1 by Douris,
they now regularly supplement dilute and glaze. Leipzig
T 3365 is by the Pan Painter, a follower of Myson.³⁵
From photographs, its badly damaged interior reveals
little besides a black lip, offset within only, and an
exergue. Akropolis 443 belonged to a cup by the Villa
Giulia Painter familiar, again, from a group of kraters
and alabastra.

The two following works fortunately survive in better
condition, for they are covered cups. On its cover,

Boston 00.356 has a white tondo framed by a narrow
white band and a red-figure laurel wreath. Unlike the
red-figure exterior, the main scene displays an elaborate
technique consisting of glaze, matte shades of red, and
numerous details in gilded relief. The cover resembles
cups in its format but it also recalls certain pyxides
in execution, in its musical open-air iconography, and
in the foliate border. The example in Delphi is less well
preserved and published. However, its cover apparently
shows a flute-playing woman within the white-ground
tondo and a symposium in the surrounding white-ground
band. Again, therefore, it proves comparable to cups
as well as to pyxides in two-dimensional projection.

The cups from the Sotades workshop mark a new
juncture. Their shape is characterized by a very fine
fabric and by wishbone handles. Furthermore, with few
exceptions, their interiors show the convention that
prevails from now on, i.e. an entirely white-ground
bowl with a subject that may be surrounded by a glaze
circle and with a more or less wide glaze band at the
lip. Produced by Sotades and the Sotades Painter, the
three cups in London exemplify the type, as well as the
unusual iconography that the workshop seemed to favor.[36]
London D 6 displays yet another Sotadean specialty, for
on the reverse it is covered with coral red. The two
examples in Brussels differ somewhat in shape and design.

While both are stemless, A 890 contains a small red-
figure tondo within the white field; A 891 has a slipped
tondo, a coral red field, and the name of another potter,
Hegesiboulos. The Six fragment may belong to a cup like
the latter one, but it does not have an exergue. Boston
13.4503 is a stemless with a coral red exterior; its
chief peculiarity lies in the picture applied during the
nineteenth century to the originally blank white interior.[37]

Like the Sotadean works previously considered, this
group of seven cups introduces an unconventional shape
and a predilection for white-ground-coral red combinations.
Moreover, all came to light in Athens,[38] suggesting that
the mastoi, phialai, white-ground cups found a local
market while e.g. the plastic vases were for export.
The three pieces in London by the Sotades Painter deserve
note for the fragile line and the pale yellowish glaze
used in the decoration; they show a blurring of subject
and background almost unparalleled on white-ground vases.
Boston 00.357 has a Sotadean shape made somewhat misleading
by the restored handles. The drawing points to a hand
outside of the workship, so that this cup may be a later
imitation.

Louvre CA 482 and 483 certainly form a pair in view
of their similar shape, size,[39] design, subject, and
execution. They may derive from Sotadean stemlesses, since
they also lack exterior decoration; on the other hand,
they reveal a richer technique with stronger polychromy,

patterned garment borders, and gilded details. They
complement each other in representing a comparable
theme set indoors and outdoors and they relate directly
to the Hesiod Painter's pyxis in Boston. Although the
style of the figurework is different and the lip has but
a thin line within, Berlin inv. 3408 may have come from
the same workshop as the Louvre examples.[40]   In any case,
these are the last white-ground cups of Sotadean form.

The works still to be discussed in this section
represent artists who specialized in cups; after the
immediately preceding interlude, most of them again
have red-figure exteriors. Strasburg University 837 and
Nicosia V 414 are isolated pieces that raise an interesting point for the potter-painter problem. They are
attributed to painters whose masters have left no white-
ground; thus, either the painters experimented on their
own or they chose to collaborate with potters who were
using the technique. The latter alternative would explain
how, at a time when white-ground was in great favor,
a painter might try it for himself once or twice but no
more; furthermore, these early classic vases suggest
that a painter who experimented with white-ground now
was less influenced by his master's example than by the
pressure of current taste. Thus, though unique within
the Boot Painter's oeuvre, Nicosia V 414 is a rather
large[41] and ambitious work; it includes e.g. the promi-

nent chair in relief as well as traces of gilded relief
for the knobs, studs, and jewelry.

The three following cups are by the Stieglitz Painter,
who is connected with Makron.[42] On the first example,
the scene covers the bowl except for a band at the lip
and consists of exquisitely fine glaze drawing supplemented by color and relief.[43] The London fragment preserves
a wreath of red-figure laurel around the slipped surface;
apart from the white painted fruit, it recalls the lid
of Boston 00.356.[44] The exterior of Oxford 1962.350
includes part of a chair which had a pelt draped across
the seat; this motif again appears on Akropolis 354 and
Dijon 1301.[45]

In mood as in execution, Florence 75409 exemplifies
the stereotype of an early classic white-ground cup. The
slipped interior has a black frame and a faintly delineated
tondo containing a domesticated Aphrodite with two hovering,
fillet-bearing Erotes. The exergue, peripheral figures
and furnishings are in glaze and dilute; against this
background, the goddess stands out with the red mantle
and closely pleated chiton that cover her ample form.
The resulting impression is one of spaciousness as well
as of balance since the alignment of the handles and
picture coincides.

The white-ground production of the Sabouroff Painter
includes several dozen lekythoi but only two cups, dated
early in his career.[46] Munich 2685 points to a potter

following Brygos.[47] Executed in glaze, added color, and
gilded relief, its representation of Hera belongs to the
tradition of gods and heroes depicted in solemn isolation rather than in a narrative context; by contrast,
the works of the Pistoxenos Painter illustrate both
genres. The rather large fragment in Prague preserves
only slip so that the interior subject here may again have
comprised a single figure.

The last, and largest, group of white-ground cups is
associated with the Pistoxenos Painter. According to
Diepolder,[48] the surely attributed pieces occur at various
points in the painter's career, although most are early.
The first three in our list, which follows Beazley's,
share two significant features: the kalos name of Glaukon
and the potter signature of Euphronios. The former provides a chronological reference to the years c. 470. The
signature furnishes unexpected evidence for Euphronios'
strong and long-lasting interest in white-ground. While
the exterior is red-figure, Berlin 2282 has a slipped
interior with a narrower than usual band at the lip and
with apparently no circle surrounding the subject. The
Tarentine example shows the same distribution of techniques, but a clearly delineated tondo within. Like its
two counterparts, the subject depicts an encounter between
two antithetical personalities. However, this work best
exemplifies the prevailing artistic temperament, for
through the maenad's sovereign calm, a traditionally

movemented scene reveals a new seriousness and depth
of characterization. Akropolis 439 is technically ambitious
because slip appears on both the inside and outside. The
latter includes horses depicted not in outline but in
matte black with incision.[49] The interior resembles the
preceding cup in the mere line which occurs at the lip;
as with Berlin 2282, the picture once had details in
gilded relief.

The best preserved, and perhaps most accomplished,
of the Pistoxenos Painter's white-ground cups is London
D 2. It is set apart by the absence of exterior decoration,
by the single figure within, and by the lack of a potter's
signature, although the "Glaukon kalos" recurs. Beneath
the painted subject, it reveals a preparatory sketch
with several significant differences in composition.[50]
According to Diepolder, London D 2 belongs with Berlin
2282 and Akropolis 439 in an early group[51] and the latter
would indeed bear witness to a versatile potter and an
ambitious painter. A fifth certainly attributed cup
exists in Ancona, but like the "probable" fragments in
Reggio, it remains unpublished.

The pieces in Samos and Boston seem to depend on
the Pistoxenos Painter's mature style as Diepolder sees
it in the Tarentine cup.[52] Boston 03.847 is decorated
inside only with a two-figure subject while its Samian
counterpart had a single Herakles within and red-figure

scenes on the outside; thus, these apparently derivative
works differ from the five main ones in design, among
other, stylistic, respects. London D 4, by the Tarquinia
Painter, belongs to the group around the Pistoxenos Painter.
The latter's influence appears both in the composition
of the interior and in the rendering of Hephaistos.
Moreover, in this work, a dramatic subject comparable
to the death of Orpheus or to Klytaimestra and Talthybios
is again given a grand and richly executed representation.
As we saw earlier, [53] the Penthesilean workshop favored
white-ground pyxides and has left us two bobbins. However,
while it produced red-figure cups in quantity, only one
fragment of a slipped covered cup remains. Decorated
by the Splanchnopt Painter, the preserved part of the
cover contains two figures from a Judgement of Paris.
Like the pyxis London D 11, for instance, it makes use
of glaze, matte color, and gilding. The virtual absence
of Penthesilean white-ground cups is noteworthy, yet the
extant piece again suggests a connection between covered
cups and pyxides. Since the oeuvres of the Pistoxenos
and Penthesilea Painters seem to complement each other
in various respects, their specialization in cups and
pyxides, respectively, conforms to the existing picture.

*63. Louvre G 109. I, Tydeus and Ismene. WG: interior.
     Philippart pl. 16. [XXXIII,2].

64. Delphi, from Delphi. I, Apollo and raven. WG: interior.

Eph. 1970, 27 ff.

65. Athens, Akropolis 429, fr., from Athens. I, (Seat back with swan's head). A, (Handle palmette). WG: interior, and exterior. Langlotz A. pl. 32; Hesp. 4 (1935), 234.

66. Athens, Akropolis 431, frr., from Athens. I, (Drapery, shield, helmet). A, (Striding figure, Hera ?). WG: interior and exterior picture surfaces. Langlotz A. pl. 32; Hesp.4 (1935), 236-237, figs. 10-11.

67. Athens, Akropolis 437, fr., from Athens. I, (Seat with drapery). WG: interior picture surface. Langlotz A. pl. 37.

68. Oxford G 544, fr., from Naukratis. I, (Horses' heads). A, (Hades). WG: interior picture surface. CV pl. 49, 4 & 14.

*69. Athens, frr., from Argive Heraion. ARV² 1558, 3. I, Dionysos and satyr. WG: interior.ΕΛ‾‾ Waldstein II pl. 68. [XXXIII,3].

*70. Athens, Agora P 43, from Athens. ARV² 1578 bottom. I, boy tuning lyre. WG: interior.ΓΕJΑΙΝΟΣΚΓΑΛΟΣJ. Hesp. 2 (1933), 225 & 229. [XXXIV,1].

71. Munich 2686, from Aegina. I, Europa on bull. A, Eros; B, (the like). WG: interior. Philippart pl. 25.

72. London D 3, frr. I, Hunter. A-B, (Lower part of four women, one male). WG: interior. Philippart pl. 26,b.

*73. Athens 2187, from Athens. I, Libation scene; figure with staff. A,(Three draped figures). WG: interior. AM 6 (1881), pl. 4. [XXXIV,2].

74. Munich 2687, from Vulci ? I, Warrior and woman. A-B, Youths and women. WG: interior. Philippart pl. 27; Jacobsthal O. pl. 85,c.

75. Athens, Akropolis 445 & Berlin 4059, frr., from Athens. I, Symposium; A, symposium. WG: interior. Langlotz A. pls. 33, 37; CV pl. 107.

76. Brauron, fr., from Brauron. I, Artemis. WG: picture surface. A.K. Beiheft I (1963), pl. 10,3.

77. Athens, Akropolis 440, fr., from Athens. I, (Top of male head). WG: interior. Langlotz A. pl. 37.

78. Athens, Agora P 10357, fr., from Athens. I, (Head of youth, forearm). WG: interior picture surface. Hesp. 32 (1964), pl. 47,10.

79. Athens, Akropolis 435, fr., from Athens. I, (Hoplite). WG: interior. Langlotz A. pl. 32.

80. Athens, Akropolis 444, fr., from Athens. I, (Youth in chariot). A, (Right leg). WG: interior picture surface. Langlotz A. pl. 33.

81. Athens, Akropolis 438, fr., from Athens. I, (Shield, with device: wheel). A, (Tendril). WG: interior, part of exterior. Langlotz A. pl. 37.

82. Athens, Akropolis 447, fr., from Athens. I, (Woman). WG: interior picture surface. Langlotz A. pl. 37.

83. Athens, Akropolis 442, fr., from Athens. I, (Woman). WG: interior picture surface. Langlotz A. pl. 37.

84. Athens, Agora P 10411, fr., from Athens. I, (Drapery, chest or basket). WG: interior picture surface. Hesp. 32 (1964), pl. 47,11.

85. London 1907.12-1.798, fr., from Ephesos. I, (Draped figure near omphalos with bird). WG: interior picture surface. Hogarth Ephesos pl. 49,6.

86. Athens, Akropolis 446, fr., from Athens. I, (WG). A, (Woman with child). Langlotz A. pl. 33.

87. Athens, Akropolis 448, fr., from Athens. I, (WG). A, (Woman). Langlotz A. pl. 33.

88. Lost, once Baron Wasberg, then Rhousopoulos, fr., probably from Aegina. I, (Veiled woman). A, (Warrior and column). WG: interior picture surface. Philippart pl. 21,a.

89. Brauron, fr., from Brauron. ARV² 1577,1bottom. I, Nike ? WG: interior picture surface. ΓΕΓιΑΡJΟΜΓοςJΚΑὐΟΓ5] retro.

90. Athens, Akropolis 430, fr., from Athens. ARV² 1579 top. I, (Top of helmet crest). WG: interior. (Hesp. 2 (1933), 228).

91. Athens, Akropolis 436, fr., from Athens. I, (WG). A, (Youth, boy). (Langlotz A. 39).

92. Lost, from Nola. I, Athena and Herakles; A-B, deeds of Herakles. WG: interior. Bull. d. Inst. 1829, 19.

The unattributed material consists mainly of fragments
from the Akropolis and the Agora; the number of fragments
certainly exceeds the number of actual cups represented.
Louvre G 109 has been associated with Euphronios since
the end of the last century.[54] In design, it recalls the
Bareiss cup as well as the Akropolis examples near Onesimos.
Due to its damaged condition, it proves difficult to
discuss. However, one result of recent cleaning has been
a reconsideration of the subject matter. M. Davies and
A. Waiblinger have independently rejected the previous
interpretation of Herakles and Eurytos in favor of Tydeus
and Ismene.

The cup in Delphi has been attributed to the Berlin
and Pistoxenos Painters,[55] but a number of features
point to an earlier colleague of Euphronios, Onesimos.
In subject, the cup recalls the youth with lyre on a
fragment in Eleusis.[56] In execution, it includes an
exergue of the type in Akropolis 432, Akropolis 433, and
Louvre G 109; with Akropolis 434, it shares a similar
treatment of the outstretched arm, hand, and phiale as
well as of drapery edges. Again, it resembles Akropolis
432 in the sandals and in the inclusion of one foot that
overlaps the delimiting borders. The flesh parts of
the youth seem also to include a considerable amount of
articulation in dilute. The present observations must
be revised on the basis of good photographs and they do

not account for the unusual stylization of the lyre's
tortoise-shell sound box. Nonetheless, in conception,
detail, and perhaps in purpose, the Delphi cup presents
significant affinities to the Onesiman pieces from the
Akropolis.

The fragments Akropolis 429 and 431 belong to cups
slipped inside and outside, and 429 has a lip offset within
only. Miss Pease differs with Langlotz in allocating the
sherds, for she associates 429 with 431 a and 431 b with
N.S. A-P 285. If her reconstruction of the latter holds,
the original work would have been exceptionally wide and
thin-walled and it would have had two superimposed scenes
on the outside.[57] The whole group of fragments shows a
precise, rather small-scale style of decoration datable
to the Leagros period. Akropolis 437 may not have had
decoration on the outside, but, as Langlotz noted,[58]
the preserved drapery suggests a Brygan hand.

Oxford G 544 appears here rather than with the later
fragments because it includes no matte color. Unlike the
exterior, the interior displays a light and sure touch
which recalls the two works in Brauron, i.e. the one
compared with the Painter of London D 15 and, even more,
the other assigned to the Stieglitz Painter. Like Oxford
G 544, the cup from the Argive Heraion stands part way
between the evidently late archaic and early classic
material. It resembles the latter in the entirely slipped

bowl and in the rather narrow band of glaze at the lip.
However, the style and technique bear out Beazley's
attribution to the "end of the archaic period."[59] The
work generally recalls Jatta 1539 by the Briseis Painter
and it may possibly belong to a late follower of the
Brygan Group.

Agora P 43 is a small cup of type C with an offset
lip; the decoration, applied inside only, makes use of
glaze, matte color, but no relief line. While the kalos
name contributes little to the dating, the piece receives
a firm terminus ante of 480 from its archaeological
context.[60] It has proven difficult to attribute stylistically,
and the existing hypotheses[61] reflect its elusive combination of an archaic spontaneity with the reflective-
ness and the technique of a somewhat later period. In
subject, mood, and certain details, it recalls the
earlier phases of Douris and a cup like London D 1.

The following pieces in our list are clearly early
classic. Munich 2686 shows the narrower lip band, the
rich polychromy and gilding, all familiar details supple-
menting the stylistic indications. Though long known and
frequently published, it remains unassigned, and in its
present damaged state, it only suggests a contemporary
of the Pistoxenos Painter's group. Athens 2187 is unique,
for it has white-ground underlying the tondo as well
as a surrounding band of figures. It represents a logical

development beyond both the usual design and Cabinet des
Médailles 603, but even in red-figure it finds few
counterparts; significantly, perhaps, those that do exist
are mainly Penthesilean.[62] The central scene makes noteworthy use of relief, e.g. for the oinochoe and phiale;
the exterior consists of a single red-figure zone.
Munich 2687 is a particularly large cup[63] with the
interior subject covering most of the surface. The
exterior might again suggest a Penthesilean, and at
the same time, collaboration between two artists; indeed,
on such a work, a painter of red-figure cups could have
joined a colleague familiar with white ground from
pyxides.

As the preceding, and other, cups of this period,
Berlin 4059 presents such a damaged interior that photographs do not sufficiently show the supplementary ornament. The existing fragments preserve an unusually cluttered
symposium which includes a dog, a suspended shield, a
couch cover with figured motifs, and carefully detailed
furnishings like the large vessel in relief. For stylistic
indications, the exterior proves more informative. A firm
attribution, however, must take into account the work's
main peculiarities: the band of palmettes around the top
of the stem[64] and the particularly ornate interior, a
recurrent feature of white-ground cups from the Akropolis.

Among the group of fragments, Akropolis 440 may well
come from a work of the Pistoxenos Painter's circle.[65]
Agora P 10357 appears about contemporary and it suggests
another dramatic encounter, as does the next piece.
Akropolis 444 indicates the general subject and composition of a further cup; its style is noteworthy for the
precise detail in the chariot fitting combined with
broader brushwork in the charioteer's cloak. Akropolis
438 might seem relatable e.g. to Akropolis 435, but it
forms part of a work slipped inside and outside. The three
following pieces each have part of a female figure; one
of these may belong with one of the male figures just
mentioned. Akropolis 442 shows the finest execution,
with white patterns on the deep red garment and with a
brooch as well as buttons in relief.

London 1907.12-1.798 stands apart not only through
its exceptional subject but also through the imprecise
delineation of the "eagle" and "omphalos"; it should
best not be discussed from Hogarth's reproduction.
Akropolis 446 and 448 are lip fragments which have slip
without decoration on the inside; their red-figure
exteriors point to lesser early classic hands who might
have specialized in Nolans or lekythoi. The fragment
once owned by Baron Wasberg has appeared in archaeological publications for almost a century.[66] However, in the
Rhousopoulos illustration, the surface appears so flat,

the features so exaggerated and beautified that either
the illustration is inaccurate or both it and the piece
are modern fabrications. For the four fragments concluding
the list, no illustrations and virtually no descriptions
exist. The Brauron example comes from a stemless which,
through the kalos name, suggests a late archaic date.
Akropolis 430 includes part of an offset lip, and according
to Miss Pease, the potting recalls Agora P 43.[67]

The series of black-figure and outline cups collected
here fills out the emerging picture of white-ground.
It reintroduces personalities like Nikosthenes and
Sotades, the Villa Giulia Painter and the Penthesilea
Group; its duration resembles that of most other shapes,
extending from the beginning of red-figure through the
end of the early classic period. However, several features
also set this material apart. While white-ground cups
occur in association with the Krokotos workshop, Nikos-
thenes-Psiax, and the Leafless Group, they actually
constitute the red-figure genre par excellence. Moreover, insofar as proveniences are known, the black-figure
and especially the early classic works tend to come from
Athens and the Greek mainland rather than from Etruria
and Magna Graecia. This fact acquires significance in
view of the high quality consistently maintained by the
outline group. The latter comprises over ninety items
displaying constant innovations in design, care and

refinement in execution; despite their relatively great
number, they seem to have been "custom made" for special
purposes, e.g. as dedications. From a qualitative view-
point, the cups with coral red differ considerably;
although they use a similar, special technique, their
decoration can also be hasty and coarse.

The most important aspect of the outline series
concerns the workshops involved. Every shape discussed
so far engaged a number of artists, some interrelated,
some not. The outline cups are no exception; in addition,
however, one single artist provides a particularly strong
sense of continuity. Euphronios may have been instrumental
in developing the slipped kylix; his influence is reflected
by the three main late archaic workshops and he collaborated with one of the major early classic painters. He
surely did not determine the evolution of white-ground
cups nor affect all of its many facets; however, his
career virtually coincides with the duration of this
genre and he gives the impression of an important, though
not always active, presence. While Psiax and Nikosthenes,
for instance, exerted their influence widely, over many
white-ground shapes, Euphronios exerted his influence
over a long period, on cups.

CHAPTER IV: Footnotes

1   For a discussion of these two workshops, cf. Ure
    Krokotos 90 ff.

2   Cf. p. 86.

3   _ABV_ 208,2 top.

4   _ABV_ 210.

5   Dr. von Bothmer has kindly shown me his notes and an
    unpublished article on the Pamphaios cup.

6   _ABV_ 235-237; ARV^2 127-130.

7   H. Bloesch, _Formen attischer Schalen_ (Bern, 1940), 62.

8   Dr. von Bothmer in notes on the Pamphaios cup.

9   ARV^2 124.

10 Bloesch 18.

11 Beazley _RG_ 61.

12 Bloesch 18.

13 Ure _Krokotos_ 101, n. 54.

14 Cf. K. Schauenburg, "Zu attisch-schwarzfigurigen
    Schalen mit Innenfriesen," _A.K._ 7 (1970), 33 ff.
    For a brief list of black-figure cups with ships
    cf. ARV^2 225.

15 Bloesch 115.

16 Their construction and manner of use is described
    in Caskey-Beazley I, 33.

17 P. 123.

18 Pp. 119 ff. and 108.

19 Bloesch 137-139.

20 London E 37 (Bloesch 64, 14; ARV^2 72,17); Vatican
    (Bloesch 65,23; ARV^2 36 below).

21 Beazley _Vases in America_ 27.

22 $\underline{ARV}^2$ 237.

23 One minor detail occurs in both the Eros here and the Triton of Eleusis 618, i.e. the neck muscle that runs from the ear to the collarbone.

24 $\underline{ARV}^2$ 330,5.

25 $\underline{ARV}^2$ 352 below.

26 Bloesch 72, 81; 82,6; 84,16.

27 Boston 13.4503 has only slip on the interior; see below p.176.

28 Bloesch 89, 4 above.

29 Dr. von Bothmer has recently examined the Villa Giulia fragment and it most likely does belong to Cabinet des Médailles 608.

30 Bloesch 72-73.

31 $\underline{ARV}^2$ 426-427.

32 This feature occurs e.g. in the Bareiss cup.

33 Cf. n. 14 for black-figure examples.

34 Cf. pp. 120-121. $\underline{ARV}^2$ 483.

35 $\underline{ARV}^2$ 550.

36 The subject of London D 7 has not yet been identified, but a noteworthy parallel occurs on a Kabeiric vase: Berlin inv. 3284. G. Bruns- P. Wolters, Das Kabiren-heiligtum bei Theben I (Berlin, 1940), pl. 27,1.

37 A. Furtwängler, Neuere Fälschungen von Antiken (Berlin, 1899), 33-36.

38 Six of the seven cups were found together in Athens in 1890. Cf. H. Philippart, "Deux coupes attiques à fond blanc," Mon. Piot 29 (1927-1928), 108.

39 E. Pottier, "Deux coupes à fond blanc," Mon. Piot 2 (1895), 40. Diameter without handles: CA 482: 14.8 cm., CA 483: 14.0; height of both: 3.6.

40 Berlin inv. 3408 has virtually identical measurements: D. 14 cm; H. 3.5.

41 D. 28.9. J.D. Beazley, Some Attic Vases in the Cyprus Museum (1948), 43.

42 ARV^2 807.

43 Its style may also recall the Brauron fragment compared by Beazley with the Painter of London D 15 (p.164,19).

44 ARV^2 827,2.

45 ARV^2 828,28 and 829,37. Dr. von Bothmer has added new fragments to the Dijon example; he also brought to my attention its relevance to the Oxford piece.

46 ARV^2 837,9 & 838,21.

47 Bloesch 87-88.

48 H. Diepolder, Der Pistoxenos-maler (110. Winckelmanns-programm, 1954), 13-15.

49 Dr. von Bothmer has observed that the preserved figure should probably be interpreted as seated.

50 P.E. Corbett, "Preliminary Sketch in Greek Vase-painting," JHS 85 (1965), 18 & fig. 1.

51 Diepolder 14.

52 Diepolder 15 and 20, n. 32.

53 Pp. 139-140 and 142.

54 Cf. bibliography in Philippart 34, no. 18.

55 I.K. Konstantinou, "Leuke Delphike Kylix," Eph. 1970,45; BCH 89 (1965), 898.

56 Eleusis 607 (ARV^2 328,115).

57 Pease North Slope 234-238, nos. 24 & 25.

58 E. Langlotz, Die antiken Vasen von der Akropolis zu Athen (Berlin, 1933), 39, no. 437.

59 ARV^2 1558,3.

60 L. Talcott, "Two Attic Kylikes," Hesp. 2 (1933), 230.

61 Cf. bibliography in Philippart 18, no. 21.

62 I owe this observation to Dr. von Bothmer.

63 D. 35.7; with handles, 44.4.

64 A similar band occurs on a cup fragment by Oltos in the Bareiss collection. Cf. also the rays at the top of the stem in Ferrara T. 18^C VP ($\underline{ARV}^2$ 882,35). I owe these parallels to Dr. von Bothmer.

65 Langlotz 39, no. 440.

66 Cf. bibliography in Philippart 97, no. 30.

67 Talcott <u>Two Kylikes</u> 228-229.

CHAPTER V: LEKYTHOI AND THE WHITE-GROUND VASES OF
OTHER SHAPES

The scope of our investigation has so far remained
within the limits defined in the Introduction. Only one
major group of white-ground vases has not been touched
upon; this chapter, therefore, deals with lekythoi that
are related to the material we have studied. The chapter
covers the black-figure and outline examples by artists
who specialized in other shapes. The limitation imposed
here excludes virtually all the white funerary lekythoi;
however, the latter engaged relatively few of the artists
who have concerned us and, furthermore, they are the
object of a monograph currently in progress.[1] Intended
as a summary and survey, the present discussion does not
aim at completeness and it makes particular use of Miss
Haspels' Attic Black-figured Lekythoi. Our interest here
lies in further elucidating the interrelation of certain
recurrent personalities and the interrelation of lekythoi
and other forms within their respective white-ground
oeuvres.

As a working hypothesis, the lekythoi of Psiax may
be considered the earliest extant white-ground examples.
The Jameson piece[2] requires no further comment. Agora P
5002[3] resembles it stylistically, but instead of ornament, the decoration below the scene consists of a
secondary frieze. These works acquire additional interest
if one reverts to Beazley's conjectured tie between Psiax

and the Amasis Painter, for among the major artists of
his generation, the Amasis Painter has left the largest
number of lekythoi.[4] The oeuvre of Psiax deserves note
also as the first of many which contains both white-ground
lekythoi and alabastra.[5]

By the last decade of the sixth century, slipped
lekythoi had become established; as we shall see, they
found some favor in red-figure workshops but now and for
some time, the black-figure production predominated.
Setting aside the Cactus Painter's two experiments,[6]
the series begins with the Gela Painter [XXXV,1].
According to Miss Haspels, the latter was active from
c. 510 well into the first quarter of the fifth century.
He decorated slipped lekythoi throughout and he followed
changes in taste, assimilating the innovations first of
the Edinburgh, then of the Athena Painters.[7] Generally
speaking, his vases consist of standard cylinders[8]
with white-ground on the body, frequently also on the
shoulder; Boston 93.99[9] and a piece in the Basle market[10]
are exceptional, with slip extending to the neck and to
the neck and mouth, respectively. In the type and disposition of ornament like palmettes and meander, the
lekythoi recall the painter's white-ground olpai rather
than his simpler trefoil oinochoai.[11] Although he also
decorated several black-figure neck-amphorae, the Gela
Painter restricted himself to few shapes; similarly,

while he adopts a subject, e.g. the Struggle for the
Tripod,[12] or an ornament currently in favor, he reveals
no particular stylistic dependence.

The Edinburgh Painter is a slightly later contemporary
who has left black-figure vases of several shapes but
only one white-ground alabastron and lekanis lid[13] in
addition to the lekythoi [XXXV,2]. He seems to have
popularized the large straight-sided lekythos, with or
without a slipped body, and his works of the latter class
introduce a new shoulder pattern comprising five, instead
of seven, palmettes.[14] These vases hardly vary from the
basic design that includes a figured scene on white-
ground, a band -- generally of dots -- above, a reserved
shoulder with the five palmettes and a row of strokes at
the junction of neck and shoulder. While Berlin 1998[15]
and Karlsruhe B 30[16] prove exceptionally elaborate, the
whole group maintains a noteworthy standard of quality.
The Edinburgh Painter belongs near, if not to, the Leagros
Group[17] and, through his serious and careful workmanship,
he resembles the late black-figure painters working on
larger shapes with white-ground.

The Sappho and Diosphos Painters were colleagues, if
not associates, within the same workshop and they follow
the Edinburgh Painter's stylistic direction.[18] However,
unlike those of other black-figure lekythos painters,
their oeuvres present technical developments directly

influenced by red-figure innovations. Their standard
shape has a rather flat shoulder, decorated with buds,
and a cylindrical body that tapers sharply to the foot,
which it joins without a fillet; according to Miss
Haspels,[19] the form corresponds to an early red-figure
type, but it also recalls the Jameson example. With few
exceptions,[20] slip occurs only on the body. The Sappho
Painter decorated the normal variety [XXXVI,1] as well
as a smaller one characterized by a stronger taper and
by a pair of confronted "barking" lions[21] on the still
flatter shoulder. Moreover, apart from three examples
in the Cock Group[22] and the Class of Athens 581,[23] he
is the first artist considered here to have painted in
colors upon a glazed rather than reserved surface (Six's
technique); while he has left fewer Six lekythoi than
the Diosphos Painter, his namepiece, the kalpis once
Goluchow, is more ambitious than anything by his colleague.
The Karlsruhe krater has shown the Sappho Painter's
skillful assimilation of red-figure ornament; insofar as
Six's technique is a black-figure equivalent to red-
figure drawing, the kalpis further suggests a preoccu-
pation with new means of representation.

The Diosphos Painter was the more prolific of the
two artists and for this reason, among others, he is the
more important to us. By virtue of his larger oeuvre,
he brings us closer to the potter(s) responsible for

the shapes and procedures of the workshop. He may have
been the main decorator, seconded e.g. by the Sappho
Painter who worked partly on the same shapes, partly
on others like the little-lions. He has left over twice
as many slipped lekythoi as his counterpart, but paid
less attention to the choice and rendering of the subjects.
By contrast, on alabastra, which he favored, he employed
relatively original solutions comprising palmettes alone
or combined with figured zones. The most noteworthy
aspects of his activity are to be seen on lekythoi
[XXXVI,2]. Thus, for example, the Diosphos Painter
produced the largest number of Six technique vases
yet attributed to one artist; as with white-ground, he
painted on a surface prepared by the potter. Although
the works may seem insignificant per se, they suggest
that this secondary workshop was seeking its own alternatives to standard black-figure as well as to red-figure.

The direct influence of red-figure becomes evident
in the Side-palmette lekythoi whose one- or two-figure
representations combine black-figure with outline. The
class centres on the pieces of the Diosphos Potter and
Painter, but it includes other shapes, e.g. a Haimonian
chimney,[24] and other artists; some of these, like the
Painter of Würzburg 517 or the Vlasto and Karlsruhe
Painters,[25] also worked in red-figure. One example,[26]
near the Sappho Painter, includes two archers who recall
the Paidikos and related alabastra. The main group consists

of the Diosphos workshop's normal and little-lion types
with slip underlying only the scene [XXXVI,3]. On
either side of the subject, they show a more or less
broad complex of circumscribed palmettes with an occasional
curling tendril or a lotus bud; here, therefore, the Diosphos Painter, or Potter, devised another use for a favor-
ite motif. The representations juxtapose a figure drawn
in outline with another figure or with attributes in
silhouette or black-figure. The procedure finds parallels
in the Bareiss cup and in works of the Athena Painter.
Besides Six's technique, the black-figure-outline combination was the Diosphos establishment's specialty;
although both occur on ordinary lekythoi, they are a
creative response to red-figure which no comparable
workshop equalled. The Sappho and Diosphos Painters
probably had most to do with the decoration; as Miss
Haspels noted, [27] their styles recall aspects of Psiax,
and such a connection may also have influenced their
technical versatility.

In the studies of Miss Haspels and Beazley, the Theseus
Painter appears among the specialists in lekythoi. While
his oeuvre includes the latter, it also contains a
significant number of skyphoi, kyathoi, and various
other shapes; the white-ground works consist of a kalpis,
oinochoai, kyathoi, and alabastra. Thus, like the Edinburgh Painter, though for different reasons, the Theseus
Painter departs from the lekythos-painter stereotype;

both could in fact be classified as "late black-figure painters of smaller pots." In view of this affinity, it is interesting that the Theseus Painter lekythoi continue the elongated cylindrical form of the Edinburgh Painter's and the limitation of slip to the body [XXXVII,1]; the younger artist may even have belonged to the other's workshop for a time.[28] However, the Theseus shape is taller, and, on the shoulder, it displays the Athena Painter's elaboration of the basic five palmette scheme. The Theseus Painter seems to have circulated among a number of establishments, e.g. those of Nikosthenes, the White Heron Group, and the Athena Painter. Since his entire oeuvre is not very large, he "spread himself thin," but at the same time, he reinforces tenuous, existing links among circles that made use of white-ground.[29]

In his over-all activity and importance to the development of lekythoi, the Athena Painter stands to the Theseus Painter as the Diosphos to the Sappho Painter. The first two artists are related both stylistically and through their use of the elongated cylinder; however, the Athena Painter was the more enterprising and prolific, as indicated by the lekythoi and by the slipped oinochoai discussed earlier. The lekythoi occur in various sizes and occasionally have slip on the shoulder as well as on the body [XXXVII,2].[30] To the decoration, they introduce three refinements which emphasize the

structure of the upper part of the vase. They have
black glaze on the neck in addition to the mouth, a pair
of horizontals framing the strokes just below, a curling
tendril and a bud issuing from the shoulder palmette
nearest the handle. While the majority of pieces is in
black-figure on white-ground, a number are decorated
with outline [XXXVII,3]. Instead of the Diosphos Painter's
programmatic light-dark contrasts, they show only accessory
details and attributes in outline.[31] These particular
works represent a lesser aspect of the Athena Painter's
oeuvre, but among black-figure lekythoi they are also
the last in the mixed technique. They lead us to one
further problem which must be mentioned, but cannot be
resolved here.

The later Athena Painter lekythoi strongly resemble
those of the Bowdoin Painter, and Miss Haspels carefully
reviews the evidence for and against equating the artists.[32]
The two groups of material correspond in shape and ornament so that they certainly come from the same workshop.
While they also share certain stylistic features, Miss
Haspels rightly emphasizes differences in the choice
and rendering of the subject matter. To his white-
ground lekythoi and oinochoai, the Athena Painter applies
a typically late archaic iconography of combats, warriors,
Dionysos and his following. The Bowdoin Painter, who
produced only lekythoi, favored Nikai, women in domestic
situations, and other, early classical, themes. If a

single artist were involved, one would have expected
some change in design, ornament, perhaps even shape
to accompany the change in subjects; with two artists,
one can imagine the potter(s) turning out vases decorated first by the Athena Painter and then by a colleague
and follower. While the dilemma therefore remains, the
material shows a noteworthy evolution from the diversified, relatively well executed late archaic oeuvre to
its similarly well represented but comparatively undistinguished successor. The Athena Painter's work
reveals less interaction with red-figure than e.g.
the Diosphos Painter's and his white-ground belongs
within the black-figure tradition.

If the Sappho-Diosphos and Theseus-Athena workshops
display a certain accomodation to contemporary progressive
developments, the Haimon workshop does not. As we have
seen, it produced a variety of shapes with slip, but apart
from the use of silhouette, it clung to the time-honored,
and increasingly debased, iconography, ornament, and
technique. The lekythoi consist of two types: one that
derives from the later Diosphos form and another with a
new "chimney" mouth [33] [XXXVIII,1]. Both classes have
light, rather than black-glazed, necks and slip on the
body, sometimes also on the neck and shoulder.[34]

The Emporion Painter was the Haimon Painter's successor,
less in a stylistic sense than through the similar char-

acter of their oeuvres.³⁵ The Emporion workshop seems
to have favored alabastra, for they show some variety
in subject matter and design. The lekythoi again include
both the calyx and chimney-mouthed classes; they recall
the Haimon Painter's not only in structure but also in
the light necks and substandard quality [XXXVIII,2].
A few with circumscribed palmettes either on the shoulder
or framing the scene heark back to the Diosphos Painter.³⁶

All major black-figure lekythos workshops used white-
ground, but with considerable variations. The Class of
Athens 581 and the Beldam Painter's work consist exclusively of lekythoi. The Gela, Edinburgh, Sappho, and
Diosphos workshops seem to have favored lekythoi, yet
they also produced vases of other types. The Theseus,
Athena, Haimon, and Emporion Painters have left the more
diversified oeuvres which represent either few shapes
abundantly or many shapes sparsely. The basic technique
throughout consists of black glaze, added color whose
use progressively diminishes, and the slip which tends
to be dense and yellowish. The relation of this white-
ground material to red-figure presents two aspects. On
the one hand, the familiar shouldered black-figure shape
emerged during the years c. 530; thus, it never existed
independently of red-figure and elements e.g. of red-
figure ornament form an integral part of its typology.
On the other hand, the various workshops responded more
or less actively and in different ways to the progressive

developments; the most evident and significant reactions
consist of technical innovations and these occur especially
in the Diosphos workshop. Generally speaking, the black-
figure lekythoi with white-ground form a self-contained
group in relation not only to red-figure but also to
black-figure vases of other shapes; they present a closely
interconnected succession which ends with the Beldam
Painter but whose functions were already being shared by
the outline examples of lesser early classical red-
figure artists.

Before the end of the sixth century, red-figure
workshops had also begun to produce white-ground lekythoi. While Psiax was the only "non-specialist" who
worked on lekythoi in black-figure, there were many
more in red-figure. As with white-ground outline alabastra, the series starts with Pasiades. Agora NS A-P
422[37] has a slipped body, a chequer pattern on what
remains of the neck, and a painter's signature incised
on the black shoulder [XXXIX,1]. The next extant example,
Berlin 2252,[38] belongs to the Syriskos Painter. It proves
most unusual for the ornament which comprises two
different crenelle motifs framing the subject and, on
the shoulder, an Eros manoeuvering among a pair of
rounded circumscribed palmettes with crisp, pointed
dependent buds. A small group of lekythoi introduces
the Painter of Munich 2774, a later archaic decorator

of pots who may be identical with the Flying Angel
Painter.[39] The works depend on the Diosphos shape and
have a slipped background for the scene and for the
interrupted meander above.

Among the contemporary workshops producing cups,
only two have left white-ground lekythoi. One piece, in
Gela,[40] is by the Brygos Painter and has unfortunately
not been republished recently [XXXIX,2]. Unlike most
of the aforementioned vases,[41] it depicts a specific narrative subject, Aeneas and Anchises. The execution seems
to include glaze applied in relief and in silhouette as
well as various tonalities of reddish brown and yellow.[42]
The two white lekythoi by Douris[43] belong, with the
cups, to the earlier phase of the artist's career [XXXIX,3].
Like the Brygan vase, they illustrate important myths:
the Sacrifice of Iphigenia, and Atalanta with three
Erotes; however, each of these representations is unique
and more elaborately rendered.[44] The pieces have slip
over most of the body as well as on the shoulder with
its circumscribed palmettes. Framed by interrupted meander
patterns, the pictures consist of four figures meticu-
lously drawn in glaze line and dilute. While the number
of slipped lekythoi is large, the Dourian examples hold
a special place among them owing to their broad pictorial
treatment of subjects still archaic in their movement and
richness of detail.

The material reviewed so far reveals a few points
of note. It suggests that white-ground outline lekythoi
developed more slowly than their black-figure counterparts. Excepting one group, they belong to workshops
which made greater use of slip on other shapes. The genre
seems to have emerged within the Pasiades and Syriskos
circles, which favored alabastra; thereafter, it was
taken up by the Brygos Painter and Douris who specialized
in cups but by no means exclusively. Compared with the
contemporary black-figure works, each of the outline
lekythoi displays a distinct and independent solution
for the decoration.

During the succeeding, early classical generation,
white outline lekythoi became the specialty of numerous
artists and workshops. As before, however, they were
produced by others as well. Three examples by the Pan
Painter exist. One, in Syracuse, [45] has a relatively
modest representation of a woman winding yarn. A second,
in the Schimmel collection, shows a woman with balls of
yarn; unlike the preceding vase, there is no ornament
below the scene. The principal piece, Leningrad inv.
2363, [46] again displays a reserved shoulder with palmettés
and a row of interrupted meanders framing the tall white
picture surface [XL,1]. It, however, is distinguished by
the representation of Artemis and a swan, magnificently
drawn and supplemented with added white. The work is
early [47] and one wonders whether the choice of technique

was not influenced by the Pan Painter's master, Myson.

Four pieces are associated with the Villa Giulia
Painter[48] whose alabastra, kraters, and cup concerned
us earlier. The two lekythoi from his hand probably form
a pair,[49] but their importance is otherwise slight. The
related examples appear more ambitious due to the floral
shoulder ornament and the added color, including white.

Since our discussion touches only on selected groups
of material, the oeuvre of the Sabouroff Painter is the
first one here that includes a great number of slipped
lekythoi -- over a hundred -- and the soon canonical
funerary iconography; contemporary artists like the
Timokrates and Inscription Painters and the Tymbos Group
were producing such vases exclusively.[50] The Sabouroff
Painter's activity focused on cups and lekythoi; two of
the former and most of the latter have slip [XL,2]. The
lekythoi illustrate the now standard design: mouth,
neck, and lower body covered with black glaze, the
shoulder and picture surface together with the crowning
pattern slipped white; as before, the ornament generally
consists of a cyma below the junction of neck and shoulder,
circumscribed palmettes with dependent buds, and some
form of meander above the scene. The Sabouroff Painter's
stylistic direction continues with the Painters of Athens
2020 and Cambridge 28.2 as well as with the Houston
Painter.[51]

During the early classic period, lekythoi and cups

were the major white-ground genres. Since production
of the former had increased significantly, the number
of non-specialists who decorated them is very small
indeed. Like the Brygos Painter and Douris in the
preceding section, the three artists considered here
also painted cups; unlike their archaic counterparts,
however, they apparently favored cups less than the
lekythoi. The coincidence of artists for the two shapes
is interesting; it unfortunately reveals nothing about
the potters, but it emphasizes that lekythoi were needed
in every range of quality while cups were only of the
best. The multiplicity of concurrent vase types and the
possibilities for observing their interrelation virtually
ends with the early classic period. Apart from the
exceptions considered earlier, lekythoi monopolize the
later fifth century production of white-ground vases
and, in the following discussion, only one personality
has appeared before.

As Beazley brought out, the oeuvre of the Achilles
Painter begins, chronologically and stylistically, in
the early classic period, but it comes to epitomize the
temperament and style of classic vase-painting.[52] While
the Achilles workshop made red-figure pots of various
shapes, it developed the white-ground lekythos type
basic both to contemporaries like the Sabouroff Painter
and to succeeding artists [XL,3]. The lekythoi served a

funerary purpose as indicated by their predominance
in graves,[53] by their iconography, and by the false
bottoms introduced to save oil.[54] Technically, they fall
into two groups: the earlier examples tend to have glaze
outlines and second white for female flesh, the later
ones lack the added white and have matte outlines;
dilute and matte colors, of course, supplement the
drawing. As with the design, none of these features
appear for the first time but the present juncture
seemed appropriate for reviewing them. The lekythoi,
however, are new with respect to the inscriptions
whose relevance to the scene is generally not evident[55]
but whose stoichedon form visually heightens the funerary-
memorial effect. More significantly, with his mastery of
line and color, the Achilles Painter created a definitive
pictorial expression for the solemn scenes of mistress
and maid, warrior and woman, or mourners at a tomb.
Through his master, the Berlin Painter, he stands within
the Euthymidean artistic tradition and certainly marks
the culmination of its concern with white-ground.

The Phiale Painter was a follower of the Achilles
Painter and although his white-ground production is
quantitatively smaller, it includes the two intact
calyx-kraters and a few lekythoi [XL,4]. The latter
continue the standard design; however, the depiction
of an outdoor setting where relevant[56] is a new feature

recalling especially the Vatican krater. Among other
contemporary decorators of pots, the Painter of Athens
1943 has left a few examples with glaze drawing;[57]
the Painter of Munich 2335 produced a large red-figure
oeuvre and white lekythoi with matte outlines, related
to those of the Bird Group.[58]

The last slipped lekythoi from non-specialist workshops represent the squat form prevalent during the later
fifth century and appearing here for the first time;
significantly, none display the funerary iconography.
Brussels A 1021[59] belongs near the Shuvalov Painter
[XLI,1]; it depicts a Nike, identified by an inscription
and seated in a rockscape like a pensive mourner. Two
exceptionally tall and elaborate examples are by the
Eretria Painter;[60] although he worked primarily on cups,
none of these has slip. Kansas City 31.80 shows two white-
ground figure zones separated by a plastic fillet with
a red-figure cyma. The subordinate shoulder section
contains Eros facing a female figure between a pair of
palmettes; the main picture presents the infant Kephalos
with his mother and four attendant personifications. In ʼ
execution, the Eretria Painter's characteristically nervous
but precise drawing conspicuously predominates over his
use of matte color. New York 31.11.13 proves even more
elaborate [XLI,2]. On the body, it has a red-figure
frieze above and below a white band illustrating two

related subjects: Achilles mourning Patroklos, and
Thetis accompanied by Nereids bringing the hero's new
armor. The slipped zone preserves traces of added color
as well as of gilded relief, which also occurs on the
red-figure scenes. The New York lekythos is by no means
exceptional in having several tiers of pictures. However,
it is unique in the use of white-ground to emphasize
one, and the central, tier among several which are
otherwise comparable; indeed, of the works we have
considered, this one most strongly recalls the many-
levelled paintings of Polygnotos and Mikon.

The final vase to be mentioned here is the fragmentary squat lekythos Leningrad TG 19 by the Meidias
Painter[61] [XLI,3]. In design, it resembles Kansas City
31.80. On the shoulder, delimited by a painted cyma, it
preserves a pair of lions and panthers;[62] below, it shows
a woman seated outdoors with attendants and Eros. Where
the other piece had a second red-figure cyma beneath
the picture, it has a meander. The Leningrad lekythos is
the sole slipped vase from a late fifth-century non-
specialist workshop. During the classic period, a few
examples still appear among groups of red-figure pots,
oinochoai, and cups; by c. 400, white-ground occurs only
with funerary lekythoi.

For the century and a half when the technique was
used, white-ground lekythoi occur in an unbroken succession.

They begin with Psiax and end, roughly, with the Triglyph Painter; in other terms, their duration coincides
with that of the shouldered shape. Of the many aspects
to this complex succession, a single one has concerned
us here, i.e. the black-figure and outline material from
workshops that also produced other slipped vases or that
did not concentrate on lekythoi. On the one hand, the
resulting picture is incomplete. On the other hand, it
isolates and highlights the relatively numerous black-
figure artists and the fewer pre-classic outline artists
who decorated lekythoi along with other shapes; it
brings out the qualitative disparity between the two
groups of painters. Finally, our discussion indicates
that the diversified outline production, like the
black-figure white-ground tradition, declines towards
the mid-fifth century and lekythoi become restricted
to specialized establishments.

CHAPTER V: Footnotes

1 By Miss D. Kurtz of the Ashmolean Museum, Oxford.

2 P. 35, no. 1.

3 P. 36, no. 7.

4 ABL 10 ff. ABV 154-155; Para. 66; cf. also D. von
Bothmer, "Three Vases by the Amasis Painter,"
Madrider Mitteilungen 12 (1971), 123 ff.

5 Cf., however, p. 100.

6 ABL 198, 4 & 6.

7 ABL 80, 82.

8 ABL 41.

9 ABL 206,5.

10 Para. 215.

11 Cf. pp. 74-75.

12 ABL 84.

13 Cf. pp. 97 & 104.

14 ABL 86-87.

15 ABL 218,50.

16 ABL 218,55.

17 ABV 476; cf. also our p. 97.

18 ABL 89.

19 ABL 94.

20 ABL 94, n. 2 & 3.

21 ABL 98.

22 Boston 10.556 (ABV 471,122).

23 Athens 12848 (ABV 503 top); Paris, Mikas (Para. 245).

24 Basle market (ARV² 303; Para. 357).

25 Cf. ARV^2 303.

26 Leningrad 671 (ARV^2 304).

27 ABL especially 101.

28 ABL 141, 145.

29 Cf. p. 158; since the Athena Painter lekythos also derives from the Edinburgh Painter's shape, the latter may provide a link to Psiax and/or Nikosthenes.

30 ABL 147.

31 ABL 111.

32 ABL 157 ff.

33 ABL 137.

34 ABL 131, 137.

35 ABL 165.

36 E.g. ABL 265, 42-46; ABV 586, 3-4.

37 ARV^2 102,1 top.

38 ARV^2 263,54.

39 ARV^2 282 below - 283 above.

40 ARV^2 385, 223.

41 Copenhagen inv. 6328 (ARV^2 283,4 above) does depict Achilles brought to Chiron.

42 O. Benndorf, Griechische und sicilische Vasenbilder (Berlin, 1883), 99.

43 Palermo, from Selinus (ARV^2 446,266); Cleveland 66.114 (ARV^2 446,266 bis; Para. 376).

44 Beazley, cited in CVA: Cleveland 1 (US 15), 1971, to Pls. 32 ff.

45 Syracuse 19900 (ARV^2 557,122).

46 ARV^2 557,121.

47 J.D. Beazley, Der Panmaler (Berlin, 1931), 24, 58.

48 Two lekythoi in Munich, ex Schoen (ARV^2 624, 86-87); New York 06.1021.134 (ARV^2 626,2); London D 20 (ARV^2 626,3).

49 R. Lullies, Eine Sammlung griechischer Kleinkunst (Munich, 1955), 34, 74-75.

50 Cf. ARV^2 chap. 40.

51 Cf. ARV^2 854-6.

52 J.D. Beazley, Greek Vases in Poland (Oxford, 1928), 49-50.

53 For relevant literary sources cf. Richter and Milne, 14. For a recent analysis of lekythos distribution to Attica, Eretria, and Magna Graecia, cf. F. Felten, Thanatos- und Kleophonmaler (München, 1971), 53 ff.

54 Miss Haspels credits the Beldam Potter with the invention of false-bottomed lekythoi (ABL 176-7). In his investigations, Dr. von Bothmer found that the innovation was taken up by the Inscription, Karlsruhe, and Sabouroff Painters and that it was used selectively through the time of Group R and the Triglyph Painter. Dr. von Bothmer also observed that the shape of the inner cylinder and the position of the vent hole vary by workshop. Cf. Noble 25.

55 A similar situation occurs on grave stelai. Cf. C.W. Clairmont, Gravestone and Epigram (Mainz, 1970), 55 ff.

56 E.g. Munich 2797 & 2798 (ARV^2 1022, 138 & 139).

57 ARV^2 1082 below.

58 ARV^2 1161 & 1168.

59 ARV^2 1213,3 top.

60 ARV^2 1248, 8 & 9.

61 ARV^2 1314,16 bis.

62 Dr. von Bothmer compares the shoulder of the loutrophoros, Louvre CA 4194 (p.143,1).

CONCLUSION

With lekythoi and the last years of the fifth century
the Attic white-ground vases end. By way of conclusion,
the development and certain major features of the
technique may be summarized. On the basis of existing
evidence, the use of white-ground began in the years
c. 530. It represents one of several contemporary
innovations affecting shape and technique; moreover,
it may have originated in one of the most decisively
experimental workshops, that of Andokides. The succeeding
development consists of two parallel, and frequently
interrelated aspects. While a number of black-figure
artists employed the new technique, the two most influential were Psiax and Nikosthenes. Whether the former
was a potter as well as a painter remains unknown. However, each is associated with certain shapes, Psiax
e.g. with lekythoi and alabastra, Nikosthenes with
oinochoai; as the kyathoi suggest, the two may also
have collaborated. Their effect extends still further
e.g. to a hydria, mastos, phiale, and to cups. Psiax
and Nikosthenes seem to dominate the picture of late
sixth century white-ground but others, of course, worked
independently, on hydriai and neck-amphorae for instance.
During the next generation, the production of black-
figure white-ground vases passed into different hands;
it shifted from artists working mainly on larger shapes

to those concerned with smaller ones, especially lekythoi.

The outline series contains no artist(s) as pervasively influential as Psiax and Nikosthenes; however, it does present several individuals and groups directly connected with specific shapes. Use of white-ground began within the Pioneer Group; it occurs on the plates and plaques associated with Euthymides and on the cups of Euphronios. From these two figures, it may be followed to others related through collaboration or influence. Thus, the Euthymidean tradition reveals a white-ground aspect appearing in decorators of large pots, i.e. the Berlin and Achilles Painters; similarly, the white-ground aspect of the Euphronian tradition manifests itself in cups of Onesimos, the Brygos Painter, Douris, the Pistoxenos Painter. The outline and slip combination prospered in unrelated workshops as well. It is characteristic of the late archaic Paidikos-Syriskos alabastra. During the early classic period, it recurs in the Villa Giulia, Penthesilean, and Sotadean workshops, among others. As indicated by the plastic vases of Sotades and the head kantharoi, the technique also served for shapes outside of the standard repertoire. The latter remained varied until the mid-fifth century; then, for another fifty years until Attic white-ground finally ceased, it consists only of funerary lekythoi and a few, isolated exceptions.

From such a survey of our subject, two important
points emerge. The white-ground technique was not,
fundamentally, exclusive. Although it tends to appear
on smaller vases and, on some shapes occurs only once,
its use was extensive; in this respect, it contrasts
with coral red and resembles Six's technique. Furthermore, the presence or absence of slip did not depend on
qualitative considerations; it served on Haimonian
mastoids and skyphoi, cups by the Brygos Painter, lekythoi of Douris and the Ikaros Painter. Indeed, it
occurs at most every level of late sixth and early
fifth century ceramic activity. This leads to our
second point. In the preparation of a vase, the potter's
rôle must have included the application of white-ground.
Such a procedure would explain the qualitative dis-
crepancies mentioned just above; it makes the slip
an adjunct of the shape and sets apart the decoration.
It would also account for recurrent features like the
use of similar shapes by different artists and the
appearance of slipped works in a variety of forms within
one workshop or in lineages of connected workshops.
According to Miss B. Cohen,[1] the technique of coral
red follows the same pattern; it engaged such potters
as Exekias, Kachrylion, and Sotades. In the study of
Attic vase-painting, the potter's rôle remains less
well understood than the painter's. However, white-

ground forms one of several secondary but self-contained groups of evidence whose interrelation with black-figure or red-figure proves most informative.

While white-ground itself is our first concern, the types of painted decoration represent another major consideration. The two basic techniques were black-figure and outline and, significantly, the artists known to us worked in one or the other but not both. Miss Haspels' "semi-outline" provided a compromise which occurs once with Euphronios and otherwise only with lekythos painters. Especially as developed in the Diosphos workshop, the combination or juxtaposition of black-glazed and outline forms represents a notable innovation; by means of the white-ground, it provided a versatile integration of black-figure and red-figure procedure. However, it does not go significantly beyond the latter.

White-ground comes into its own with the polychromy that emerged in the early classic period. It offered a neutral surface and the greatest possible contrast to the drawing, painting, and details in relief. Its effectiveness can be appreciated by comparing e.g. the Penthesilea Painter's red-figure Amazonomachy in Munich[2] with his slipped pyxis and bobbin in New York or with the Pistoxenos Painter's slipped cups. The first piece displays an exceptional amount of added

color and gilding which originally appeared even stronger;
nonetheless it lacks clarity and impact on account of the
reserved forms and black background. White-ground polychromy may have been fostered in part by the influence
of monumental painting. In any event, it enhanced pictorial effects, as shown by the "mythological" type of
pyxides or by the Phiale Painter's kraters and lekythoi; it also heightened the expressiveness e.g. of
lekythoi, for the reds and ochres of the Achilles Painter,
the greens and purples of Group R create an effect in
coloristic terms comparable to the respective drawing
styles. Such vase-painting, in the literal sense,
grows out of the use of added color in black-figure and
early red-figure as well as of dilute in varying con-
sistencies. It is, however, something new, brought
about by the accomodation of slipping and painting
techniques.[3]

A third consideration basic to an understanding of
our subject and concerning both potter and painter
regards the function of white-ground. Most often, slip
seems to serve no precisely identifiable purpose, but
occasional exceptions occur. On both black-figure and
outline vases, it may provide a means of articulation,
emphasizing part of the shape and/or of the decoration;

the two are rarely separate. To cite only a few examples, slip stresses part of the structure in the Bareiss Lykomedes hydria, the New York Andokides amphora, the Euthymidean plates; it influences the decoration in the Goettingen Painter column-krater, the Methyse Painter volute-krater, the Eretria Painter lekythos in New York. White-ground may stand for other materials: metal in the Leningrad Lykomedes hydria and perhaps the Syriskos Painter aryballos, alabaster in alabastra, stone in the Aischines base. On black-figure works, particularly those of inferior quality, the technique often seems to exist for variety only. To outline, it provided a background that enhanced effects of glaze, as in the Bareiss cup or the Munich Brygos, and of color. With lekythoi, it may even have come to symbolize their purpose.

The function of white-ground presents a further aspect that has not been introduced here because it would entail examination of and experimentation on the objects themselves. The problem concerns the quality of the slip as it affected the use of a vase, particularly of cups. It arises with the increasingly bright but fragile white which comes into use towards the mid-fifth century. The unresistent surface may not have caused difficulties with lekythoi, which served mainly as dedications, or with kraters, pyxides, and other shapes slipped on their exterior surfaces. How-

ever, its occurrence e.g. on the Pistoxenos Painter's
cup in London raises questions concerning the raison
d'être of such pieces if they were not employed for
drinking. The impermanent white appears relatively
late in the history of white-ground; it in no way
changed the actual use of slip, but may have hastened
the latter's disappearance from all utilitarian shapes.
Despite their technical shortcomings, the lekythoi continued to exist because they met an ongoing demand.
Therefore, here as throughout its history, the presence
of white-ground depended not only on the possibilities
it offered but also on the shapes with which it was
used.

CONCLUSION: Footnotes

1   Forthcoming article in <u>Marsyas</u>.

2   Munich 2688 (<u>ARV</u>^{2} 879,1); color illustration in
    Robertson 115-116.

3   One of the most "aceramic" developments was the
    use of certain matte unfired colors, applied
    after the shape with its slip had been fired.
    Cf. Noble 64-65.

SELECTED BIBLIOGRAPHY AND LIST OF ABBREVIATIONS

A. Abbreviations of Serials and Handbooks

AA	Archäologischer Anzeiger in the Jahrbuch des Deutschen Archäologischen Instituts
A.A.	Ars Antiqua (Lucern), sale catalogue
ABL	Haspels, C.H.E. Attic Black-figured Lekythoi. Paris, 1936.
ABV	Beazley, J.D. Attic Black-figure Vasepainters. Oxford, 1956.
AJA	American Journal of Archaeology
A.K.	Antike Kunst
AM	Mitteilungen des Deutschen Archäologischen Instituts, Athenische Abteilung
Ant. Class.	L'Antiquité classique
Anuari	Anuari: Institut d'Estudis Catalans
Arch. Class.	Archeologia classica
ARV^1	Beazley, J.D. Attic Red-figure Vasepainters, first edition. Oxford, 1942.
ARV^2	Beazley, J.D. Attic Red-figure Vasepainters, second edition. Oxford, 1963.
AZ	Archäologische Zeitung
B. Ap.	Berlin Museum, Gerhard Apparatus
BCH	Bulletin de correspondance hellénique
BMFA	Bulletin of the Museum of Fine Arts, Boston
BMMA	Bulletin of the Metropolitan Museum of Art, New York
BSA	Annual of the British School at Athens
Bull. d. Inst.	Bullettino dell' Instituto di Corrispondenza Archeologica
Cl. Rh.	Clara Rhodos

CV	Corpus Vasorum Antiquorum (especially sections III H, III I, III J)
Delt.	Archaiologikon Deltion
EAA	Enciclopedia dell'Arte Antica
Eph.	Ephemeris Archaiologike
Fasti	Fasti archaeologici
Hesp.	Hesperia
Hesp. Art Bull.	Hesperia Art Bulletin (Philadelphia)
HSCP	Harvard Studies in Classical Philology
JdI	Jahrbuch des Deutschen Archäologischen Instituts
JHS	Journal of Hellenic Studies
Journ. Walt.	Journal of the Walters Art Gallery, Baltimore
M.M.	Münzen und Medaillen (Basle), sale catalogue
Mon. Ant.	Monumenti antichi per cura della Reale Accademia dei Lincei
Mon. Ined.	Monumenti inediti pubblicati dall'Instituto di Corrispondenza Archeologica
Mon. Piot	Monuments et Mémoires (Fondation Piot)
N. Sc.	Notizie degli Scavi di Antichità
Para.	Beazley, J.D. Paralipomena: Additions to Attic Black-figure Vase-painters and Attic Red-figure Vase-painters. Oxford, 1971.
R.I.	German Institute, Rome
Riv. Ist.	Rivista dell'Istituto Nazionale d'Archeologia e Storia dell'Arte
RM	Mitteilungen des Deutschen Archäologischen Instituts, Römische Abteilung
Stud. Etr.	Studi etruschi
Trudy	Trudy Otdela Antichnogo Mira

B. Other Books and Articles

Albizzati, C. Vasi antichi dipinti del Vaticano. Rome, 1925-39.

Anderson, J.K. Handbook to the Greek Vases in the Otago Museum. Dunedin, 1955.

Angermeier, H.E. Das Alabastron. Giessen, 1936.

Arias, P.E., Hirmer, M., Shefton, B. A History of Greek Vase-painting. New York, 1961.

Aurigemma, S. Il R. Museo di Spina. Ferrara, 1935 (first edition) and 1936 (second edition).

Bartoccini, R. and de Agostino, A. Museo di Villa Giulia. Milan, 1962.

Beazley, J.D. "The Antimenes Painter," Journal of Hellenic Studies 47 (1927), 63ff.

-----. Attic Black-figure: A Sketch. London, 1928.

-----. Attic Black-figure Vase-painters. Oxford, 1956.

-----. Attic Red-figure Vase-painters, first edition. Oxford, 1942.

-----. Attic Red-figure Vase-painters, second edition. Oxford, 1963.

-----. Attic Red-figured Vases in American Museums. Cambridge, 1918.

-----. Attic White Lekythoi. London, 1938.

-----. "Charinos," Journal of Hellenic Studies 49 (1929), 38ff.

-----. Corpus Vasorum Antiquorum: Oxford 1 (Great Britain 3). Oxford, 1937.

-----. The Development of Attic Black-figure. Berkeley, 1951.

-----. Greek Vases in Poland. Oxford, 1928.

-----. "Little-master Cups," Journal of Hellenic Studies 52 (1932), 167ff.

-----. Paralipomena: Additions to Attic Black-figure Vase-painters and Attic Red-figure Vase-painters. Oxford, 1971.

-----. Potter and Painter in Ancient Athens. London, 1946.

-----. Review of _Les coupes attiques à fond blanc_ by H. Philippart, _Gnomon_ 13 (1937), 289ff.

(-----). _Select Exhibition of Beazley Gifts to the Ashmolean Museum._ Oxford, 1967.

-----. _Some Attic Vases in the Cyprus Museum._ London, 1948.

----- and Magi, F. _La Raccolta Benedetto Guglielmi._ Rome, 1939.

Benndorf, O. _Griechische und sicilische Vasenbilder._ Berlin, 1883.

Bieber, M. _Entwicklungsgeschichte der griechischen Tracht._ Berlin, 1934.

Bloesch, H. _Formen attischer Schalen._ Bern, 1940.

Blümel, C. _Antike Kunstwerke._ Berlin, 1953.

Boardman, J. "A Name for the Cerberus Painter," _Journal of Hellenic Studies_ 75 (1955), 154ff.

-----. "Painted Funerary Plaques and Some Remarks on Prothesis," _Annual of the British School at Athens_ 50 (1955), 51ff.

-----. "Painted Votive Plaques and an Early Inscription from Aegina," _Annual of the British School at Athens_ 49 (1954), 183ff.

-----. "Some Attic Fragments: Pot, Plaque, and Dithyramb," _Journal of Hellenic Studies_ 76 (1956), 18ff.

----- and Pope, M. _Greek Vases in Cape Town._ Cape Town, 1961.

Bothmer, D. von. _Amazons in Greek Art._ Oxford, 1957.

-----. _Ancient Art from New York Private Collections._ New York, 1961.

-----. "Andokides the Potter and the Andokides Painter," _Bulletin of the Metropolitan Museum of Art, New York_ (February, 1966), 201ff.

-----. "Aspects of a Collection," _Bulletin of the Metropolitan Museum of Art, New York_ (June, 1969), 425ff.

-----. "New Vases by the Amasis Painter," _Antike Kunst_ 3 (1960), 71ff.

Boulter, C.G. "Graves in Lenormant Street, Athens," _Hesperia_ 32 (1963), 113ff.

Bruhn, A. "Greek Vases in the Ny Carlsberg Glyptothek," From the Collections 2 (1939), 113ff.

Buschor, E. Attische Lekythen der Parthenonzeit. Munich, 1925.

-----. Grab eines attischen Mädchens. Munich, 1941.

Cambitoglou, A. The Brygos Painter. Sydney, 1968.

Caskey, L.D. and Beazley, J.D. Attic Vase Paintings in the Museum of Fine Arts, Boston. Oxford, 1931-63.

Collignon, H. and Couve, L. Catalogue des vases peints du Musée National d'Athènes. Paris, 1902-4.

Cook, R.M. Greek Painted Pottery. London, 1960.

Corbett, P.E. "Preliminary Sketch in Greek Vase-painting," Journal of Hellenic Studies 85 (1965), 16ff.

Cornelius, H. Elementargesetze der bildenden Kunst. Leipzig, 1908.

Demangel, R. "Un nouvel alabastre du peintre Pasiadès," Monuments Piot 26 (1923), 67ff.

Diehl, E. Die Hydria. Mayence, 1964.

Diepolder, H. Der Pistoxenos-Maler. Berlin, 1954.

Eisman, M. "The Nikosthenic Workshop as the Producer of Attic Kyathoi," American Journal of Archaeology 74 (1970), 193.

-----. "The Theseus Painter, the Marathon Tumulus, and Chronology," American Journal of Archaeology 75 (1971), 200.

Fairbanks, A. Athenian White Lekythoi. New York, 1907 and 1914.

Feytmans, D. Les vases grecs de la Bibliothèque Royale de Belgique. Brussels, 1948.

Fiorelli, G. Notizia dei vasi dipinti rivenuti a Cuma. Naples, 1857.

Frel, J. Řecké Vázy. Prague, 1956.

-----. "Choix de vases attiques en Tchecoslovaquie," Sborník Národního Musea v Praze 13 (1959), 232ff.

Frickenhaus, A. "Griechische Vasen aus Emporion," Anuari: Institut d'Estudis Catalans 2 (1908), 195ff.

Fröhner, W. La collection van Branteghem. Brussels, 1892.

-----. La collection Tyszkiewicz. Munich, 1902.

Furtwängler, A. Beschreibung der Vasensammlung im Antiquarium. Berlin, 1885.

Gabrici, E. "La prevalenza del commercio attico a Cuma," Monumenti antichi 22 (1913), 449ff.

-----. "Il santuario della Malophoros a Selinunte," Monumenti antichi 32 (1927), 5ff.

García y Bellido, A. Los hallazgos griegos de España. Madrid, 1936.

-----. Hispania Graeca. Barcelona, 1948.

Gardner, E.A. A Catalogue of the Greek Vases in the Fitzwilliam Museum, Cambridge. Cambridge, 1897.

Gardner, P. Catalogue of the Greek Vases in the Ashmolean Museum. Oxford, 1893.

Gerhard, E. Trinkschalen und -Gefässe des Königlichen Museums zu Berlin. Berlin, 1848-50.

Ghali-Kahil, L. Les enlèvements et le retour d'Hélène. Paris, 1955.

-----. "Quelques vases du sanctuaire d'Artémis à Brauron," Antike Kunst Beiheft 1 (1963), 5ff.

-----. "Loutrophore à fond blanc au Musée du Louvre," Antike Kunst Beiheft 4 (1967), 146ff.

Gjerstad, E. et al. The Swedish Cyprus Expedition. Stockholm, 1934-37.

Gorbunova, X.S. and Peredolskaya, A.A. Mastera grecheskikh raspisnykh Vaz. Leningrad, 1961.

Graef, B. and Langlotz, E. Die antiken Vasen von der Akropolis zu Athen. Berlin, 1925-33.

Grünhagen, W. Erlangen:Antike Originalarbeiten der Kunstsammlung des Instituts. Nürenberg, 1948.

Gullini, G. "La coppa di Taranto del maestro di Pentesilea," Archeologia classica 3 (1951), 1ff.

Hartwig, P. Die griechischen Meisterschalen. Stuttgart, 1893.

Haspels, C.H.E. Attic Black-figured Lekythoi. Paris, 1936.

Heydemann, H. Die Vasensammlungen des Museo Nazionale zu
Neapel. Berlin, 1872.

Hogarth, D.G. Excavations at Ephesus: The Archaic Artemesia.
London, 1908.

Holmberg, E. "Three White-ground Vases," Collection Hélene
Stathatos, III. Strasbourg, 1963, 155ff.

Hoorn, G. van. Choes and Anthesteria. Leyden, 1951.

Hoppin, J.C. A Handbook of Attic Red-figured Vases.
Cambridge, 1919.

-----. A Handbook of Greek Black-figured Vases. Paris, 1924.

Inghirami, F. Pitture di vasi etruschi. Fiesole, 1852.

Jacobsthal, P. Göttinger Vasen. Berlin, 1912.

-----. Greek Pins. Oxford, 1956.

-----. Die melischen Reliefs. Berlin, 1931.

-----. Ornamente griechischer Vasen. Berlin, 1927.

Jahn, O. Beschreibung der Vasensammlung. Munich, 1854.

Jucker, I. Aus der Antikensammlung des bernischen historischen
Museums. Bern, 1970.

Karydi, E. "Ein Skyphos aus dem Kerameikos," Athenische
Mitteilungen 77 (1962), 105ff.

Khanenko, B. Collection: antiquités de la région du Dniepre.
Kiev, 1899-1907.

Klein, W. Die griechischen Vasen mit Lieblingsinschriften.
Leipzig, 1898.

Konstantinou, I.K. "Leuke Delphike Kylix," Ephemeris
Archaiologike 1970, 27ff.

La Borde, A. de. Collection de vases grecs de M. le Comte
de Lamberg. Paris, 1813-28.

Langlotz, E. Griechische Vasen in Würzburg. Munich, 1932.

-----. Zur Zeitbestimmung der Vasenmalerei und der gleich-
zeitigen Plastik. Leipzig, 1920.

-----. et al. Sammlung Freiherr Max von Heyl. Helbing

(Munich) 30 October 1930.

Lau, T. et al. Die griechischen Vasen. Leipzig, 1877.

Licht, H. Sittengeschichte Griechenlands. Dresden and
Zürich, 1925-28.

Lullies, R. Griechische Kunstwerke. Sammlung Ludwig,
Aachen. Düsseldorf, 1968.

-----. Eine Sammlung griechischer Kleinkunst. Munich, 1955.

----- and Hirmer, M. Griechische Vasen der reifarchaischen
Zeit. Munich, 1953.

Marconi, P. Il Museo Nazionale di Palermo. Rome, 1932.

Masner, K. Die Sammlung antiker Vasen und Terracotten im
K.K. Oesterreich. Museum. Vienna, 1892.

Merlin, A. "Pégase et Chrysaor sur une pyxide attique du
Musée du Louvre," Mélanges G. Glotz. Paris, 1932, 599ff.

Milne, M.J. "Peleus and Akastos," Bulletin of the Metropolitan Museum of Art, New York (June, 1947), 255ff.

Mingazzini, P. Vasi della Collezione Castellani. Rome, 1930.

Morrison, J.S. and Williams, R.T. Greek Oared Ships.
Cambridge, 1968.

Murray, A.S. and Smith, A.H. White Athenian Vases in the
British Museum. London, 1896.

Nicole, G. Catalogue des vases peints du Musée National
d'Athènes, supplément. Paris, 1911.

Noble, J.V. The Techniques of Painted Attic Pottery. New
York, 1965.

Orsi, P. "Gela," Monumenti antichi 17 (1906), 5ff.

-----. "Megara Hyblaea," Monumenti antichi 1 (1890), 689ff.

Papaspiridi, S. "Eleusiniaka Angeia," Archaiologikon Deltion
9 (1924), 1ff.

Payne, H.G.G. Necrocorinthia. Oxford, 1931.

Pease, M.Z. "The Pottery from the North Slope of the
Akropolis," Hesperia 4 (1935), 214ff.

Pellegrini, G. Catalogo dei vasi antichi dipinti delle

collezioni Palagi ed Universitaria. Bologna, 1900.

-----. Catalogo dei vasi greci dipinti delle necropoli felsinee. Bologna, 1912.

Perrot, G. (and Chipiez, C.). Histoire de l'art dans l'antiquité. Vols. 9 and 10. Paris, 1911 and 1914.

Peters, K. Studien zu den panathenäischen Preisamphoren. Berlin, 1942.

----- and Hundt, A. Greifswalder Antiken. Berlin, 1961.

Pfuhl, E. Malerei und Zeichnung der Griechen. Munich, 1923.

Philippart, H. "Les coupes attiques à fond blanc," L'Antiquité classique 5 (1936), 5ff.

Pottier, E. Vases antiques du Louvre. Paris, 1897-1922.

Poulsen, F. Vases grecs récemment acquis par la Glyptothèque Ny Carlsberg. Copenhagen, 1922.

Raubitschek, I. The Hearst Hillsborough Vases. Mainz, 1969.

Richter, G.M.A. Attic Red-figured Vases: a Survey. New Haven, 1958.

-----. "A Kyathos by Psiax in the Museo Poldi-Pezzoli," American Journal of Archaeology 45 (1941), 587ff.

-----. "The Menon Painter and Psiax," American Journal of Archaeology 38 (1934), 547ff.

-----. "Psiax," American Journal of Archaeology 43 (1939), 645ff.

----- and Hall, L. Red-figured Athenian Vases in the Metropolitan Museum of Art. New Haven, 1936.

----- and Milne, M.J. Shapes and Names of Athenian Vases. New York, 1935.

Riezler, W. Weissgrundige attische Lekythen. Munich, 1914.

Robertson, M. Greek Painting. Geneva, 1959.

Roebuck, C. "Pottery from the North Slope of the Akropolis, 1937-1938," Hesperia 9 (1940), 141ff.

-----, "White-ground Plaques by the Cerberus Painter," American Journal of Archaeology 43 (1939), 467ff.

Rolley, C. Catalogue des vases grecs du Musée d'Auxerre.

Auxerre, 1959.

Sacken, E. von and Kenner, F. Die Sammlungen des K.K. Münz- und Antikenkabinets. Vienna, 1866.

Schaal, H. Griechische Vasen und figürliche Tonplastik in Bremen. Bremen, 1933.

Schauenburg, K. "Zu attisch-schwarzfigurigen Schalen mit Innenfriesen," Antike Kunst Beiheft 7 (1970), 33ff.

-----. "Zu 'Irrtümern' in der griechischen und etruskischen Vasenmalerei," Festschrift G. von Lücken. Rostock, 1968, 765ff.

Schefold, K. Meisterwerke griechischer Kunst. Basle, 1960.

Sichtermann, H. Griechische Vasen in Unteritalien aus der Sammlung Jatta in Ruvo. Tübingen, 1966.

Smith, C.H. Catalogue of the Greek and Etruscan Vases in the British Museum, III. London, 1896.

-----. Edinburgh Museum of Science and Art. Catalogue of a Collection Presented by Sir Hume-Campbell. Edinburgh, 1877.

-----. The Forman Collection. Sotheby 19 June 1899.

Smith, H.R.W. New Aspects of the Menon Painter. Berkeley, 1929.

Strong, E. Catalogue of the Antiquities of Lord Melchett. Oxford, 1928.

Talcott, L. "Two Attic Kylikes," Hesperia 2 (1933), 217ff.

-----. "Vases and Kalos-Names from an Agora Well," Hesperia 5 (1936), 333ff.

Thimme, J. "Griechische Salbgefässe mit libyschen Motiven," Jahrbuch der staatlichen Kunstsammlungen in Baden-Württemberg 7 (1970), 7ff.

Truitt, P. "White-ground Pyxis and Phiale, ca. 450 B.C.," Bulletin of the Museum of Fine Arts, Boston 67 (1969), 72ff.

Ure, A.D. "Krokotos and White Heron," Journal of Hellenic Studies 75 (1955), 90ff.

Ure, P.N. Sixth and Fifth Century Pottery from Rhitsona. London, 1927.

Vanderpool, E. "Some Black-figured Pottery from the Athenian Agora," Hesperia 15 (1946), 120ff.

Vos, M.F. Scythian Archers in Archaic Attic Vase-painting. Groningen, 1963.

Waldhauer, O. Kratkoe opisanie sobraniya antichnikh raspisnikh Vaz. St. Petersburg, 1914.

Waldstein, C. The Argive Heraeum. Boston, 1902-5.

Walters, H.B. Catalogue of the Greek and Etruscan Vases in the British Museum, II. London, 1893.

Watzinger, C. Griechische Vasen in Tübingen. Reutlingen, 1924

Zahn, R. "Kleinigkeiten aus Alt-Athen," Die Antike 1 (1925), 273ff.

-----. "Altertümer auf Stift Neuburg bei Heidelberg," Archäologischer Anzeiger 1893, 187ff.

Zannoni, A. Gli scavi della Certosa di Bologna. Bologna, 1876.

Plate I

1. Athens, Akropolis 611. (I.A. p. 27).

2. Louvre F 117. (I.B.1. p. 31).

Plate II

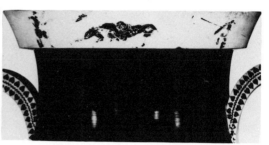

2. Detail, New York 63.11.6.

1. New York 63.11.6. (I.C.1. p. 33).

3. Louvre F 203. (I.C.2. p. 33).   4. Louvre F 203.

Plate III

1. Paris, Jameson. (I.D.1. p. 35).　　2. Leningrad 381. (I.D.2. p. 35).

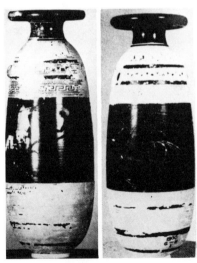

3. London 1900.6.-11.1.
(I.D.4. p. 35).

4. Würzburg 436.
(I.D.5. p. 36).

Plate IV

1. Basle inv. 421. (I.D.6. p. 36).

2. Dresden ZV. 1780. (I.E.3. p.40). 3. Basle, Bloch. (I.E.5. p. 40).

Plate V

1. Copenhagen 111. (II.A.2. p. 48).

2. Würzburg 312. (II.A.3. p. 48).

3. Leningrad 2366. (II.A.9. p. 49).

4. Detail, Leningrad 2366.

Plate VI

1. Once Darmstadt,
   Max von Heyl.
   (II.A.11. p. 49).

2. Louvre CA 4716. (II.A.13. p. 49).

3. Louvre CA 4716.

Plate VII

1. Louvre F 374. (II.B.2. p. 54).

2. Vienna 3607. (II.C.5. p. 56). 3. Maplewood, Noble. (II.C.10. p. 57).

Plate VIII

1. London B 631.
   (II.D.2. p. 63).

2. London B 632.
   (II.D.3. p. 63).

3. Havana, Lagunillas. (II.D.9. p. 64).

Plate IX

2. Leipzig T 428. (II.D.15. p. 64).

1. New York 46.11.7. (II.D.13. p. 64).

3. Berlin 1969.3. (II.D.17. p. 64). 4. Villa Giulia. (II.D.32. p. 71).

Plate X

1. Bibliotheque Royale 6.
   (II.D.40. p. 71).

2. Basle market (M.M.).
   (II.D.49. p. 72).

3. Harvard 1927.154. (II.D.54. p. 72). 4. Osnabrück. (II.D.65. p. 73).

Plate XI

1. Karlsruhe B 32. (II.E.1. p. 80).

2. Once Swiss market. (II.E.2. p. 81).

Plate XII

1. Leningrad
   (II.F.6. p. 82).

2. Munich 1986. (II.F.23. p. 83).

3. Munich 2003. (II.G. p. 87).

Plate XIII

1. Frankfurt, V.F. β 316.
   (II.H.5. p. 88).

2. London B 681. (II.I.3. p. 89).

3. Ny Carlsberg inv. 2759. (II.I.8. p. 90).

4. Once Geneva market. (II.I.15. p. 90).

Plate XIV

1. Once Barcelona, Montaner.   2. Gerona 9.   4. Gerona 806.
   (II.J.8. p. 95).   (II.J.10. p. 95).   (II.J.23. p. 96).

3. Havana, Lagunillas.   5. London B 669.
   (II.J.16. p. 96).   (II.J.26. p. 96).

Plate XV

1. Maplewood, Noble.
   (II.K.7. p. 101).

2. Louvre.
   (II.L.1. p. 102).

3. London B 678.
   (II.M.4. p. 103).

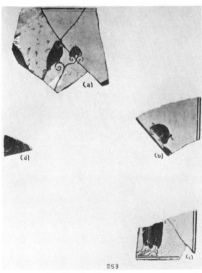

4. Athens, N.S. A-P 2073a-c & 1774d.
   (II.N.2. p. 105).

Plate XVI

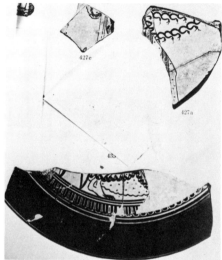

1. Adria Bc 64.10.
   (III.A.1. p. 119).

2. Athens, Akropolis 427.
   (III.A.4. p. 119).

3. New York 91.1.462.
   (III.B.3. p. 122).

Plate XVII

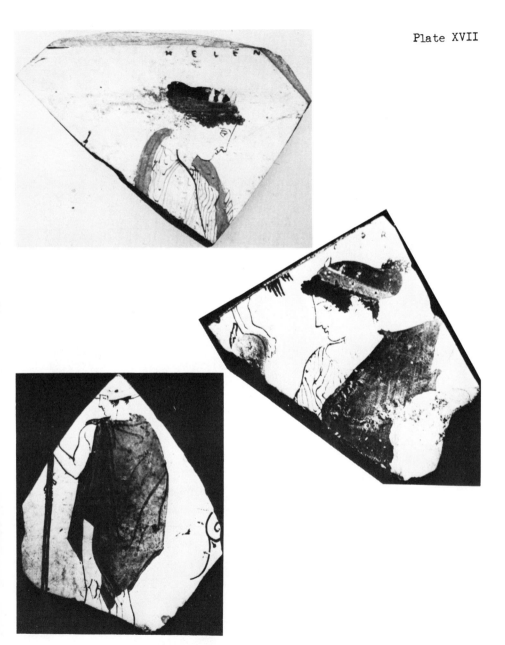

Cincinnati 1962.388. (III.B.6. p. 122).

Plate XVIII

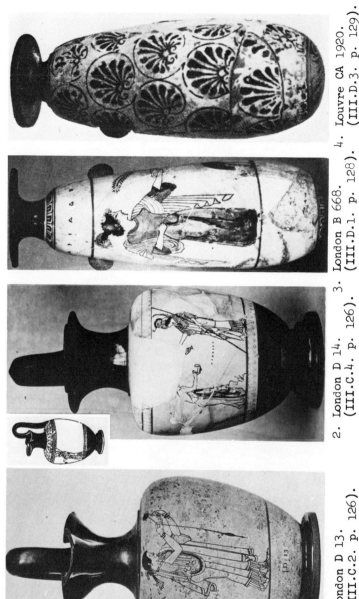

1. London D 13.
   (III.C.2. p. 126).

2. London D 14.
   (III.C.4. p. 126).

3. London B 668.
   (III.D.1. p. 128).

4. Louvre CA 1920.
   (III.D.3. p. 129).

Plate XIX

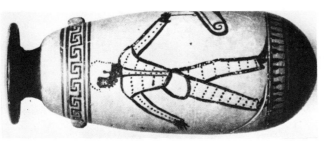

1. Berlin inv. 3382   2. Berlin inv. 3382.   3. Louvre CA 2515.
   (III.D.17. p. 130).   (III.D.40. p. 131).

Plate XX

1. Boston 98.887. (III.E.1. p. 136).

2. Berlin 2261.
(III.E.9. p. 137).

3. Dresden ZV. 54. (III.E.18. p. 138).

Plate XXI

1. New York 28.167.
   (III.F.2. p. 141).

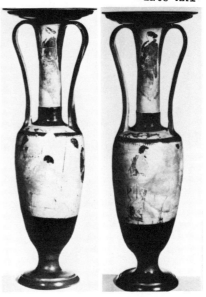

2. Louvre CA 4194.
   (III.G.1. p. 143).

3. Taranto 4553.
   (III.G.2. p. 143).

4. Boston 65.908.
   (III.G.4. p. 143).

Plate XXII

1. London D 8. (III.H.2. p. 154).

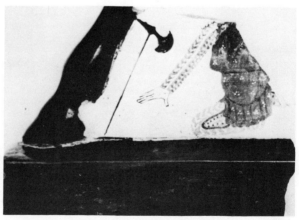

2. Louvre SB 4138 & 4151. (III.H.7. p. 145).

Plate XXIII

1. Boston 98.928. (III.I.1. p. 147).

2. Boston 98.928.

3. Tarquinia 6845. (III.I.4. p. 147).

4. Leningrad. (III.I.8. p. 148).

Plate XXIV

1. New York, Jan Mitchell. (IV.A.3. p. 155).

2. New York, Jan Mitchell.

3. Stockholm, Medelhavsmuseet 1960:12. (IV.A.8. p. 156).

Plate XXV

2. London B 679.

1. London B 679.
(IV.A.14. p. 156).

4. Athens 408.

3. Athens 408.
(IV.A.19. p. 157).

Plate XXVI

2. Gotha 48. (IV.B.2. p. 162).

1. Greenwich, Bareiss. (IV.B.1. p. 162).

3. Gotha 48.

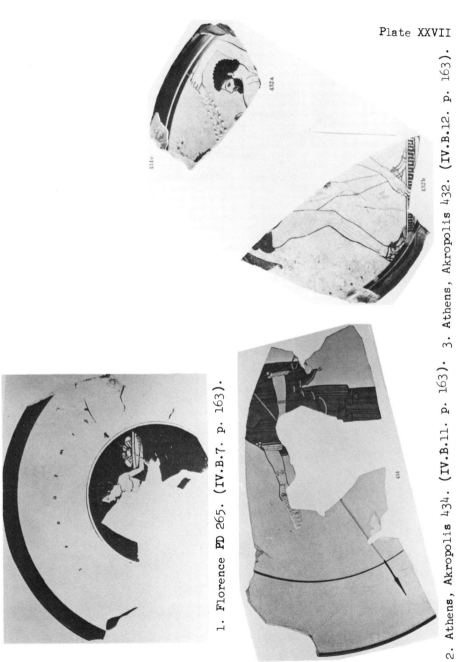

Plate XXVII

1. Florence PD 265. (IV.B.7. p. 163).

2. Athens, Akropolis 434. (IV.B.11. p. 163). 3. Athens, Akropolis 432. (IV.B.12. p. 163).

Plate XXVIII

3. Detail, Cabinet des Médailles 608. (IV.B.23. p. 164).

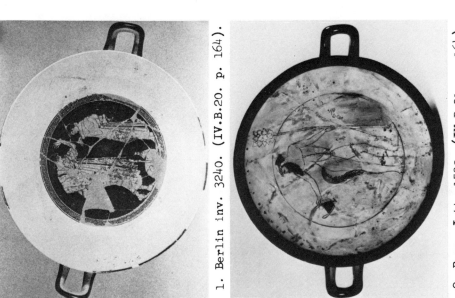

1. Berlin inv. 3240. (IV.B.20. p. 164).

2. Ruvo, Jatta 1539. (IV.B.21. p. 164).

Plate XXIX

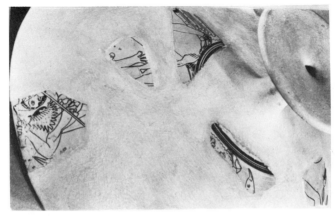

3. London D 1.

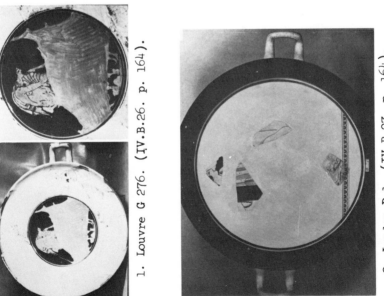

1. Louvre G 276. (IV.B.26. p. 164).

2. London D 1. (IV.B.27. p. 164).

Plate XXX

1. Boston 00.356. (IV.B.32. p. 171).

2. London D 6. (IV.B.34. p. 172).

3. Brussels A 891. (IV.B.38. p. 172).

Plate XXXI

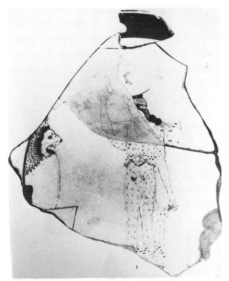

1. Brauron. (IV.B.47. p. 172).

2. Florence 75409. (IV.B.50. p. 173).

Plate XXXII

1. Athens, Akropolis 439.
   (IV.B.54. p. 173).

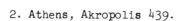

2. Athens, Akropolis 439.

3. London D 4.
   (IV.B.61. p. 174).

Plate XXXIII

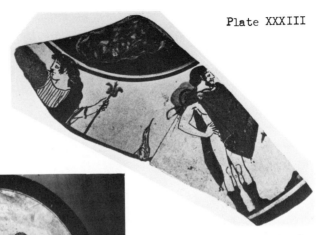

1. Athens, Akropolis 589.
   (IV.B.62. p. 174).

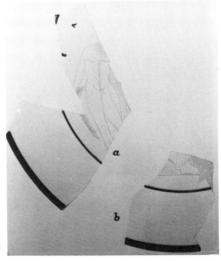

2. Louvre G 109. (IV.B.63. p. 181).

3. Athens. (IV.B.69. p. 182).

Plate XXXIV

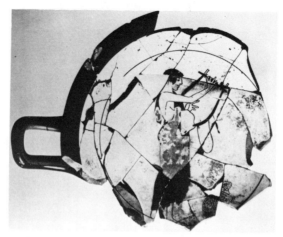

1. Athens, Agora P 43. (IV.B.70. p. 182).

2. Athens 2187. (IV.B.73. p. 182).

Plate XXXV

1. Palermo. (V. p. 196).

2. Athens 1130. (V. p. 197).

Plate XXXVI

1. New York 41.162.29. (V. p. 198).

2. New York 66.11.4.
(V. p. 199).

3. New York 06.1070. (V. p. 200).

Plate XXXVII

1. Germany private.
(V. p. 201).

2. Princeton.
(V. p. 201).

3. New York 08.258.28.
(V. p. 202).

Plate XXXVIII

1. Göttingen 21.
(V. p. 203).

2. Vienna 3644.
(V. p. 204).

Plate XXXIX

1. Athens, Agora A-P 422. (V. p. 205).   2. Gela. (V. p. 206).

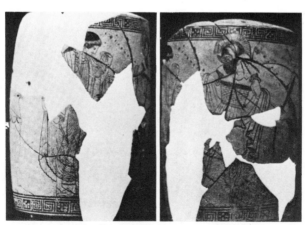

3. Palermo. (V. p. 206).

Plate XL

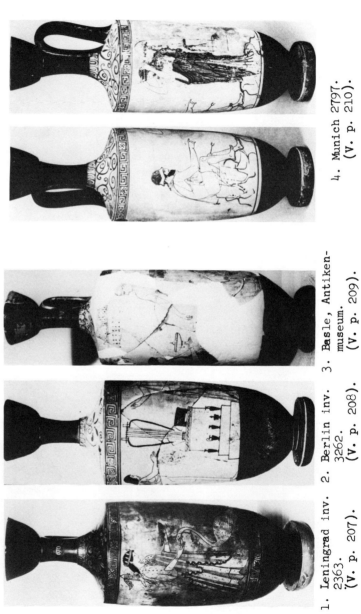

1. Leningrad inv.   2. Berlin inv.   3. Basle, Antiken-   4. Munich 2797.
   2363.   3262.   museum.   (v. p. 210).
   (v. p. 207).   (v. p. 208).   (v. p. 209).

Plate XLI

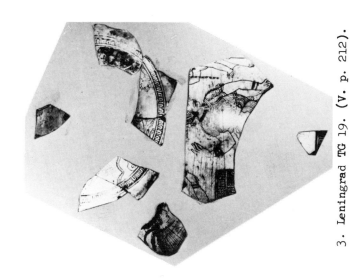

3. Leningrad TG 19. (V. p. 212).

1. Brussels A 1021. (V. p. 211).

2. New York 31.11.13. (V. p. 211).